Tomáš Frydrych, Ph. D. (2000) in Old Testament, University of Edinburgh, is tutoring Old Testament at University of Edinburgh and working as a Translation Consultant for World Bible Translation Center, Fort Worth, T X.

LIVING UNDER THE SUN

SUPPLEMENTS

TO

VETUS TESTAMENTUM

EDITED BY
THE BOARD OF THE QUARTERLY

H.M. BARSTAD – PHYLLIS A. BIRD – R.P. GORDON
A. HURVITZ – A. van der KOOIJ – A. LEMAIRE
R. SMEND – J. TREBOLLE BARRERA
J.C. VANDERKAM – H.G.M. WILLIAMSON

VOLUME XC

LIVING UNDER THE SUN

Examination of Proverbs and Qoheleth

BY

TOMÁŠ FRYDRYCH

BRILL

LEIDEN · BOSTON · KÖLN

2002

This book is printed on acid-free paper.

Die Deutsche Bibliothek – CIP-Einheitsaufnahme

Frydrych, Tomáš:
Living under the Sun ; Examination of Proverbs and Qoheleth / by Tomáš
Frydrych. – Leiden ; Boston ; Köln : Brill, 2002
　(Supplements to Vetus testamentum ; Vol. 90)
　ISBN 90-04-12315-6

Library of Congress Cataloging-in-Publication Data

Library of Congress Cataloging-in-Publication Data is also available

ISSN　0083-5889
ISBN　90 04 12315 6

PRINTED IN THE NETHERLANDS

To Linda

(Proverbs 31:31)

TABLE OF CONTENTS

PREFACE

The present book is based on my PhD thesis with an identical title, submitted at the University of Edinburgh in August, 2000. It stems from my interest in wisdom literature, and, in particular, in its significance and implications for OT theology, which was sparked by Professor Bruce Waltke during my time at Regent College (Vancouver, B.C.). In recent years a number of scholars have expressed a desire to accord wisdom literature a more significant place in the formulation of wisdom theology; the present work is intended as a contribution to this effort.

The principal aim of this study is to formulate the worldviews that lie behind the books of Proverbs and Qoheleth in a manner that would allow a comprehensive, and yet transparent comparison, and further, to consider the nature of their similarities and differences, as well as plausible explanations for these. Two principal theses will be put forward in due course: first, that the wisdom phenomenon is best understood in terms of a quest defined by aims and methodology, rather then simply being seen as a discourse defined by its topics, literary forms or vocabulary, and second, that the by no means insignificant differences in the two worldviews are caused primarily by differing socio-economic conditions from which the two books stem.

A number of people were instrumental in producing this book. I would like to express my thanks to my PhD supervisor, Dr Peter Hayman, who spent countless hours discussing with me various questions pertaining to my research. I wish to thank Drs Katharine Dell and David Reimer for the insights provided during the examination of the original thesis, and Douglas Briton for his comments on the work in its later stages. I am grateful to Prof. André Lemaire for accepting this book for publication in *Supplements to Vetus Testamentum*, as well as for his valuable comments on the early form of the manuscript. My further thanks go to Mattie Kuiper of Brill Academic Publishers for her patient assistance in the publication process. Last, but by no means least, I wish to thank my wife Linda, without whose support, encouragement and help this book would never have materialised.

The difficulties that the present study deals with are by no means trivial and have been around for over two millennia. I do not presume that the answers I attempt to provide are final or flawless; what I hope for is that this study will stimulate further debate, opening the door for a new way of approaching the old problems of wisdom.

Falkirk, 19 September 2001

LIST OF ABBREVIATIONS

Literary Sources

BDB	Brown, Driver, Briggs, 1979
BHS	Elliger and Rudolph (eds), 1990
BibInt	*Biblical Interpretation*
BSac	*Bibliotheca Sacra*
BTB	*Biblical Theology Bulletin*
BZAW	Beihefte zur Zeitschrift für die alttestamentliche Wissenschaft
CBQ	*Catholic Biblical Quarterly*
CBQMS	Catholic Biblical Quartely Monograph Series
ConBOT	Coniectanea Biblica - Old Testament series
HAR	*Hebrew Annual Review*
HUCA	*Hebrew Union College Annual*
IBS	*Irish Biblical Studies*
IEJ	*Israel Exploration Journal*
ITC	International Theological Commentary
Jas	Jastrow, 1996
JBL	*Journal of Biblical Literature*
JJS	*Journal of Jewish Studies*
JNES	*Journal of Near Eastern Studies*
Joü	Joüon, 1993
JQR	*Jewish Quarterly Review*
JSOT	*Journal for the Study of the Old Testament*
JSOTSup	JSOT Supplement Series
JSP	*Journal for the Study of Pseudoepigrapha*
JSS	*Journal of Semitic Studies*
JTS	*Journal of Theological Studies*
KBL-2	Koehler and Baumgartner, 1985
KBL-3	Koehler and Baumgartner, 1994
L&S	Liddell and Scott, 1940
NIV	New International Version
OBO	Orbis Biblicus et Orientalis

RB	*Revue Biblique*
RSV	Revised Standard Version
SBLDS	Society of Biblical Literature Dissertation Series
SBLMS	Society of Biblical Literature Masoretic Studies
SBTh	Studies in Biblical Theology
SJOT	*Scandinavian Journal of the Old Testament*
SR	*Studies in Religion*
SVT	Supplements to Vetus Testamentum
TWOT	Harris, Archer, Waltke, 1980
TynBul	*Tyndale Bulletin*
TZ	*Theologische Zeitschrift*
UF	Ugarit-Forschungen
VT	*Vetus Testamentum*
WMANT	Wissenschaftliche Monographien zum alten und neuen Testament
WOC	Waltke and O'Connor, 1990
ZAW	*Zeitschrift für die alttestamentliche Wissenschaft*
ZThK	*Zeitschrift für Theologie und Kirche*

Textual Witnesses

𝔐	Masoretic Text
L	Leningrad Codex
𝔊	Septuagint
𝔊º	Origen's recension of Septuagint
𝔗	Targume
𝔖	Peshita
ℭ	Cairo Geniza Texts
𝔙	Vulgate
α'	Aquila
ϑ'	Theodotion
σ'	Symmanchus
Amen.	The Instruction of Amenemopet

Other Abbreviations Used

ANE	Ancient Near East
BH	Biblical Hebrew
cs.	Construct form
EBH	Early Biblical Hebrew
fs	Feminine singular
impv.	Imperative
inf.	Infinitive
infa.	Infinitive absolute
infc.	Infinitive construct
K	Ketib
LBH	Late Biblical Hebrew
MH	Mishnaic Hebrew
ms	Masculine singular
pass.	Passive
pl.	Plural
ptc.	Participle
Px	Prefix conjugation
Q	Qere
sfx	Suffix
sg.	Singular
Sx	Suffix conjugation

CHAPTER I

INTRODUCTION

Wisdom and Theology

When the similarity of Prov 22:17ff. with the Egyptian *Instruction of Amenemope* came to light in the early 1920s, it triggered scholarly interest in biblical wisdom, until then standing on the periphery of OT studies. The surge in wisdom research reached serious proportions after World War II, so that it is now possible to speak of wisdom studies as a specialised discipline.[1] Yet, historically the impact of wisdom literature on theological deliberation has been, and still remains, rather limited. Often, wisdom is almost completely ignored by the theologian, and even scholars who pay greater attention to it have major difficulties when it comes to giving it a place in their overall OT theology. To mention only a few, Eichrodt's massive work (1967, published in German 1933) dedicates to wisdom a mere dozen pages, Vos (1973, first published 1948) ignores wisdom literature altogether, and recent works by Childs (1985, 1992) allocate to wisdom books fewer than three pages without actually seriously considering the real theological significance of wisdom texts.[2] The most significant effort to date to give wisdom a legitimate place in OT theology remains that of von Rad (1962, 1972), who felt the need to return to wisdom in a separate volume after publishing his OT theology. Yet, while this volume is an extensive treatment of OT wisdom *per se*, wisdom still does not fit logically into von Rad's theological framework.

The source of the theologians' difficulties is twofold. The first one is related to a wider problem of OT theology and its methodology,

---

[1] It is not my intention to present a complete and exhaustive survey of the present state of the study of Proverbs and Qoheleth here, and even less of the whole of wisdom. Such overviews can be readily found elsewhere, and there is no need to repeat what others have done with skill and lucidity. For the Book of Proverbs, an exhaustive overview of the academic research can be found in Whybray (1995); for Qoheleth see for instance Murphy (1992); for wisdom theology see Perdue (1994), Martin (1995), Dell (1997).

[2] Childs is more concerned with questions about the role of wisdom in the formation of the canon, than wisdom theology *per se*.

namely, the question whether there is a single key concept around which OT theology could be organised, and if so, what it is; the number of such pivotal ideas proposed in the past speaks for itself. The details of the discussion surrounding this issue are not of an immediate interest to this study,[3] with the exception of the fact that in virtually all cases the theological paradigms are built around the OT legal/prophetic traditions alone. Thus, the difficulties with OT wisdom literature, characterised by notable lack of interest in any of Israel's national traditions and only limited occupation with cultic[4] matters, are easily conceivable.

The problem of certain perceived tension between wisdom and the legal and prophetic traditions of the Hebrew bible is by no means new; efforts to unite the two types of traditions are already present, as will be argued in the present work, in the epilogue to Qoheleth, and even more clearly in Ben Sira. The modern solution for this tension most often, as has already been indicated, amounts to silently ignoring it, but for example Gunneweg (1993) goes as far as arguing that wisdom is a foreign body to the OT, centred around the Egyptian concept of Maat, which is irreconcilable with Yahwistic piety, a view which I disagree with; my own examination of the possible use of the Egyptian material in Prov 22:17ff. leads me to the conclusion that the Egyptian concepts have not been accepted blindly by the Israelite sages, but rather both the content and the form were modified to suit the new background; the sages' belief in orderliness of the world is set within a Yahwistic framework of its own, as it will be argued in chapter 4.

At the other end of the spectrum attempts have been made to establish closer formal links of wisdom material with the legal and prophetic traditions. Thus, Wilson (1984) argued that the outlook of Proverbs, and in particular of Prov 1–9, is closely related to the deuteronomistic perspective, listing a number of points of contact between certain proverbial statements and those found in Deuteronomy. However, while there are some formal similarities in the language and formulations found in the two books, it will be argued later that proverbial Yahwism

---

[3] An overview can be found in Hasel (1991).

[4] The term *cult* will be used throughout this study in a very broad and generic sense. The reader should understand by it a set of formal rituals and practices the sole, or at least principal, purpose of which is to mediate between a human being and a deity. I wish to impose no further constrains on the term, i.e., these rituals could be private or communal, mediated by other persons or without a mediator, centralised or not.

is a Yahwism of a very peculiar type, quite distinct from the Yahwism of the prophetic and legal traditions of the OT, and that makes deuteronomistic origins of Proverbs, including Prov 1–9, questionable; an explanation for the formal similarities is more likely to lie in traditions and customs common to both the proverbial sages and the deuteronomists. A further notable attempt to bridge the gap between these different traditions is that of Harris (1995), who argued for dependency of some of the material in Prov 1–9 on the Joseph story and passages from Jeremiah. However, I personally find the suggested parallels unconvincing.[5]

While the theologian's first problem is largely one of methodology and, as Perdue (1994:34) pointed out, it is essentially external to the textual tradition, the second problem is rooted in the material *per se*. The fundamental obstacle lies in the fact that it appears to be extremely difficult to formulate an 'umbrella' theology for the OT wisdom corpus that would be comprehensive, yet, adequate. In turn, the lack of such a formulation makes it difficult to incorporate wisdom into the larger OT theology. Perdue (1994:341) captures it well as he writes:

> Renderings of the theology of wisdom literature need to be written and refined. Regardless of the interpretative paradigm, articulations of the faith of the sages are necessary. Otherwise, the literature will not be taken seriously in formulations of comprehensive Old Testament and biblical theologies.

This problem is not simply a question of the 'centre of gravity' of wisdom thought (for Wisdom theology faces a methodological problem similar to that of the larger OT theology[6]). The real problem lies in

---

[5] The link between Prov 1–9 and the Joseph story depends on repetition of very common Hebrew vocabulary, while at the same time the differences between the allegedly parallel stories are significant. Thus, in the Genesis account Joseph does not appear to be the innocent man of Prov 1:18–19, who has been ambushed without cause, and Judah's surety for Benjamin is a surety for a blood relation, not, as in Prov 6:1–5, for a 'neighbour'. When we take into account the fact that Proverbs offers generalised schemes of human behaviour, it seems more likely that the Joseph story partially fits the scheme than to assert that the paradigm was derived from it. Likewise, the suggested parallels between Prov 1:20–33 and Jer 7 & 20 hinge on very common vocabulary, and the similar setting of the two stories, rather than literary dependence, appears to be a more feasible explanation for the common features.

[6] The three most commonly suggested centres of gravity for wisdom thought are anthropology, cosmology and theodicy. A fourth proposed approach builds around a diachronic shift from earlier anthropologically-oriented wisdom to a later wisdom focusing on cosmology and theology; the discussion has been well summarised by Perdue (1994:34–48), with whom I am inclined to agree that the most fruitful approach

the fact that the seeming naiveté of Proverbs, the disillusionment of Job, and the pessimism of Qoheleth, appear to share far less common theology than vocabulary. Thus, most of the present studies in theology of wisdom look on the individual texts in relative isolation without seriously dealing with the dialogue which these texts create within the OT.[7]

The internal tension among the OT wisdom texts is often perceived along diachronic lines as the so called *crisis of wisdom*.[8] Behind this phrase hides the notion that the wisdom texts attest to a diachronic shift from a naïve and grossly inadequate perception of the world by the earlier sages toward a more realistic picture painted by the later texts. While I am convinced, and will argue later, that the diachronic element is critical to understanding this tension, the standard crisis theory in my view does not account for the textual data, and fails to even consider the possible origins of the problem. Crüsemann's (1984) attempt to understand the shift of perspective in terms of a change in the social structures is in my view on the right track, although the view that it is the exile that is the primary cause of the development may need reconsidering later on. The critical question is not so much what made Qoheleth and Job part with the proverbial outlook, but what made the proverbial sages take such a seemingly naïve stance in the first place.

The above analysis of the two-fold problem associated with theology of wisdom leads to the following two conclusions. First, if wisdom literature is to have a meaningful place in OT theology, there is a need for a fresh start, that would include consideration of wisdom in the actual process of building the theological framework, as has been pointed out by Perdue (1994:19–34). As of the moment, as far as I am aware, no OT theology treats the wisdom corpus as material on a par with the legal and prophetic traditions. Second, it is necessary to move from considering the OT wisdom texts as isolated entities to examining

---

is in retaining a synchronic tension between the anthropological and cosmological perspective on creation.

[7] It can be further observed that often 'wisdom theology' is essentially the theology of Proverbs, with the other texts being marginalised. Thus, for instance, Zimmerli (1978) more or less reinterprets Qoheleth and Job in the light of Proverbs, and similarly von Rad's (1972) understanding of wisdom is based primarily on Proverbs.

[8] Among scholars who adopted this approach one may mention for instance Crenshaw (1985:370, 1988b:51) and Loader (1986:8–11), but objections have been raised by von Rad (1972:238) and more recently Murphy (1995:233).

the effects of their juxtaposition; without this larger synthesising step wisdom literature is bound to remain on the periphery of OT theology.[9]

The Aims and Method of the Present Study

The present work stems from the need for a more synthetic view of OT wisdom just outlined. It is obvious that for the synthesis to have any real value, it can only be attempted after a thorough exegetical analysis, on the basis of which the different perspectives that these texts represent could be examined and related to each other. The present study is intended as a step in that direction, looking in detail at two of the OT wisdom texts, Proverbs and Qoheleth, and examining closely their views: the similarities, the differences and the probable causes of these. The principal focus will be on the analysis of the two perspectives, with only a few limited comments and suggestions concerning the implications for formulation of wisdom theology. At the same time, it has to be acknowledged that the theological questions are reflected in the chosen methodology. Notably, my main interest is in understanding the perspectives of the books in their present shape. This is not to imply that I consider these books monolithic compositions each written by a single author, nor that the questions pertaining to the history of their formation are of little importance. In fact, it will be seen that the analysis of the perspectives represented by the present shape of the texts has some bearing on our understanding of their origins.

Which Text?

The deliberate choice to look at each of the two books from a synchronic perspective is closely related to the question of choosing the text to work with. Since the biblical material is not represented by a uniform textual tradition, before any study of it can be carried out, a decision needs to be made about the identity of the texts that are going to be considered, as well as the overall text-critical strategy. Three prin-

---

[9] Of the more recent works, Perdue (1994) has come closest toward the formulation of a wisdom theology proper. Carrying out a rather careful examination of the entire OT and apocryphal wisdom corpus in its own right, he demonstrated that creation is a central theme in all of the examined wisdom texts. Yet, Perdue himself does not attempt any significant degree of theological synthesis, i.e., he does not formulate wisdom theology as such. In addition, because he concentrates largely on the theme of creation and its anthropological and cosmological aspects, he does not offer a sufficiently comprehensive formulation of the worldviews of the individual books.

cipal options are open to any interpreter: to use one particular textual tradition, to use an eclectic text, or to use a text of one of the principal traditions occasionally corrected in the light of other textual witnesses. The choice is largely determined by the character of the material available and the purpose of the study. From the perspective of a theologian the former approach has the advantage of being able to claim close continuity with a community of faith that the text represents, but it ignores a number of issues stemming from the lack of uniformity of the textual witnesses. In biblical studies the third approach is the most common (although the principal text and the degree with which the resulting corrected text nears one of the other two ends of the spectrum vary). This third approach will also be employed here. The principal tradition will be that of 𝔐 with the intention being to stay as near to that textual tradition as reasonably possible, but not to the extent of ignoring the nature of the formation and transmission of ancient texts. This approach should allow the claim of continuity to be mostly retained, without having to entirely ignore the reality of varying textual traditions; my principal interest is not in the text *per se* but in the mindset that brought it into being.

The details of the textual situation in the case of the two books differ significantly, therefore, the specifics of the text-critical strategy adopted here will be somewhat different for each of them. The textual situation is relatively simple in the case of Qoheleth. The versions in their present form appear to stem from the same tradition as 𝔐, and show serious attempts to stay as close to the received tradition as possible. Thus for instance in the case of 𝔊, the translation is extremely rigid, even rendering the particle אֶת־ by the preposition συν, and further, where the translator did not understand the meaning of the Hebrew text, he typically rendered the words as literally as possible, even though the resulting Greek may not make much sense.[10] As far as 𝔐 of Qoheleth is concerned, it appears that a number of common scribal errors entered the text as we have it, but often these are not reflected in the versions which can be used to correct them.[11]

---

[10] This led some scholars to the conclusion that the text preserved in 𝔊 is not the original 𝔊 translation, but a secondary replacement. Thus for instance Gordis (1955a:126) suggested that the present text of 𝔊 of Qoheleth is the first version of Aquila's translation.

[11] Unfortunately, attestation of Qoheleth among the Dead Sea Scrolls is limited, but the evidence will be used for text-critical purposes where available; for detailed information see Muilenburg (1954) and Ulrich (1992).

In the case of Proverbs the situation is more complicated. The text of 𝔊 differs significantly from that of 𝔐, both in respect of the arrangement of the material and of the actual content. To some extent this is due to differences in the translator's Hebrew *Vorlage* (Tov, 1990), but there are other, and more critical factors at play. A recent extensive study by Cook (1997) demonstrates significant intentional reworking of the text by the translator, who is concerned that the overall intentions of the Hebrew text, rather than its minute details, are carried over into the Greek. The translation reflects its Hellenistic milieu in three important ways. First, the translator seeks to produce a good Greek text, and thus, the material often needs to be adjusted to conform to the demands of Greek style. Second, the translator intends to make clearer some of the basic views of the Hebrew book, and avoids possible misunderstandings by getting rid off numerous ambiguities found in the Hebrew text. Finally, the translator strives to distance the wisdom of Proverbs from Hellenistic views, and to that end he brings into the translation a number of Hellenistic traditions to expose them as incompatible with true wisdom. As a result 𝔊 of Proverbs has much more pronounced religious colouring than the Hebrew text. Overall, 𝔊 of Proverbs represents a quite separate tradition, stemming from different circumstances and addressing different concerns, one that deserves study in its own right. At the same time its value for text-critical purposes when dealing with the Hebrew text is limited, and it has to be used with caution (Cook, 1997:334). Since 𝔊 seems to have influenced the other major versions at least to some extent, equal care needs to be taken when their variant readings are evaluated.[12]

The outline of the basic text-critical strategy needs to be accompanied by a few notes on my view of the text of the two books from a more macroscopic perspective. Until recently it has been taken for granted that the sayings collected in Proverbs are mutually unrelated, to the extent that some commentators felt free to rearrange the material according to their own schemes.[13] However, this approach has been seriously challenged in recent years. Of the greatest significance in this respect is the work of Van Leeuwen (1988), who suggested that the literary context in Proverbs intentionally substitutes the lost life-context,

---

[12] For instance 𝔖 often tends to conflate the texts of 𝔐 and 𝔊 although on a number of occasions the translator understood the Hebrew text better than the translator of 𝔊.

[13] An example *par excellence* of this approach to the book is the commentary by McKane (1970).

i.e., the *Sitz im Leben* had been consciously replaced by *Sitz im Buch*, and, therefore, the context has to be considered carefully when interpreting the book.[14] The implications of this newly gained insight are far reaching—the whole is more than the sum of its parts. At the same time, this new perception of the book should not obscure the fact that the nature of the petty sayings is such that they have to be understandable in relative autonomy, i.e., the primary source of meaning in the collections is the individual saying. A juxtaposition of selected sayings can focus the meaning of the sayings in a particular direction (individual sayings are often open to a number of related, but not necessarily identical interpretations, and can be applied to different situations in life), or the juxtaposition can add certain additional nuances; there are a number of cases in Proverbs where this is detectable. On the other hand, as far as I am able to see, the book does not display any homogenous overall strategy for organisation of the material; it remains first and foremost a collection of sayings.

Concerning the composition of Qoheleth, numerous attempts have been made to date to identify a meaningful literary structure in the book that would aid its interpretation. The sheer number of the various schemes perceived by different interpreters would seem to point in one direction—there is no obvious and carefully constructed literary framework to Qoheleth proper (i.e., Qoh 1:2–12:8). This is not to say that the text is a random collection of sentences; there are smaller identifiable units, held together by common themes and catchwords and the analysis of these and of the grammatical forms shows a shift of emphasis between the first and second half of the book.[15]

The key issue for the overall interpretation of the book is the relationship between Qoheleth proper and the epilogue.[16] While it is widely acknowledged that the views of the two differ, the theological significance of this juxtaposition is not normally addressed in OT theologies, and the theologian often accepts one or the other as the overall voice

---

[14] Another example of context-oriented approach to the book of Proverbs is Saebo (1986).

[15] This matter will be addressed further in chapter 2.

[16] The opinions of commentators on the origins of the epilogue differ; it is most often seen as coming from a different hand than the core of the book, but Fox (1977), for instance, argued otherwise. Further, it has been suggested that there are in fact two epilogues in the book, Qoh 12:9–11 and Qoh 12:12–14. This is possible in the sense that the two sections could have originated separately. However, no attempt is made in the second section to distinguish its voice from that of the earlier portion. Thus, on the literary level, the entire epilogue represents a single voice.

of the book. However, Sheppard (1977:184–89) argued that the epilogue cannot be seen as a simple theological corrective to the book's scepticism, but instead that it has a wider canonical function giving a singular focus to the entire wisdom corpus, and at the same time limiting its extent. Although I am not completely convinced about the latter assertion, which Sheppard developed later on (1980), I agree with him that the epilogue is not a simple theological corrective. It should be observed that the epilogue thinks highly of Qoheleth and his wisdom, and, thus, it is unlikely that it is intended as an outright rejection of the rest of the book. In addition, the epilogue is too brief to have been intended as a serious rebuttal of Qoheleth's views. Yet, quite clearly, the epilogue cannot be perceived as a straightforward endorsement of the core of the book, leaving the question of its purpose wide open.

Wilson (1984) argued that the epilogue is intended to form a frame with Prov 1:1–3, which is meant to serve as a hermeneutical key for the two books, essentially to do with divine demand for justice and divine judgment with respect to fulfilment of this obligation. While I find Wilson's argument unconvincing at a number of points,[17] I am of the opinion that both Sheppard and Wilson are correct in detecting in the epilogue what might be called canonical forces, by which I mean evidence of attempts to bring together traditions that are quite different from each other, namely wisdom and the traditions that revolve around the cult.

When interpreting the book as a whole, it is necessary to pay attention to the formal literary relationship between the core of the book and the prologue/epilogue. The text indicates clearly by the shift from first person to third person references to the persona of Qoheleth that the two voices are to be seen as distinct from each other. Thus, in the following chapters, I will treat the two voices of Qoheleth and the epilogist as voices in their own right.[18]

---

[17] I have already expressed reservations about the claims of deuteronomistic origins of Prov 1–9 and without it the implicit reference of the epilogue to Proverbs is untenable. Overall, Wilson in my view fails to appreciate the fundamental difference between the perspective of the epilogist on the one hand and both the views of Proverbs and Qoheleth on the other, a difference which I will attempt to demonstrate in due course.

[18] For a recent extensive treatment of the epilogue and various interpretative issues see Christianson (1998:96–114).

Examining the Worldviews

Having explained the basic approach to the textual tradition adopted in the present study, I wish to outline the way in which the analysis of the text will be carried out. The intention is to formulate a worldview for each of the two books; by *worldview* I mean an overall and comprehensive set of beliefs about the world and one's place in it which informs, if not dictates, one's behaviour. I have decided to use the term *worldview* quite deliberately. It is common in biblical studies to speak of *theology* of a book when referring to its overall perspective. Although I have used the term this way so far, e.g., referring to *theology of wisdom*, I do not find the terminology entirely satisfactory, partly because sometimes it is necessary to speak of theology in a narrower sense of views concerning God, partly because I feel that using the term in the broad and loose sense does in fact prejudice the enquiry by forcing theological issues where none might be present. In my view neither Proverbs, nor Qoheleth are principally theological works; they have to *reckon with* theology, but they are not *about* theology.

Since, as I have also already indicated, my primary interest at this moment is in the synchronic voice of each of the two books, the examination of the worldviews will be carried out along the lines of the intentions detectable in the composition of the books. In considering the worldview of Proverbs, the book will be treated as speaking with a single voice, for this appears to have been the editorial intention. Where Qoheleth is concerned, the situation is, as was already noted, different. Since the voice that speaks in the epilogue expresses views that appear to be different and independent from those of Qoheleth proper, I will be looking for two separate worldviews. Obviously, due to the brevity of the epilogue, it will not be possible to formulate a complete worldview of the epilogist, but only some of its elements. However, since, by the nature of the text, these will be the points where the two perspectives differ most significantly, the incompleteness will not have serious consequences for the present study.

The key methodological issue is how to formulate the worldviews of the two books. First of all, it is important that the perspectives of the two texts are examined and expressed in terms that are native to them, rather than using concepts that are borrowed from other OT traditions. In addition, there are two conflicting requirements on the formulation itself. On the one hand, it has to be sufficiently comprehensive, i.e., the formulation should cover all the essential issues that the texts are concerned with; failure to do so would call into serious question the general validity of the conclusions reached. On the other hand, the formulation must allow a reasonably transparent comparison of the two worldviews. This requires that the discussion is limited to a relatively small number of clearly defined issues, for too large a number of categories would necessarily lead to a fragmentation of the overall picture. Also, since the ultimate aim of the study is to relate the two worldviews to each other, in deciding what the key issues in the two books are, relative rather than absolute significance has to be considered. What may appear to be a major issue in one book, may not appear so in the other. Yet, from the point of view of the comparison, an absence or near absence of a particular issue from one of the worldviews might be just as revealing, and therefore significant, as an emphasis would be. Therefore, the issues considered for each book must be the union, in the mathematical sense of the word, of the key concerns of the two texts.

For practical reasons, it is useful to draw a distinction between the cognitive part of a worldview, i.e., what a person thinks of the world, and its practical element, i.e., how in practical terms this cognitive perspective projects itself into the person's behaviour; both Proverbs and Qoheleth have the latter of these in mind, and to some extent I will be attempting to derive the abstract perspectives from the practical ones.

In the case of Proverbs, a distinction can be made between three main types of conduct that the book addresses: behaviour within the context of human relationships, behaviour within the context of relationship with God, and, occasionally, behaviour with consequences largely limited to the self. Thus, it is necessary to examine the proverbial social and anthropological views, including the sages' ethics,[19] and the book's theological perspective. Closely related to the latter is the larger cosmological framework that the text represents, and material with implicit or explicit cosmological implications is scattered all over the book. It is, therefore, necessary to look also at the sages' cosmology. Further, we have to appreciate that Proverbs is not simply a rule book, but that the desired behaviour is an informed one, as is shown by the high concentration of cognitive vocabulary throughout. This fact requires that we also examine the sages' epistemology.

---

[19] Throughout this work I will use the term *ethics* with the very basic sense of system of values that governs the way how a person's behaviour is, or should be, affected by the presence, needs or interests of other people.

Turning to the latter book, the types of behaviour that Qoheleth examines fit under the same three rubrics used above, although the mutual proportions of these are different, and the behavioural considerations are mainly from the perspective of an impact on the self, so that the term ethics can be used with reference to the book only with caution. Similarly to Proverbs, the book is also interested in an informed behaviour, as is shown by the frequent occurrence of the root ידע, so that the question of epistemology is no less important. As far as the epilogue of Qoheleth is concerned, some significant aspects of the epilogist's worldview are implied in spite of its brevity. Thus, his comments about Qoheleth, his work and the wisdom enterprise in general reveal certain views concerning knowledge, the process through which it is acquired and its value. Further, all of these comments show a certain theological perspective that informs the epilogist's epistemology, and offer insight into the code for proper behaviour to which he adheres.

Overall, the cognitive element of the worldviews that we find in these books can be formulated under the categories of epistemology, theology, cosmology, anthropology and social perspective. The two books will be discussed along these lines in chapters 3–5, and in chapter 6 I will present a summary of the practical code of conduct that the two books derive from their respective understandings of the world.

One of the potential dangers of treating the two books merely under the five isolated rubrics is losing the sense of the overall picture. In order to avoid this, the detailed analysis of the worldviews of the two books in chapters 3–6 is preceded by a chapter that presents a more coherent, albeit only sketchy, image of what is happening in the two books, the concerns they stem from, the questions they address, and the ways they go about doing so. The detailed discussion of the individual aspects of the two worldviews in chapters 3–6 should be understood as always having an implied reference to this overall framework.

Additional Notes

A few notes on the format of the following chapters, are called for. In order to argue the case, it is necessary to quote the text of Proverbs and Qoheleth frequently, and some of the material used has a direct bearing on discussion of several different aspects of the worldview, and will, therefore, figure several times in the text. For the sake of the reader and the fluency of the argument it was deemed more practical to repeat such passages, rather than to back-reference them. However, the textual notes that accompany these are included only once. This is normally on the first occurrence of the given material, except for situations where a shorter piece of text is used in one place, but the same text is found later within a larger quote. In such cases the textual notes accompany the larger text. In all cases, however, appropriate page references are given. It should be further noted that the text-critical notes are by no means exhaustive; for reasons of physical space and readability only textual variants that were considered significant for the sake of the argument were included. The grammatical terminology used throughout the study is that found in WOC.

CHAPTER 2

THE WISDOM ENTERPRISE

What kind of world hides behind the two biblical books of Proverbs and Qoheleth? This is a question which is at the very heart of the present enquiry. However, it must be made clear from the outset, that in asking this question I am not looking for answers of an historical nature, i.e., how and when these books were born, nor am I principally asking about their *Sitz im Leben*, i.e., what immediate purpose did they serve the community that produced and used them. Rather, I am enquiring about *the kind* of people that these books represent, their concerns, aspirations, joys and struggles; about *the kind* of world in which they belong. In the following chapters I will deal in detail with a number of individual elements of this world and the place of humans in it; at present I wish concentrate on the basic question of what these books are all about. Thus, I will attempt to sketch an elementary framework for looking at these texts, one which will serve as the starting point for the detailed examination found in the later chapters.

What is Wisdom?

The Problem of Defining Wisdom

The question of what our two books are about is closely related to the wider question of what is wisdom, one which has been the subject of a considerable debate. This has been sparked initially by von Rad's (1953) identification of the Joseph narrative as a wisdom material. Von Rad's lead in widening the notion of what constitutes wisdom was then followed by a number other scholars, who perceived wisdom influence in a large number of other OT texts from all sections of the Hebrew canon.[1]

However, this broad perspective on the wisdom tradition is not without difficulties. When the definition of wisdom is loosened to accommodate a broad variety of material, it becomes virtually meaningless

---

[1] Extensive bibliographical information can be found in Crenshaw (1969:129).

to speak of wisdom literature as such. This led to criticism of the von Rad's school of thought from two different directions. On the one hand, Crenshaw (1969), after consideration of the methodological issues, argued for the need to maintain distinction between the 'classical' wisdom texts, such as Proverbs and Qoheleth, and the other so called wisdom texts.[2] On the other hand, Whybray (1974) went further, arguing not only that 'the interests of scholarly investigation are not served by the application of the word "wisdom" to every manifestation to use one's brains in ancient Israel [*sic*]' (p. 3), but also that there is no coherent wisdom phenomenon found in the OT, only a loose *intellectual tradition*.[3]

While Whybray's work exposes the difficulties in identifying wisdom material on the grounds of subject, form and vocabulary, it contains certain methodological flaws, notably the disputed texts, such as the Joseph narrative, are considered to be wisdom material from the outset, and, thus, the question whether wisdom can be defined narrowly, or only in broad terms, is prejudged. Further, the loose concept of intellectual tradition that Whybray arrives at is of no more practical use than the watered-down definition of wisdom which he is so critical of. Even though the traditional categories of subject, form and vocabulary, if applied systematically, may not be enough to distinguish the 'classical' wisdom texts from other OT material, it is difficult to deny that three books of Proverbs, Job and Qoheleth are distinct from much of the rest of the OT, and yet, similar to each other; the difficulties that these texts pose to the OT theologian due to their lack of interest in Israel as a nation, redemptive activity of God and the cult have already been pointed out in the Introduction and witness to the distinctiveness of these texts.

However, Whybray is, in my view, on the right track when he starts looking at wisdom outwith the confines of a literary genre. I wish to suggest that the central question with respect to wisdom is not one of forms and vocabulary, but rather the question of what wisdom is really about. By this I do not mean simply what type of subjects we find in wisdom literature, but rather what aspirations hide behind the texts and what methodology is used to achieve them. It is these categories that differentiate between a scientist and a philosopher, between a

---

[2] For a more recent and comprehensive rebuttal of von Rad's analysis of the Joseph story see also Weeks (1994:92–109).

[3] A similar view of wisdom was expressed more recently by Weeks (1999).

preacher and a biblical scholar, i.e., among smaller segments of a broad intellectual tradition. In our attempt to understand what it is, if anything at all, that distinguishes books such as Proverbs and Qoheleth from the rest of the OT, and that unites them with each other, we need to look through the literature at the quest which produced it, a quest with aims and procedures.

In my opinion the distinction between the quest *per se* and the texts that represent it, i.e., the distinction between *wisdom* and *wisdom literature*, holds the key to the understanding of the relationship between the wisdom tradition and other traditions attested in the OT. The books such as Proverbs or Qoheleth are not the wisdom quest *per se*, they are merely its products, vehicles for communication of its concerns, questions and conclusions. As McKenzie (1967:2) noted,

> We study wisdom literature because that is all we can study; but we do not by this study learn what was the living tradition of wisdom.

The fact that writing and composing are only occasionally mentioned by the two books shows quite clearly that the wisdom undertaking does not revolve around literary forms. Yet, the view that the wisdom quest is in principle the exercise of producing these texts is not uncommon, and led in the past to treating Proverbs, in particular, as a scribal by-product. Such an attitude obscures the profound nature of the concerns that these texts represent.

Consequently, I will approach Proverbs and Qoheleth as deposits of a wider quest. As a starting point I will take Crenshaw's (1969:132) definition of the wisdom undertaking as 'the quest for self-understanding in terms of relationships with things, people, and the Creator'. This definition can be applied fully to both books, *self-understanding* being its key term. Wisdom, as we find it in Proverbs and Qoheleth, is not simply about making and stating observations, nor is it about formulating rules. It is about penetrating beyond that which is observed and comprehending it, and in particular, about understanding the place that a human being has in the world. This is reflected in the contemplative nature of these texts and their focus on the generalised rather than the specific. Here lies a fundamental difference between material such as Proverbs or Qoheleth on the one hand, and texts such as the Joseph narrative on the other. While many other OT texts may have an educational purpose, they do not combine the contemplative with the generalisation; narratives may lead to contemplation, but present specific cases, while legal and cultic materials typically present generalisations but, being principally prescriptive, lack the contemplative element driven by a desire for understanding.

While Crenshaw's definition of wisdom is fully applicable to our two books, it does not describe comprehensively what is happening in Proverbs and Qoheleth; it lacks at least two critical ingredients. First, it does not provide the answer to the question of the purpose of such a search. Neither in Proverbs, nor in Qoheleth, as we will see later, is self-understanding the ultimate goal; rather it is only a means to a more tangible end. Its purpose is to live; the wisdom of our sages is not simply about understanding who they were but also about making the most of that understanding, about getting the most out of life. I, therefore, wish to propose that a more adequate description of the wisdom of Proverbs and Qoheleth is *a quest for self-understanding in terms of relationships with things, people and the Creator, and for self-realisation in the context of these relationships*.

The second component lacking in Crenshaw's definition has to do with methodology. In our search to understand the material in front of us we need to go deeper than merely attempting to understand the aims that hide behind these books. It is not enough to know what the wisdom thinkers were broadly doing, we also need to understand *how* they carried out the quest for understanding, and our definition of the wisdom undertaking should reflect this. The *how*-question can be further separated into two narrower issues. The first of these concerns the epistemological perspective of the sages, the basic processes through which they obtained and evaluated their data, i.e., how they got to their self-understanding. This in itself is a complex matter which I will leave aside for the moment and return to in the next chapter. The second sub-question concerns the methods that the sages used to get from the raw knowledge, i.e., the self-understanding, to fulfilling their aim, i.e., the self-realisation, and it is this question that I will concentrate on now. However, before we take a closer look at the two books, one further issue needs to be addressed.

Two Modes of Human Thought

I would like to draw a distinction between two rather different modes of thought. The first mode is *exact*; to understand a phenomenon means to be able to describe fully the mechanics of it, to describe it *as it really is*. The search for understanding then is a search for complete comprehension. Such a concept of understanding is common in the exact sciences, but can be found outside of this arena, for instance in dogmatics. While to an educated twenty-first century reader this might seem the 'normal' mode of thought, it is one that is rarely applied by ordinary people to normal problems in the real world. Instead, most of the time we operate with a different mode of thought, one that I will call *practical*. Within the practical mode we settle for understanding that is only partial. There is a variety of reasons why we do that: sometimes simply because the imprecision we are ignoring may not be significant enough for the given purposes, or, a more complete understanding becomes too complex to be practically applicable, or the exact mode is too elusive. Sometimes we do this automatically without much thought, for instance when we use imprecise terms such as calling something 'red' or 'blue'. On other occasions we choose the practical mode very deliberately, for instance the equations used in engineering disciplines are almost always simplifications of the equations used by theoretical scientists. However, in both situations, if the imprecision of our approach was pointed to us by an external observer, we would not feel the need to revise our approach.

This brings us to the principal difference between the two modes, which is not in the fact that one is exact and the other is not, for the mere conviction that something is in a particular way does not guarantee it to be so; even in the exact sciences perspectives develop and come to be modified from time to time, sometimes radically. The key difference lies in the attitudes that accompany the two modes, in the fact that in the latter case the imprecision is at least tacitly acknowledged and considered acceptable, while in the former case imprecision is a fundamental flaw that has to be avoided and overcome when it is discovered. Thus, these two modes of understanding need to be evaluated differently, and the answer to the question whether the two books ahead of us approach the world in the former or the latter manner will fundamentally influence our view of them. Consequently, it is worthwhile to consider some of the basic characteristics that distinguish the latter approach from the former.

At the heart of practical knowledge is a paradigm. By a paradigm I mean a theoretical system which describes a behaviour of some other, real system, and is used to predict the state of the real system on the basis of some input data. However, the theoretical system, i.e., the paradigm, is always simpler than the real system. For example, the student of BH learns vowel patterns of different Hebrew stems and the endings of the verbal suffix conjugation. This allows her to create an appropriate suffix conjugation form when given the root, the stem, the person and the grammatical gender. While this paradigm may seem overwhelming to the student at first, it saves her memorising all possible forms of all possible roots for all the stems. As is obvious from this example, the simplification of a paradigm is achieved by exploiting patterns of behaviour exhibited by the real system.[4]

A second property of a paradigm is closely linked to the first one. A paradigm, because it is simpler than the real system, only produces results that are an approximation of the true state of the real system. For example, the basic paradigm for formulating the past tense of an English verb works well with most verbs, but there are some 300 cases where it produces incorrect results. The imprecision of a paradigm can be approached in two basic ways. The first option is for the exceptions to be listed, i.e., the student is made to memorise a list of the irregular English verbs. The second alternative is to look for ways of improving the paradigm to cover the exceptions. Thus, when, for example, the rules of vowel contraction are added to the basic paradigm for conjugating a Greek verb, it can be applied to contracted verbs, which otherwise would have to be treated as exceptions. While this second approach may seem to be the better solution by far, its shortcoming resides in the fact that as the complexity of the paradigm increases, its practical usability diminishes; the strength of a paradigm resides in its simplicity. In the real world a compromise will always be necessary between a paradigm's precision and complexity; a good English textbook will make use of the fact that within the group of irregular verbs there are subgroups formed along the same patterns, but will not try to overcomplicate the matter.

Yet, sometimes there are cases where one can neither improve the paradigm nor list the exceptions. Notably, this holds true for real systems that are not entirely deterministic. In such cases the users of the paradigm simply have to acknowledge that it does not always work to a complete satisfaction. As an example we can take a train timetable; the timetable does not guarantee that our train will arrive at the specified time, but hopefully, in some countries more than in others, it gives us

---

[4] That such a conjugation table is a paradigm and not the real system itself is clear from the fact that the native speaker is likely to be fluent in the language and entirely able to decline and conjugate long before he or she might even come across a grammar book. It is now commonly recognised that grammar is descriptive rather than prescriptive, i.e., grammar is a paradigm, a theoretical system attempting to describe the real system, i.e., language.

a reasonable prediction of what will happen. The key question with respect to a paradigm describing a non-deterministic system is how often it does produce satisfactory results. For such a paradigm to serve its purpose, the frequency and impact of its errors must be within certain limits. When the errors get outside of what the users for whom the paradigm was intended consider reasonable, the paradigm will fall out of use. In the previous sentence the clause *the users for whom the paradigm was intended* needs to be emphasised; the validity, and consequently, the value of a particular paradigm can only be apprised from the point of view of its intended purpose. This point is of great importance and we shall return to it shortly.

The imprecision of a paradigm and the way in which it is handled brings us to a further, and rather important characteristic of a paradigm: paradigms are formulated to serve a purpose, and are entirely subject to it. A typical paradigm has two aims, an immediate aim and a broader aim. The immediate aim concerns the modelling of the real system, the broader aim has to do with exploiting the knowledge of the behaviour of the real system. The real value of the paradigm resides not in it being able to serve the immediate aim, but precisely in it facilitating reaching the broader aim. A conjugation table will have as its immediate aim facilitation of conjugating and parsing a verb. While some linguists may find this to be an exciting exercise *per se*, it is not the ultimate reason why conjugation tables are created (although a first year BH student may think otherwise). The broader aim is to enable one to learn to use the language correctly and effectively. Here lies one of the principal differences between a practical paradigm and a scientific theory; the value of a scientific theory does not reside in its potential for immediate practical utilisation, but in the very fact that it provides understanding of a particular phenomenon.[5]

The intended purpose of a paradigm is closely related to another aspect of the nature of paradigms, one which stems directly from the fact these are simplifications: an individual paradigm is meant to be used under a specific, and sometimes rather limited, set of circumstances. It is quite common to have several different paradigms describing the same real system and serving the same purpose but intended to be used in different situations. Thus, a typical grammar of biblical

---

[5] True, science can often be driven by utilitarian forces, but these tend to hinder rather than encourage the scientific enterprise and are external to it.

Hebrew will present a number of distinct paradigms for conjugating verbs, each of which applies to only a limited group of verbal roots. If the conditions under which a paradigm is meant to be used are not satisfied, it will produce an incorrect result. Yet, this has nothing to do with the quality of the paradigm, and cannot be used to disregard the paradigm as flawed.

In addition to these basic characteristics of a paradigm, one further issue needs to be considered: a question of *reversibility*. Some paradigms are reversible, i.e., from a state of the real system it is possible, using the paradigm, to derive the input conditions that led to such a state. The way present participles are formed in English can serve as an example of such a paradigm. When one encounters an English word ending in *-ing* it can be surmised with a significant degree of certainty that it is a present participle and the present stem can be found by removing the ending. On the other hand, the paradigm for forming the regular plural of an English noun is not reversible. When one is presented with a form that ends in *-s*, it is not possible to determine without additional information whether it is a plural form of a noun, a third person singular verb in the present tense, or whether the *-s* is a part of the stem itself. In general, real systems where distinct inputs can produce identical outputs and systems that are not entirely deterministic will be described by paradigms that are not reversible.

The discussion of the differences between exact and practical approaches to knowledge and the basic characteristics of paradigms was lengthy, but hopefully the reader will come to appreciate shortly that being aware of these is rather important for the task at hand. In conclusion of this discussion, the nature of paradigms can be summarised as follows: a paradigm is a simplification or reality with a two-fold purpose, carrying with it a systematic error, which, however, is considered insignificant for the particular purpose; a paradigm is intended for specific users and is to be applied under specific conditions; the primary function of a paradigm is to predict the real system, and only some paradigms can be used in the reverse direction.

Having explained what I mean by practical, or paradigmatic, understanding, I can now return to our two texts. It should be obvious, that our understanding of what is happening behind the scenes of theses books, and indeed our judgement about their value will be significantly different if we see them as an expression of a quest for exact type of knowledge, or merely practical understanding. Thus, before we go any further in our analysis of these texts, we have to answer the question whether the enterprise reflected in them is, or is not, paradigmatic in the sense outlined above. It is, if it satisfies the following two conditions: (1) it is understood by the respective books that the depiction of the world they offer is incomplete but the possible error is considered of only limited significance under the specific circumstances; (2) the two books offer understanding with a practical end in mind and the value of this understanding is in its practical application. To answer the question postulated here, we will now take a closer look at the key characteristics of the perspectives found in the two books.

An Outline of the Proverbial Perspective

The Basic Structure of the Proverbial Worldview

The overall framework of the proverbial perspective reflects the three distinct elements contained in Crenshaw's definition of wisdom: the relationships with things, people and the Creator. Yet, these are not addressed in equal proportions. Relatively little attention is given to the understanding of the relationships with things, and the examination of the relationship with God is also fairly limited and largely implicit. Instead, the proverbial emphasis lies quite heavily on understanding the principles on which relationships between people are based.

At the heart of the proverbial perspective is a world polarised into two camps. This polarisation is all inclusive, there are no other types of people, or more precisely, as will become clear in a moment, of responsible adults. One camp is perceived as positive, the other as negative. I will refer to the positive as *the wise* and to the negative as *the fools*. In reality, the terminology is more complex and a number of distinct expressions are associated with both groups. The following paragraphs will take a brief look at the most important of these in order to delimit the two groups more clearly. However, before I do so, a more general comment on the nature of wisdom vocabulary is needed.

Even a brief glance at the book of Proverbs, and OT wisdom texts in general, reveals that the wisdom tradition uses certain characteristic vocabulary. We can distinguish two groups of lexemes in particular: words that are exclusive to Proverbs/OT wisdom literature, and words attested elsewhere, but used with an increased frequency in Proverbs/OT wisdom.[6] While these two groups deserve special atten-

---

[6] By 'OT wisdom literature' I mean here the three OT books available in Hebrew

tion, we need to resist the temptation to automatically label either of these vocabulary sets as *technical*. The fact that a lexeme is exclusive to the traditional OT wisdom corpus does not necessarily mean that it was not used in other contexts, only that it is *not attested* so in our body of texts, which is relatively small and specialised; this factor should be taken into consideration before we identify such unique words or phrases as *technical*.[7] Similarly, a high frequency of a lexeme in the wisdom corpus does not mean that it belongs to the technical vocabulary of wisdom, or that occurrences of such a word outside of this corpus indicate wisdom influence.[8] A distinction is necessary between what is *typical* vocabulary, and what is *technical* vocabulary in the proper sense, i.e., vocabulary used with a sufficiently distinct, or refined, sense from

---

broadly agreed to be wisdom literature, i.e., Proverbs, Qoheleth and Job, and the so-called wisdom psalms.

[7] The assumption that *exclusive* to our body of texts equals *technical* is in the background of the argument about the *Sitz im Leben* of Proverbs by Shupak (1987). Having identified 14 expressions that are exclusive to the wisdom corpus, she attempts to ascertain their equivalents in Egyptian instructions and school texts, and argues that these indicate that both the Egyptian material and the biblical wisdom texts have the same *Sitz im Leben*. Yet, it is questionable whether many of these expressions should be considered technical. For instance, since the adjective חֲסַר is not exclusive to wisdom and לֵב is the ordinary word for *mind*, it is conceivable that the expression חֲסַר לֵב could have been a common one. Similarly, since חֵמָה is regularly used in the sense *anger* and אִישׁ is commonly used in 'converting' nouns into adjectives (WOC 9.5.3b), the assumption that the phrase אִישׁ חֵמָה is a technical wisdom expression is dubious; the vivid imagery of both קַר רוּחַ and קְצַר רוּחַ is easily conceivable and could hardly have been limited to the wisdom circles; the references to *beating* and *rod*, are more likely alluding to the upbringing of children in general rather than indicate a school setting. In a later study (1993) Shupak becomes more cautious about pinpointing *Sitz im Leben* on the grounds of similarities with Egyptian material, and she identifies only eight biblical expressions related to Egyptian literature. Four of these are in her view adapted to Hebrew style and usage and four are direct translations. The value of the former category is in my view doubtful, since one has to question whether the signs of adaptation are not signs of independence. Of the latter category אִישׁ חֵמָה and קַר רוּחַ were already addressed. The third expression is תֹּכֵן לִבּוֹת, which Shupak believes is an epithet for God. Yet, in Prov 21:2 this is not an epithet, but predicate + object, and further, this phrase is not fixed, for in Prov 16:2 we find רוּחוֹת instead of לִבּוֹת. Considering that the verb תכן is used with reference to moral judgement elsewhere in the OT [1 Sam 2:3; Ezek 18:25, 29; 33:17, 20], it appears unlikely that this particular construction is necessarily of an Egyptian origin. This leaves only one of the terms, תַּחְבֻּלוֹת, as a feasible Egyptian import, and so the overall evidence for an extensive Egyptian influence on the tradition's terminology is weak.

[8] A similar view is expressed by Whybray (1974:75) and more recently by Weeks (1994:90).

that found in non-wisdom texts. Only a limited number of words found in Proverbs are truly technical.[9]

The lexemes used to define the polarity wise/fools can be divided broadly into two groups: those with primary reference to abilities or skill, such as חָכָם or כְּסִיל, and those with mainly ethical connotations, such as צַדִּיק and רָשָׁע. As will be noted below, the two types of words are used differently in the book, but this should not obscure the fact that the referent of the corresponding words from either group is the same, i.e., חָכָם and צַדִּיק have the same type of a person in mind, and similarly, כְּסִיל and רָשָׁע have an identical referent. This is most clearly seen where these terms, or their synonyms, are found in parallelism [e.g. Prov 9:9; 11:30; 13:9; 23:24].

The derivatives of the root חכם, of which the adjective/noun חָכָם is the most common representative, feature prominently in the depiction of the bi-polar world. The meaning of חָכָם, as used in the OT outside of the wisdom books, can be broadly placed into two categories. First, in the more general sense, it denotes that a person possesses a certain skill, most often a cognitive one, but not exclusively [e.g. Exod 31:6]. This meaning is ethically neutral. It denotes a proficiency, which can be put to both good and bad use, although the former is more common.[10] The ethically-positive English *wise* is a somewhat limping equivalent; the range of meanings of the Hebrew word is broader.

Second, the plural form חֲכָמִים is used on a number of occasions with reference to the royal advisors, both at Israelite and foreign courts. The view that these wise men should be identified with a professional group, namely the palace advisors, was most extensively advocated by McKane (1965). With Whybray (1974), I have reservations about McKane's argument at a number of points, which leave the whole case untenable.[11] At the same time, Whybray's (1974:15–31) argument

---

[9] The book of Proverbs, and the Wisdom literature in general, are preoccupied with the cognitive. Consequently, there is a great concentration of words describing this side of human/divine nature. Yet, many of these expressions appear throughout the Hebrew bible with the same meaning and without any wisdom connotations. For a complete survey of the distribution in the OT of the vocabulary common in wisdom texts see Whybray (1974:75–154). Whybray shows that most of the common wisdom expressions cannot be considered technical in any real sense; unfortunately he fails to notice the distinct use of some vocabulary in Proverbs (see the following discussion of חָכָם and פֶּתִי).

[10] See 2 Sam 13:3ff. for an example where wisdom is clearly void of any positive ethical connotations.

[11] McKane depends heavily on the assertion that 2 Sam 16:23 implies that prophecy

for there not being any professional use of the word חָכָם in the OT is not convincing either. While not all the passages where the technical use is commonly assumed need to be understood so, on some occasions a major degree of exegetical ingenuity is necessary to make the text to conform Whybray's thesis.[12] My own view is that there are places where the term חֲכָמִים is used in a professional sense [e.g. Jer 18:18], but that this use needs to be identified cautiously. The key question concerning the references to the royal advisors is that of precedence; are these men called wise because they are the king's advisors, or are they the king's advisors because they are wise? In other words, is it a title derived from the position, or is their position a result of their ability expressed by the title? The answer to this question can only by obtained from the wisdom tradition itself, for it is there where the self-identity of the wise is expressed.

In the book of Proverbs we find a similar twofold distribution of the meaning of the root חכם. Most occurrences are of the first type, referring to skill. However, closer examination of the semantics shows that the actual sense has been significantly narrowed, so that it is possible to speak of a technical usage. It should be noted that most occurrences of the word in the book are in context describing what a חָכָם does, i.e., the thrust of the book is to define what it means to be wise. The adjective then does not designate a person with just any skill, but someone who lives according to the principles expressed in the book, and has an understanding of the consequences of human actions that agree with the book's perspective [e.g. Prov 10:14; 13:20; 14:3, 16; 15:31–32]. Wisdom in Proverbs is not so much about intellectual knowledge or abilities, but rather, it is a *commitment* to a way of life,

---

and wisdom were two parallel and competing systems of guidance in Israel during the early monarchy (pp. 55–58). He, however, fails to notice that the statement of 2 Sam 16:23 refers exclusively to Ahithopel, but clearly not to Hushai. Consequently, this is not a statement about the office or profession, but about the exquisite abilities of an individual. The assertion that the same dualism is also to be seen in 2 Sam 14:17, 19; 19:27 is equally unconvincing. Further, McKane's claim that עֵצָה is a technical word of the secular wisdom was convincingly refuted by Whybray (1974:132–33), who pointed out that this claim requires that the wise would be *a priori* identified as the palace politicians, thus begging the question. In many of the passages interpreted by McKane as an apologetic against wisdom, the vocabulary is more likely to be due to the topic of the discourse, with the polemic aimed more generally than at a specific and narrow class of palace professionals.

[12] A prime example is Whybray's seven-page discussion of Jer 18:18 which reaches the conclusion that the verse is a pejorative numerical saying concerned with excessive talking (pp. 24–31).

one which is often depicted by the metaphor of walking along a path [e.g. Prov 4:10–19; 15:10; 23:19]. This metaphor captures an important characteristic of proverbial wisdom; for the proverbial sages being wise is not merely a present static state, but it is a continual dynamic process. Thus, even though one can be designated as wise, such a person is always in the process of becoming wise, heading up the path of wisdom. In other words, the person who is referred to as חָכָם in the proverbial sense has a desire and striving for improvement and perfection [e.g. Prov 1:5; 9:8–9; 12:15; 25:12]. The 'path of wisdom' from which the proverbial חָכָם does not deviate is rather narrow, but I will leave the detailed discussion of its limits for chapter 6.[13]

Alongside this basic sense of חָכָם, the plural form חֲכָמִים is quite clearly used in a still narrower sense in Prov 1:6. Here the surrounding vocabulary shows that it designates people involved with the literary forms found in the book, quite clearly those who formulate and pass on the principles that constitute wisdom. That this sense of חֲכָמִים is not the same here as the basic one outlined above is indicated by the fact that the book in its quest to impart wisdom, i.e., to form a חָכָם, does not directly encourage the literary activity which is explicitly associated with the חֲכָמִים. The basic distinction between these two uses is that the former one is adjectival/descriptive, the latter is nominal. This distinction is better carried over into English if חָכָם in the broader sense is rendered as *a wise person* while חֲכָמִים in the narrower sense as *the sages*. There are two other places where this usage is, in my view, attested in the book [Prov 24:23; Prov 22:17[14]], although on other occasions it is also possible [e.g. Prov 15:12].

---

[13] For further treatment of the path metaphor see Habel (1972), and, in particular, Van Leeuwen's (1990) discussion of the already-not-yet dimension of Proverbial wisdom and the liminality of Proverbial worldview.

[14] In Prov 22:17 𝔐 reads הַט אָזְנְךָ וּשְׁמַע דִּבְרֵי חֲכָמִים while 𝔊 has Λόγοις σοφῶν παράβαλλε σὸν οὖς καὶ ἄκουε ἐμὸν λόγον. I am inclined to think that the Hebrew text originally read דִּבְרֵי חֲכָמִים הַט אָזְנְךָ וּשְׁמַע דְּבָרַי and once דִּבְרֵי חֲכָמִים became displaced, דְּבָרַי was omitted. Since it is quite clear that a new collection of material starts at this point (note the change in form after the introduction of vv. 17–21), it is likely that *words of wise* was originally its title. Whybray (1974:48–54) objects to interpreting the occurrences of חֲכָמִים in the superscriptions as references to a class of professionals. His argument is that if Prov 22:17 is in fact a transposed superscription, then it is a prosaic text, and we would expect an article with the noun. From the lack of the article Whybray infers that the phrase should be rendered *words of clever ones*. The same rendering is then by analogy applied to Prov 1:6 and 24:23. Yet, if in case of Prov 22:17 we are dealing with a textual corruption, we have to allow for the possibility that the article dropped out when the superscription was transposed into the poetry. In addition, it is likely that the

There is no direct additional indication in the book who these sages were. Yet, one of the central notions in Proverbs is that wisdom is available to all who show interest, and the content of the book is almost generally applicable, with no exclusive focus on any social class or otherwise defined group. While there is some indication of association of wisdom with the court, this is insufficient to fully identify the wise with the court advisors.[15] In the absence of an attempt by the sages to clearly identify themselves as anything other than the wise, it is necessary to conclude that this is their primary identity; they represent a certain intellectual movement, the concerns of which were with broad understanding of humanity, not just with politics. However, my use of *intellectual movement* differs from that of Whybray's (1974:57ff) *intellectual tradition*, in that I am convinced that while the wise cannot be identified exclusively with any other group found in the OT (e.g. palace politicians), they still represent a clearly defined entity of their own, and more importantly, they thought of themselves as a clearly distinct group, albeit not necessarily formally organised. This seems to be quite clear from the proverbial superscriptions that I have already mentioned, and the comments about the person of Qoheleth and the work of other sages that we find in the epilogue of the latter book [Qoh 12:10–11].

---

perceived lack of article is more a case of English than Hebrew usage. The plural form of the adjective could have been perceived in certain contexts by the native speakers as intrinsically definite (WOC 13.4a). Since the general contrast *definite- indefinite* in Hebrew is that of identity vs. class (WOC 13.2b), the lack of the article does not mean that the expression cannot designate a specific group. After all, the translation suggested by Whybray (*clever ones*) also denotes a specific group—the distinction of this rendering is not so much in the absence of the article, but in different semantic understanding of the word, and I have pointed out earlier that חָכָם in Proverbs does not simply mean *clever, intellectually capable.*

[15] I am inclined to give some historical currency to the statement about Hezekiah's court in Prov 25:1, as I am not aware of any more satisfactory explanation for its presence. The proposal that the reference to Hezekiah is to give more weight to the text by calling upon the authority of a legendary wise man and a patron of wisdom (Weeks, 1994:41–46) suffers from the lack of Hezekiah's reputation for wisdom in the surviving tradition and, more critically, from the fact that the collection is not actually ascribed to Hezekiah himself, but to some anonymous men at his court. Similarly, the textual evidence for the claim that the reference is due to intertextual links between the collection and the record of Hezekiah's reign in 2 Kgs (Carasik, 1994) is insufficient. This argument hinges on two roots, שׂכל and בטח, of which the former does not appear at all in Prov 25–29, and both of which are more frequently associated with David than Hezekiah. The whole superscription is construed in such a way that Hezekiah's name does not have in it any other than temporal value, indicating that even if its historical value cannot be taken for granted, in the circles that preserved the book its contents were associated with the royal court.

The second most important word associated with the wise is the already mentioned צַדִּיק. In contrast to the previously discussed term חָכָם, most of the occurrences צַדִּיק in the book are in contexts that depict what happens to a person. In other words, the book is not attempting to define what it means to be צַדִּיק, the word being used in Proverbs with the same basic sense it has elsewhere in the OT.[16] Its meaning needs to be seen against the background of life in a community; צַדִּיק is a person who shows integrity in dealing with others and who works for the well-being of the community. Such a person shows also integrity in the relationship with the deity, but Stigers may go too far when suggesting that צַדִּיק is 'the man who ... tries to preserve the peace and prosperity of the community *by fulfilling the commands of God* in regard to others' (TWOT, p. 1879, italics mine). Being צַדִּיק is not so much about fulfilment of religious obligations, but about personal identification with what is right, an identification which the community knows it can rely on.

While this is the principal meaning of the word in the book, there is a number of proverbs that address what we might want to call the legal process, i.e., situations in which a third party is required to adjudicate a conflict between some other parties. In such sayings the word צַדִּיק is used with a much narrower scope, its reference being limited to the rightness of a party in the particular conflict. This forensic use is best translated to English as *innocent* [Prov 17:15; 18:5; 24:24].[17]

The examination of the lexica used in the book to refer to the fools possibly casts even more light on the nature of the polarity of the proverbial world than the terms that designate the wise. The basic word for a fool in Proverbs is כְּסִיל. It should be observed that just as being wise is not about intellectual abilities, similarly being a כְּסִיל is not to do with lack of capabilities. Rather, the state of folly is one entered of one's own volition. This is not to say that there is no intellectual dimension to being a fool, for the כְּסִיל is intellectually lazy, showing disdain for knowledge [Prov 1:22]. Further, he lacks the genuine desire of the wise people to move on, to improve, and instead is complacent [Prov 1:32].

---

[16] It is perhaps worth noting that there are more occurrences of צַדִּיק in the book than there are of חָכָם. Yet, the mentioned pattern of usage is in harmony with the perception that most readers will gain from the book, namely, that wisdom, rather than righteousness, is its principal topic.

[17] There a few additional terms used to refer to the wise largely synonymous with the two main words discussed. Among those belong נָבוֹן, a parallel to חָכָם, and יָשָׁר parallel to צַדִּיק.

This complacency manifests itself in a number of different ways. The כְּסִיל lives merely for the present [Prov 21:21]. He is stubborn and unteachable, his intellectual life being entirely self-centred, he will not seek advice of others [Prov 18:2] and refuses to accept any correction [Prov 17:10]. At the same time, his trust in his own abilities knows no limits [Prov 28:26], to the extent that he is unable to learn even from personal experience [Prov 26:11]. Instead of having sensible aspirations and being prepared to work hard to achieve them, the כְּסִיל is an unrealistic and unfocused dreamer [Prov 17:24].

Yet, the fool is not simply living in a way that the proverbial sages do not consider sensible, but the term is ethically coloured in Proverbs. כְּסִיל is bent on evil [Prov 10:18; 13:19] from which he derives pleasure [Prov 10:23]. He has no self-control whatsoever [Prov 29:11], and shows a tendency to initiate conflicts [Prov 18:6]. He even lacks respect for his closest relations [Prov 15:20].

A second frequent designation of the fool is לֵיץ, usually translated as *mocker*. This word underlines a subset of the characteristics of the fool that we have already seen with the word כְּסִיל. The basic traits of לֵיץ are pride and insolence [Prov 21:24] demonstrated in his refusal to admit a fault and accept correction [Prov 9:8; 13:1; 14:9; 15:12]. Since those who try to correct him receive hostile treatment, without their correction being heeded, the sages are of the view that any effort made to rebuke a mocker is wasted. In the light of what has been said so far, it comes as a no surprise that the mocker is seen as a perpetual source of conflicts in the community [Prov 22:10].

One additional word from the other terms used to refer to the fool by the proverbial sages that is worth of mentioning is עָצֵל. This is a person who is lazy, a sluggard [Prov 6:9–11; 26:14] who has all sorts of ridiculous excuses to avoid work [Prov 22:13; 26:13]. Alongside כְּסִיל and לֵיץ, עָצֵל also portrayed as one who considers himself smarter than anyone else [Prov 26:16], and his behaviour is sometimes described with a healthy dose of irony [Prov 26:15]. It should be noted that laziness is not seen merely as an attitude that is self-destructive, but ultimately also as one that is detrimental to others [e.g. Prov 10:26].

The three words discussed so far, כְּסִיל, לֵיץ, and עָצֵל, stand roughly in antithesis to חָכָם, and are ultimately used to define what it means to be wise through negation. They all point primarily to a flawed understanding of, or a blatant disregard for, the way the world is (or more precisely, the way the proverbial sages believed it to be). However, when antithesis is to be created with the ethically loaded צַדִּיק, the book uses the term רָשָׁע, or sometimes the impersonal רֶשַׁע, *wickedness*, which is typically employed with indirect personal reference [e.g. Prov 10:2]. Overall, the root רשע, with almost 80 occurrences, is the most common one in the book, and the adjective רָשָׁע is the most common personal attribute used by the sages. Similarly to the use of צַדִּיק, the book does not generally attempt to define the meaning of the word, with about three quarters of the occurrences found in statements depicting what happens to such a person.

From those statements that are descriptive, it can be surmised that רָשָׁע has certain clear affinities with the other terms used to designate the fool already discussed. For instance, such a person does not accept correction [Prov 9:7], is self-confident [Prov 21:29] and his views are of little value [Prov 10:20]. However, the main connotation of the word is that of evilness. The speech of רָשָׁע is perverse and destructive [Prov 10:32; 11:11; 12:6; 15:28]. Such a person is deceptive [Prov 11:18; 12:5], cruel and merciless [Prov 12:10; 21:10], and does not hesitate to pervert the course of justice to achieve his own ends [Prov 17:23]. Further, not only רָשָׁע adheres to no ethical standards himself, but he also dislikes people who show integrity [Prov 29:27]. His attitudes toward others ultimately project themselves back into his own life, and he suffers from paranoia in fear for his own safety [Prov 28:1]. It can be observed that רָשָׁע is not necessarily a person who does not engage in formal worship, but on the account of his unethical behaviour, the proverbial sages believe that his religious practice is of no value [Prov 15:8–9]. Finally, it should be noted that just as it was the case with the antithetical צַדִּיק, רָשָׁע can be used in a legal context, with a much narrower forensic sense *guilty* [Prov 17:15; 24:24].

As we look at the vocabulary employed to describe the bi-polarity of the proverbial world, a pattern emerges. The words without primary ethical connotations such as חָכָם or כְּסִיל are used mainly in statements which describe human activity, while the words of chiefly ethical significance, i.e., צַדִּיק and רָשָׁע are used largely in statements that describe the consequences of human behaviour. This pattern is more significant than the initial impression might be. It is well known that the force of the proverbial admonition rests on association between certain actions and their consequences,[18] yet, it follows from the observations made that the two groups of lexemes play a different role in the this associ-

---

[18] The nature of this association will be discussed in some detail in chapter 4.

ation, the one being linked to the behaviour and the other to its consequences. Thus, the authority of the book rests largely on the ethical
vocabulary, since it is mainly the ethical lexemes that are linked with
the consequences of human behaviour, in turn used to motivate the
reader to accept the sages' teaching.[19]

The bipolarity wise/fools lies at the heart of the proverbial perspective, but in itself is not sufficient to outline it. As will be discussed in
chapter 4, this bipolarity is not just a convenient and simple way of
describing the human society, but rather the sages believed it had been
engraved deep into the fabric of the entire world, by divine design.
They had an unshakable conviction that the God who created this
world, and has a complete control over it, unequivocally favours the
wise and righteous just as much as he detests the fools and evil people
[e.g. Prov 3:33; 10:3; 15:29]. As a result of the role that God plays, the
world of the proverbial sages is regular and predictable and those who
follow the path of wisdom will succeed in it and prosper.

The Aims of Proverbs and the Working Parameters of Proverbial Wisdom

Having considered the basic structure of the proverbial worldview, I
will now turn in greater detail to the question of what end the sages
pursued. In order to understand the aim of the book of Proverbs, we
first need to deal with another lexical term which does not fit into the
otherwise strictly bipolar classification of people as wise or fools, the
פֶּתִי. This word occurs only twice in the OT outside of the wisdom texts
with the basic sense of one who is simple, naïve, not entirely responsible
for his or her actions.[20] In wisdom material the sense is more narrowly
defined. The פֶּתִי is an individual who is immature in the sense that he
is untrained in wisdom.[21] Such an individual has a double identity in
Proverbs. He is not a fool *per se*, yet, has a natural inclination toward
foolish behaviour and is easy to trick because he lacks experience [Prov
14:15; 22:3; 27:12]. Thus, he is sometimes listed alongside the fools [Prov

---

[19] It has been suggested in the past that the two groups of words come from
distinct traditions, the former from an older, secular wisdom, the latter from a later
theological/Yahwistic reworking of the originally secular tradition (McKane, 1970:10–
22). I will return to this issue in chapter 6, where we will be in a better position to
evaluate this view (p. 176).

[20] The non-wisdom occurrences are Ezek 45:20; Ps 116:6. Note the parallel with אִישׁ
שֹׁגֶה in Ezek 45:20.

[21] Outside of Proverbs it is found in the wisdom psalms 19:7 and 119:130, in both
cases of someone being educated (חכם used in the former case, בין in the latter).

1:20–33; 14:18]. However, this natural leaning can be overcome through learning and discipline; he has the potential to become wise, and so is sometimes found alongside this other group [Prov 1:2–6; 19:25].

The possibility of moulding the פֶּתִי into a wise person is what principally distinguishes him from those who are classed as fools. This can be seen well in the following passages:

> Who is correcting a mocker receives an insult and who rebukes the wicked comes to harm. Do not rebuke a mocker, so that he does not hate you, rebuke a wise person and he will love you. [Prov 9:7–8]

> [If] you beat the mocker then the immature becomes prudent, but rebuke a learned person, and he gains [even more] knowledge. [Prov 19:25]

Rebuking a fool, in this case designated as a mocker, is a pointless exercise, for the fool is incorrigible, and the former of the two texts advises against it in no uncertain terms. Instead it encourages to invest such an effort into those who are wise, and will gratefully accept correction and learn from it. The latter text takes a very similar attitude, excepts it acknowledges that a public rebuke of a mocker can serve as a deterrent for the פֶּתִי, who will learn from it.

The fool is unlikely to be reformed not because he is less capable than the פֶּתִי, but because, in contrast to the פֶּתִי, he has already decided that he does not want to pursue wisdom. The transformation of a פֶּתִי into a fool is captured in the following passage:

> Until when will [you] immature love immaturity? (But[22] scorners revel in laziness, and fools will always hate knowledge.) Should[23] you turn to my rebuke, see, I would pour out to you my spirit, I would reveal to you my words. Since I called and you refused [to listen], since I stretched my hand, and no-one was paying any attention, since you neglected all my advice and did not wish to accept my rebuke, I also will laugh at your disaster, and will mock [you] when your calamity comes—when your calamity comes like a storm (and your disaster will come upon you as a hurricane!), when distress and agony come upon you.

> Then they will call me, and I will not answer; they will seek me—they will not find me. This is because they hated knowledge, and did not

---

[22] The shift to 3rd person shows that the sluggards and fools are not addressed by Wisdom, and requires disjunctive rendering of the conjunction ו. The B and C colons are best understood as an independent proverb used as a parenthetical comment (cf. Emerton, 1968).

[23] Px best understood in modal sense, cf. McKane (1970:274) who treats the verse as a conditional clause without a conditional particle.

choose the fear of Yahweh. They did not wish to accept my advice, and rejected all my rebukes, and [so] they will eat from the fruit of their ways, and they will be sated from their own cleverness.[24] For the apostasy of the immature will kill them, and the carelessness of the fools will destroy them. But who obeys me, will dwell securely, and sleep without a nightmare. [Prov 1:22–33]

Wisdom is here addressing a group of פְּתָיִם who are about to become fools. In v. 22a Wisdom speaks directly to the immature; in contrast to that, the fools are only mentioned indirectly in the third person. The second person address in v. 23ff. is also directed at the simple, since the categorical statement of v. 22c about the fools' persistent attitude to knowledge indicates that the glimmer of hope contained in v. 23 can only refer to the פְּתָיִם.

The climactic point in the story is the arrival of the disaster. In the pre-disaster section [vv. 22–28] there is some hope for the simple which, in spite of the fact that they appear to be nearing the critical point rapidly, makes it worthwhile for Wisdom to address them. With the arrival of the disaster the situation changes dramatically. The פְּתָיִם must now bear the consequences of their folly, they are no more spoken to in the second person, but only spoken of in the third person just as the fools were earlier on; they are now considered fools.

The critical failure of the פְּתָיִם is their מְשׁוּבָה [v. 32]. This rare word in the OT[25] is found parallel to רָעָה [Jer 2:19] and פֶּשַׁע [Jer 5:6], but it is not synonymous with them. The basic sense of מְשׁוּבָה is relational, it has to do with abandoning a person. Elsewhere in the OT God is the person walked out on, but it is clear from the use of this word in the marriage metaphor of Jer 3:6ff. that on its own מְשׁוּבָה does not have an exclusively religious frame of reference. In our passage it refers to the פְּתָיִם abandoning the speaking Wisdom. By the act of מְשׁוּבָה the simple become fools, and when they try to get hold of Wisdom later on, she has turned to a new audience for which the once פְּתָיִם, now suffering fools, become a deterring example. Thus, we can see in this passage both a distinction between the פְּתִי and the fool, but at the same time

---

[24] מוֹעֵצָה is mostly used in negative contexts, but the noun itself can have positive connotations [cf. Prov 22:20].

[25] In 𝔐 found in Hos 11:7; 14:5; Jer 2:19; 3:6, 8, 11, 22; 5:6, 8; 14:7; Prov 1:32. In the Vorlage of 𝔊 possibly also in Ezek 37:23. It was further proposed for Prov 12:28 in place of 𝔐 נְתִיבָה (e.g. KBL-2), but this cannot be easily accounted for as a scribal error, whether audible or visual.

a very close natural affinity of the two groups; it takes no effort for the
פֶּתִי to become a fool.[26]

What then is the aim of Proverbs? The book's explicit intention is
to make a wise person out of the immature [Prov 1:2–6]. The פֶּתִי
is an uncommitted youth [e.g. Prov 7:7], who has reached a point of
adulthood where he has to assume responsibility for his life, and it is
this character to whom the sages' turn as their primary audience [Prov
1:4,[27] 22; 8:5; 9:4]. This young man finds himself in the world divided
among the wise and the fools, where both try to 'recruit' him for their
side. The first nine chapters of the book are essentially a polemic of
the wise which is meant to convince the פֶּתִי that wisdom is the only
way forward and that he can only ignore it at his own peril. To achieve
this, various witnesses are brought in to testify to the benefits of wisdom
and the shortcomings of folly: the father, the grandfather,[28] and even
Wisdom herself. All of them paint vividly the serious consequences of
following one or the other; it is made clear to the reader that the choice
between wisdom and folly is a choice between life and death.

Yet, as I have pointed out previously, wisdom in Proverbs is not so
much about knowing as about a commitment to a way of life, i.e., about
doing through knowing. The following verse can serve as an illustration
of this point:

> A prudent person sees trouble and takes cover, but the simple walk on
> and get punished. [Prov 22:3]

It is not the seeing that distinguishes between the prudent and the
simple, it is the action that follows; the proverbial wisdom is supposed
to enable one to live and prosper. Thus, on a different level, the aim of

---

[26] It should perhaps be mentioned that the proverbial sages do not think it impossible for a fool to abandon his ways and to embark on the way of wisdom [Prov 8:5], they merely hold little hope that he will decide to do so.

[27] Note how in Prov 1:2–6 the purpose of the book is denoted by the repeated construction לְ + infc. Verse 5, in light of its deviation from this pattern, should be understood as a parenthetical comment—the book is for the simple, but even those already wise can learn from it.

[28] Prov 4:4ff. Note how the previously singular vocative *my son* changes into pl. *sons* in Prov 4:1 and back to sg. in Prov 4:4. This is a rhetorical device which is intended to distinguish the voice of the father from that of the grandfather's address to the father. This understanding is further supported by the fact that the next occurrence of בָּנִים [Prov 5:7] is directly preceded by וְעַתָּה indicating the present flow of the discourse is being interrupted; since the topic remains the same, change of speaker is the best explanation for the interruption (cf. Delitzsch, 1982a:105)

the book is not merely to impart wisdom, but through wisdom to foster success in life.

From our discussion so far, we can see that there is a twofold aim behind the proverbial wisdom. On the immediate plain the book wishes to impart knowledge about the world and to make the simple people into wise. Yet, behind this immediate aspiration lies a more tangible end, the desire to succeed and to be happy. It is further true that in Proverbs the tangible benefits of being wise provide the main source of motivation to follow the path of wisdom, and therefore, the value of wisdom hinges significantly on its usefulness in achieving the broader aim. In this respect, therefore, proverbial wisdom fits into the practical, paradigm-centred way of thinking outlined earlier in this chapter.

Admittedly, this depiction of the proverbial wisdom is somewhat simplified. In reality the value of wisdom does not rest solely on the practical benefits that it is supposed to provide. The situation is complicated by the relationship between wisdom and God, which will be discussed in chapter 4; while the material aspects of success are very pronounced in the book (most comprehensive picture being painted in the poem about the woman of valour in Prov 31:10–31), hoarding wealth is not construed as the sole purpose of life [e.g. Prov 23:4], nor is material prosperity an aim with the highest priority, as will be seen in chapter 5. I am inclined to think that the pronounced material emphasis found on the surface of the book is largely due to the intended audience, the פֶּתִי. The immature youth of the days past is unlikely to have been much different from the young person of the present, who is rarely interested in abstract arguments about the value of knowledge and education, but rather asks about tangible benefits that the required effort will lead to. In response to this the sages sought to present their view of the world in a manner that such a youth would find attractive. In other words, they built a paradigm that could be considered useful by the intended audience. By declaring the פֶּתִי as the intended addressee, the book defines for itself a context within which its perspective is to be understood, namely, it should be seen as an introduction to wisdom for this youth, as an elementary paradigm, not as an attempt to deal exhaustively with the enigmas of life.[29]

---

[29] That Proverbs is essentially a beginner's primer of wisdom has long been observed. Jerome, for instance, stated: 'Solomon wrote his three books, Proverbs, Ecclesiastes and the Canticle, in order to instruct mankind in the three stages of the spiritual life. Proverbs taught men how to live virtuously in the world and was meant for begin-

In conclusion of the present examination of the basic aims of the book of Proverbs it is possible to say that the proverbial approach to reality satisfies the second criterion which we set for identifying the paradigmatic mode of thought, namely, there is a two fold aim behind the proverbial framework, one of imparting knowledge and succeeding through such knowledge, and the value of proverbial wisdom is derived from its ability to fulfil the broader, practical objective of successful life. This would suggest that indeed the proverbial approach is paradigmatic, but we still need to consider whether it satisfies the other criterion set forward earlier, namely, whether the proverbial depiction of the world is understood by the sages themselves to be simplified but adequate for their own purposes.

How Complete is the Proverbial Picture?

When one first reads through the proverbial material, the world which emerges is very black and white: the wise prosper and the fools come to destruction, over and over again. Is this the whole picture, or are there indications in the book that the sages were aware that such an understanding is subject to exceptions? A closer reading shows that indeed some exceptions are at least implied, if not explicitly stated. Consider the following proverb:

> A poor person who walks in his integrity is better than one with twisted lips and who is a fool.[30] [Prov 19:1]

There are two types of people depicted here; the one is explicitly described as poor and honest, the other as deceitful and foolish. However, the antithetical parallelism implies further characterisation. The antithesis is established by the contrast honest/deceitful, but the other two attributes, poor and fool, are not directly related to each other and imply that their antonyms are gapped in the corresponding halves of the verse. Thus, the full characterisation of the two is a wise, honest, yet poor person on the one hand, and a foolish, deceitful and rich person

---

ners. Ecclesiastes taught them to despise the things of the world as vain and fleeting and was meant for the *proficientes*. The Canticle told initiates of the love of God.' (Smalley as quoted in Murphy, 1982:331–32).

[30] 𝔐 כְּסִיל; 𝔊 ܥܒܕ, i.e., עָשִׁיר, but the texts of the 7a1 family read ܣܟܠܐ, supporting 𝔐, although it is possible that this a result of harmonising the text with the Hebrew. I am inclined to agree with Toy (1899:368), that the alternative reading represented by 𝔊, is probably the result of smoothing the parallelism and harmonisation with Prov 28:6.

on the other. In other words this saying acknowledges that the combination wisdom/poverty is possible and not necessarily undesirable.

Admittedly, sayings of this type are scarce in the book. Yet, the premise about prosperity of the wise and destruction of the fools has to be reiterated again and again. This suggests at least indirectly that in the real world to which the sages are addressing themselves, this principle might not always be so obvious, and therefore, persistent reinforcement is required. Consider the following passages:

> My son, should the sinners try to seduce you, do not go! Should they say: 'Come with us, let us lie in wait for blood, let us lie in ambush for an innocent person even though he gave us no cause. Let us swallow them alive—like Sheol,[31] and in one piece,[32] like those who descend to the pit. We will find all sorts of precious things, we will fill our houses with spoil.' [Prov 1:10–13]

> Righteous person will not be made to stagger for ever, and the wicked ones will not inhabit [the] land. [Prov 10:30]

> Luxury is not appropriate for a fool, how much worse for a servant to rule over princes. [Prov 19:10]

> Do not lie in ambush for the property of the righteous, as a wicked person does, do not plunder his home. For the righteous falls seven times and rises [again], but wicked people will be brought down by disaster. [Prov 24:15–16]

> Muddied spring and damaged fountain: a righteous person crawling before a wicked person. [Prov 25:26]

These sayings, and other like them, only make adequate sense if in the sages world at least occasionally those who ambush the innocent fill their pockets with loot, the righteous stagger, the wicked have the upper hand and fools live lives of luxury. Thus, there are both explicit and implicit indications that the proverbial sages were aware that the picture of the world they paint is not entirely accurate.

There is an additional aspect of the sages teaching that has some bearing on the issue. From the opening paragraph of the book it transpires that the intention of Proverbs is not simply to impart a set of rules, but rather, that the sages aim to equip the simple *to understand* the words of the wise in their different forms [Prov 1:6]. To put it differently, it is the stated intention of the book to foster the ability to scrutinise different perspectives, suggesting that there is

---

[31] Or: *let us swallow them as Sheol swallows life* (McKane, 1970:221).
[32] I follow here McKane (1970:269), who sees here implied reference to Mot.

legitimate wisdom even outside Proverbs. A person who is perceived as wise can still learn and grow in wisdom. If being wise had simply meant acquiring the specific set of rules contained in the book, there would have been no way that the wise could have become any wiser from the same book. Yet, the prospect of a wise person learning from Proverbs is explicitly acknowledged [Prov 1:5]. Proverbial wisdom is, therefore, not a fixed body of doctrine, but rather a process of active interaction among the wise helping each other to grow in wisdom [e.g. Prov 9:8; 17:10]; the concept of wisdom in Proverbs is that of an ongoing and fundamentally collective quest for understanding.

Therefore, we can conclude that the proverbial perspective is genuinely paradigmatic in the sense defined earlier, having pragmatic thrust and being aware of its limits. Consequently, theological dogmatism is not an adequate explanation for the fact that the exceptions to the proverbial scheme of things are expressed in the book only in a subtle manner. Partly this is, as it has been already suggested, due to the focus on the simple. However, any paradigm is valid only when the exceptions to it are relatively insignificant with respect to its aim. In this context, the primary addressee is not an adequate explanation for lack of wider acknowledgement of disparity between the proverbial perspective and the reality of the world; it is improbable that the sages insisted on the simple gaining this particular perspective only to have to abandon it shortly. Thus, if, from our contemporary experience, the book appears to be very naïve, we must resist the temptation to see it is a product of a primitive or dogmatic mind. Rather, we should first examine the possibility whether the book might not have originated in conditions where the reality was much closer to the proverbial scheme of things than it is today, and I will argue in chapter 5 that this is in fact the case.

The Reversibility of the Proverbial Paradigm

I now wish to turn to the question whether the basic paradigm, as presented in the book of Proverbs, is understood to be reversible or not. It has been pointed out above, that one of the marks of success in the perspective of this book is material prosperity. If the righteous accumulates wealth, is it equally true that the wealthy person is righteous? The answer to this question in Proverbs is no, for it is possible to obtain wealth by dishonest means, and, as it was pointed out a short while

ago, there can be poor people among the wise; the sages unequivocally consider poverty resulting from person's honesty to be preferable
to wealth gained by deception [Prov 16:19; 19:1; 28:6;]. It is therefore
quite clear that the proverbial paradigm as it is presented in the book is
irreversible.

This should not be surprising since the real system with which the
book deals is acknowledged not to be fully deterministic, for God
directs it at his pleasure [e.g. Prov 16:9; 21:1], as we will see in greater
detail in chapter 4. However, the irreversibility of the paradigm is not
stressed in the book. This is most probably due to close relationship
with the fact that the paradigm is not entirely adequate, and stress-
ing it would be contra productive to the book's overall effort to motivate the young man to follow its advice. Consequently, it is easy to
overlook this fact and it is not necessary to provide lengthy proof that
paradigms very similar (if not identical) to the proverbial one were perceived as an exact depiction of the world and treated as reversible
already in antiquity: Job's friends and Ps 37 serve as suitable examples.

Formal Expression of the Paradigm

Finally, a brief note is appropriate on some of the literary features of the
book relating to the paradigm. The book is made up of two formally
distinct bodies of material: the initial nine chapters, and the rest of the
book. The former is characterised by longer units that tend to have a
narrative line, while the latter is made of several collections of short
sayings, that are sometimes grouped into sections using different poetic
techniques, based on sound or catchwords,[33] but, as I have pointed out
in the Introduction, still retaining their overall autonomy.

While the formal differences between Prov 1–9 and Prov 10–31 are
striking, there is one other issue that distinguishes these two sections,
and which is, in my view, of much greater significance. It can be
observed that the collections of sayings found in Prov 10–30 have one
particular purpose: they introduce the reader to what it means to be
wise. Thus, they depict what the wise people do, what the fools do,
what the righteous do, what the wicked do. In contrast, almost all of the
initial nine chapters are filled with calls to acquire wisdom at all costs
and to be wise, but they contain relatively little of practical instruction,

---

[33] See in particular McCreesh (1991) and Van Leeuwen (1988).

the main exception being the warnings against strange women. In other words, it is virtually impossible to build a picture of what wisdom is from these chapters. This character of the opening section of the book implies that they serve primarily as an introduction to the wisdom enterprise and are intended to motivate the simple to become wise. The way of wisdom itself is then expressed in the form of the short sayings that follow.

These shorter sayings can be classified according to their form into two types, that of *wisdom sentence* and that of *instruction*. The former is characterised by use of indicative mode, the latter by imperative mode (McKane, 1970:3). Yet, this formal distinction should not be pressed too far when the function is considered, for it is only significant on the level of locution with both forms having the same illocutionary force; both are intended to make the addressee act, or not act, in a certain way. The sometimes made assertion that the indicative sentences arc mere dispassionate statements of observation without any implied judgement is untenable. Austin (1962) argued convincingly that it is not possible to distinguish constantive and performative[34] statements on the grounds of grammatical criteria, such as verbal mood (p. 53–66), reaching the conclusion that all speech is performative by function, and that no human speech, with the possible exception of swearing, has merely constantive value (pp. 132–46). That this is so in the case of the contrast between *wisdom sentence* and *instruction* can be demonstrated, for instance, in Prov 23:24–25, where a wisdom sentence [v. 24] is followed by a proverb which is almost identical with it, except that it has the form of an instruction [v. 25]; the illocutionary forces of both of these verses are undoubtedly identical.

Since much of the proverbial perspective is expressed through these very short sayings which provide limited context, their interpretation can sometimes be difficult. In particular, this is true about the use of different verbal conjugations, and so a few notes on the syntax of the proverbial verb are in place.[35] Many of the short sayings are intended

---

[34] By *performative* Austin means statements that do not merely acknowledge, but seek to accomplish something in the real world through the statement. For instance the performative phrase 'I declare you a man and wife' is intended to institute a legally binding relationship, rather than merely inform. In contrast *constantive* statements are such that do no intend to cause a change the external reality.

[35] These notes on the use of verbal conjugations are not meant to be exhaustive, but rather indicate the direction which will be taken in the following chapters. For a wider

to depict universal truths about the way the world is. English uses the
present tense to express such gnomic notions, the proverbial Hebrew
uses perfective conjugations to achieve the same, such as in:

צַדִּיק מִצָּרָה נֶחֱלָץ וַיָּבֹא רָשָׁע תַּחְתָּיו: [Prov 11:7].

The righteous *gets rescued* from trouble, and it *comes* upon the wicked
instead.

The non-perfective conjugations are then used to express other than
gnomic notions, notably, repetitive aspects of human or divine behaviour, such as in

בֵּן חָכָם יְשַׂמַּח־אָב וּבֵן כְּסִיל תּוּגַת אִמּוֹ: [Prov 10:1]

A wise son *continues to bring* joy to his father, but a foolish son is his
mother's grief

On other occasions non-perfective conjugations have a modal sense, for
instance

אַכְזְרִיּוּת חֵמָה וְשֶׁטֶף אָף וּמִי יַעֲמֹד לִפְנֵי קִנְאָה: [Prov 27:4]

Anger is cruel and rage is a flood, but who *can withstand* jealousy?,

or denote simple future, as in:

זֹרֵעַ עַוְלָה יִקְצָר־אָוֶן [Prov 22:8A].

Who sows wickedness *will harvest* evil

The different nuances of the non-perfective tenses in the proverbial
material can be quite significant, as in Prov 26:27:

כֹּרֶה־שַּׁחַת בָּהּ יִפֹּל וְגֹלֵל אֶבֶן אֵלָיו תָּשׁוּב:

Who digs a pit may/will fall into it, and who rolls a stone, it may/will
roll back over[36] him.

This saying gains quite a different sense if the prefix conjugations are
understood as having a modal sense (i.e., *may fall ... may role back*),
instead of being taken, as they usually are, as simple futures. In this
particular case the former is more likely what was initially intended, for
the way proverbs similar to this one are used by Qoheleth [Qoh 10:8–
9] suggests that our saying is more about occupational hazards than
sinister schemes.[37] At the same time, to restrict the interpretation of the

---

discussion one should consult the standard grammars, and in particular the treatment
in WOC (30.5.1, 31.3, 33.3.1) on which I am drawing heavily.
   [36] אֵלָיו וֹת requires such a rendering in the context, cf. 𝕲.
   [37] See note 71 on p. 195.

proverb to this particular reading alone would be a mistake, for the power of a proverb as a literary form resides principally in two things: brevity and openness to reinterpretation.

It needs to be appreciated that the brevity of the proverbial literary forms chosen as the primary means through which the paradigm is expressed has important implications for our understanding of it. As a result of the pettiness of the sayings, none of them contains a full picture of reality; rather each individual saying offers a mere glimpse at the world from a particular, and narrow, angle. The paradigm is constructed as a kaleidoscope, where the whole image of the world is created by a combination of the glimpses that the individual proverbs offer, and is more than a simple sum of the parts. Consequently, as the paradigm is examined, it is necessary to focus on the intended whole, not on the individual sayings in isolation. This is perhaps most important where different sayings stand in tension with each other. These should not be considered as contradictory, but rather as complementary, trying to express reality that is more complex than a single saying can capture.

An Outline of Qoheleth's Perspective

The Basic Structure of Qoheleth's Worldview

Just as is the case with Proverbs, the basic framework of Qoheleth's worldview contains the three key elements from Crenshaw's definition of wisdom, the relationships with things, people and the Creator. Yet, these are represented in different proportions than we found them in Proverbs. While the proverbial paradigm places greatest emphasis on the understanding of the human to human relationships, in Qoheleth there is much more stress on the interaction between the larger world and human beings, with particular attention being paid to the role played by God in this interaction.

For all practical purposes, Qoheleth's perspective can be labelled theo-cosmological. The critical environment in which human life is taking place is not the human collective, but the impersonal world. Human experience is determined mainly by factors that are external to humanity, and out of human control, subject merely to the divine whim. Yet, even though Qoheleth concentrates heavily on the issue of the unpredictability of God's involvement, divine activity in the book is rarely direct; most often it is mediated by the design of the cosmos. A detailed examination of the nature of the cosmos as it is perceived by Qohelcth will be carried out in chapter 4, but essentially at the heart of Qoheleth's wisdom lies a picture of a world which by the divine design has a natural tendency toward equilibrium between what is in some sense bad and detrimental to human beings, and that which is good and beneficial for them. Within this equilibrium every single positive event has its corresponding negative counterpart and this pairing ensures that no substantial and lasting accomplishment is possible in the course of human life. To some extent there is a similarity with the proverbial perspective, both being based on a bipolar arrangement of the world. Yet, in contrast to the proverbial paradigm that revolves along what is essentially an ethical dichotomy, where good and evil people are treated in a different manner, the polarity postulated by Qoheleth is ethically neutral, affecting all people equally.

This understanding of the world has major implications for Qoheleth's view of wisdom. While for the proverbial sages wisdom was equal to identification with what is right and just, as far as the quest for success and prosperity is concerned, in Qoheleth's world, which does not differentiate between the righteous and the wicked, ethical questions loose any significance. In a sense, wisdom becomes pure science. At this point Qoheleth betrays his wisdom heritage, for as we will see in chapter 6, even though this is what he understands about the world, he is reluctant to endorse behaviour that does not care about ethical issues, and in fact it is quite clear that he considers the very nature of the cosmos evil, on the account of its ethical neutrality.

The Aims of Qoheleth's Quest and Its Working Parameters

Determining the aim of Qoheleth's undertaking is slightly more complicated than in the case of Proverbs. Qoheleth's inquiry is introduced by the question *what profit is there for a human being in all his labour which he carries out under the sun* [Qoh 1:3]. This is clearly a rhetorical question. Rhetorical questions can serve two distinct purposes. They can either be declarative, making a statement which is equivalent to the implied answer, or they can be introductory, serving as a headline focusing the following discourse. While in this case the reader has his suspicion what the answer to the question is to be (especially in the light of the preceding verse), it is my understanding that this question functions mainly as an introductory one and is, thus, rightly identified by Ogden (1987b:28) as a programmatic question.

The key word of this question is יִתְרוֹן, more or less an accountant's term, referring to that which is left over when all the transactions are added up, a *profit*. In itself יִתְרוֹן does not have any special theological significance in the book, and it certainly does not refer to an advantage in the afterlife (*pace* Ogden, 1987b:22–26), for Qoheleth is unable to shed any light on what happens after one dies, and, as we will see later (p. 111), expresses serious doubts about the possibility of a meaningful existence after death. Rather than imposing a singular point of reference on יִתְרוֹן, one needs to appreciate that it is used in the book in its generic sense but in two distinct contexts. On the one hand it is found referring to a profit generated by a person's activities throughout their entire life, on the other hand it refers to a short-term gain associated with a particular undertaking in a particular time. In the case of the programmatic question יִתְרוֹן is modified by the phrases *in all his work*, and *under the sun*. The latter phrase, and the synonymous *under the heavens*, is Qoheleth's way of referring to the spatial and temporal sphere in which human life happens. It is an arena exclusive to the living, the unborn have not yet entered it, while the dead have no share in it anymore.[38] We can see, therefore, that the יִתְרוֹן about which Qoheleth is asking in the programmatic question is the result of adding up all of a person's undertaking during the person's lifetime—Qoheleth's quest starts as a search for some absolute gain from life.

However, Qoh 1:3 does not apply to the entire book. As the equilibrious picture of the world outlined above begins to emerge out of Qoheleth's inquiry in the first half of the book, it becomes obvious that no absolute and lasting advantage can be achieved; the divinely enforced balanced nature of the world precludes it. The ultimate conclusion with respect to the question of Qoh 1:3 reached by Qoheleth is summarised in the word הֶבֶל. This term poses serious difficulties to the translator, for there is no single English equivalent that would fully capture its sense and its precise significance has been widely debated. In my view the best analysis of the meaning is that of Miller (1998) who argues that הֶבֶל with its original meaning *vapour* is used by Qoheleth as a symbol that encapsulates the notions of insubstantiality, transience and foulness, summarising Qoheleth's evaluation of human experience.[39] In relationship to יִתְרוֹן and its antonym חֶסְרוֹן, surplus and

---

[38] The makeup of Qoheleth's cosmos will be discussed in detail in chapter 4 (p. 107ff.).

[39] This understanding, however, does not resolve the problem of English rendering.

deficit, הֶבֶל is Qoheleth's term for nothingness—human beings produce nothing of lasting value, whether positive or negative, there is no absolute יִתְרוֹן.

Yet, while the world leans toward the outlined equilibrium in the long-term run, it allows for temporary imbalance. Joy is not necessarily instantaneously followed by sorrow, just as not all people die at the point of birth. The temporary asymmetry allows for a temporary gain, and so instead of being forced to abandon the search for יִתְרוֹן altogether, Qoheleth is able to refocus his enquiry. The original programme is transformed into a less ambitious one, captured by the question *who knows what is good for a human being while he is alive, during the limited number of days of his absurd living* [Qoh 6:11]. There are good reasons to believe that the original search for absolute advantage was never intended as a serious option, for the presence of the framing negative inclusio of Qoh 1:2 & 12:8 shows an immediate prejudice about fruitfulness of such a search. Yet, this broader-aimed quest was necessary both to justify the legitimacy of limiting the wisdom quest to a search for an answer to the less ambitious programmatic question of Qoh 6:11, and to lay down foundations for the basic answer that Qoheleth is going to give to it. The wider question of Qoh 1:3 displays Qoheleth's affinity with other wisdom texts, while the shift to the limited question of Qoh 6:11 reflects his departure from the wisdom ideal as found, for instance, in Proverbs. The overall aim of Qoheleth's quest then lies within the boundaries redefined at Qoh 6:11; he is looking for ways to maximise any temporary success.

What then does Qoheleth perceive as success in life? Similarly to Proverbs, material welfare is at the centre of Qoheleth's understanding of it. However, wealth *per se* is not identified with success, and it constitutes much less a mark of a person's status in Qoheleth's mind than it does in the proverbial association wise-wealthy. Qoheleth's principal emphasis is on the ability to enjoy one's resources, and any striving

---

Common translations include *meaningless* (NIV), *vanity* (RSV), *absurd* (e.g. Fox, 1989) and one commentator even proposed a somewhat shocking, yet not entirely inadequate, rendering *shit* (Crüsemann, 1984). Since no English word covers the various semantic nuances with which הֶבֶל is used in the book, one has to either use different words to translate it in different context, and so destroy the link this lexeme creates throughout the book, or use a single English term, with the result that the translation is occasionally too wooden. For the present purposes, the latter alternative was deemed preferable, and I have decided to adopt Fox's rendering *absurd*, which provides a reasonably accurate sense throughout, with the exception of Qoh 3:18–22 where *passing* was used instead.

for possession is only 'legitimised' by the prospect of enjoyment; the effort to succeed and gain property is seen as a painful one and only the resulting enjoyment can make it worthwhile [Qoh 2:22–24]. Situations in which one is not able to enjoy the product of one's endeavour are perceived as deeply tragic [Qoh 6:1–3]. In other words, Qoheleth does not advocate hoarding wealth for its own sake, it is only a means to an end. Indeed, excessive possessions have their pitfalls [Qoh 5:10–11], and it matters more to have a good reputation and maintain it throughout one's life than to be rich [Qoh 7:1]. Further, it is worth noting that Qoheleth does not perceive success in purely individualistic terms. Rather, he prefers situations where achievement and material resources can be enjoyed in the company of others, solitude is depressing and degrading [Qoh 4:7–12]. Thus, in spite of Qoheleth's focus on the individual, he perceives that people are ultimately social creatures, and success requires that their social needs be met.

Again, we can see that the whole search that Qoheleth undertakes is driven by practical concerns. For Qoheleth, the value of knowledge is explicitly located in its practical benefits. In fact, in contrast to Proverbs, Qoheleth entirely relativises the value of wisdom as a mark of success; his perception of wisdom is nowhere near to the elevated imagery of Dame Wisdom as found in Prov 8. Wisdom is not much more for him than a tool through which one's resources can be manipulated and maintained [Qoh 7:11–12[40]], and it is entirely human in nature. Thus, while in certain contexts Qoheleth affirms the superiority of the combination wisdom/poverty to that of folly/wealth [Qoh 4:13], without access to the resources wisdom does not constitute success in Qoheleth's eyes [Qoh 6:7–9] and can be virtually worthless.

---

[40] I prefer to render Qoh 7:11A 'wisdom *with* inheritance is good'. Crenshaw (1988:138) renders עִם by *as* on the basis of Qoh 2:16. However, in 2:16 the הַכֹּל indicates that the force of the thought is more associative than comparative, and since Qoheleth regularly uses כְּ to express comparison [e.g. Qoh 2:15] without a clear indication that comparison is intended it is preferable to render *with*. Fox (1989:231) quotes Job 9:26; 37:18 as examples of עִם used comparatively, but both cases are questionable. Ogden (1987b:108) adds the equivalence of *wisdom* and *money* in v. 12 as a supportive argument for reading *as*, but there clearly is no equivalence between wisdom and riches in Qoheleth's mind, since he has stated previously [Qoh 6:7–9] that wisdom cannot guarantee wealth. If v. 11 is rendered as suggested above, then it serves as a qualifying statement for the assertion of v. 12, where wisdom is not a guaranteed source of riches *per se*, but a suitable tool that can help to multiply and preserve wealth. This is in harmony with the explicit affirmation of v. 12b that wisdom can preserve the life of those who possess it, which quite clearly is not intended as a claim that the wise do not die; wisdom is no more equivalent to riches than it is to life.

That, however, does not mean that Qoheleth rejects wisdom. On the contrary, he loathes folly [Qoh 10:2–3, 12–15]. On many an occasion he sees little difference between the fool and the wise, but not on a single one does he suggest that it is better to be a fool [e.g. Qoh 2:13–14; 9:16–18]; he identifies with the wise. To cover up the enigmatic and painful elements of human experience by ignorance satisfies him even less than having to admit the ultimate failure of wisdom. He chooses the frustration and pain of knowledge over the ease of inanity, and the epilogist grasps this, when he describes him as a sage [Qoh 12:9–10].

Qoheleth's wisdom is set within certain limiting boundaries. His investigation is based entirely on experience and the ability to experiment. He refuses to speculate about those issues that he personally cannot examine, notably about the question of a meaningful afterlife and the possibility of achieving a lasting benefit from life that would reach beyond the point of death. As we will see later, he subscribes to the traditional OT idea of Sheol, a shapeless existence in oblivion, but at the same time, he is aware of not being able to verify this understanding, and leaves the issue at least theoretically open. This should not, though, obscure from us the fact that the depiction of the world which he offers is strictly limited to the here-and-now; the points of birth and death are the basic boundaries within which Qoheleth's wisdom applies. This earth-bound, yet, cautious position should be respected. On the one hand it allows the reader to incorporate the book into belief-systems that may not entirely share Qoheleth's sceptical position, such as it was possible for the first century rabbis to include it among their canonical texts. On the other hand, it should also prevent the interpreter from imposing such external solutions as the concept of after-death judgement on the internal tensions within the book. It is only then that one can begin to get to grips with the person of Qoheleth and his world.

Adequacy of Qoheleth's Picture of the World

We find in the book a conviction that the quest for understanding cannot be completed, the world is not fully comprehensible and never will be because God intended for it not to be:

> Then I saw [concerning] every activity of God, that a person is not able to find out [about] the activity which is happening under the sun, no matter how much a person may work to search [it] out, yet, he cannot

find [it] out, and even if the sage should say that he knows, he cannot find [it] out. [Qoh 8:17][41]

The quote shows an acute awareness that the sage must be careful with what he claims. The specific expression of one's wisdom is always short of reality, and it is the reality which remains the ultimate object of Qoheleth's investigation. Qoheleth of all people is least in danger of confusing his theories with the tangible world.

Having seen that Qoheleth's search for understanding is driven by practical application from which the value of wisdom is solely derived, and having seen that he is aware that even the conclusions of his experience cannot be considered the final word, it is possible to say that Qoheleth's approach to wisdom is also paradigmatic in the sense defined earlier, even though the composition of the book is such that the process of progressing from observation to a paradigm is not always immediately obvious. The fact that this is what Qoheleth is doing can be illustrated by the following example where a specific case is turned into a general paradigm:

> There was a small city and few men in it, and a great king came to it, and surrounded it, and built against it massive ramparts.[42] And he found in it a poor person,[43] [who was] wise, and could have rescued[44] the city by his wisdom, but not a single person remembered this poor person. And I said: Wisdom is better than strength, but the wisdom of a poor person is despised, his words are not listened to. [Qoh 9:14–16]

---

[41] For textual notes see p. 153.

[42] Reading with two Hebrew manuscripts, 𝔊, σ', 𝔖, 𝔙, מְצוּרִים.

[43] The subject of the verb is not clear. I am inclined to agree with Fox (1989:261–2) that the subject is the king from v. 14, but Fox's rendering *and in it he [the king] apprehended a man ... and he ... saved the city* is impossible in the context, because if the man was apprehended in the city, it had to be already taken—too late to be rescued. Driver (1954:231) proposes to read מָצָא pointing out the post-biblical מָצוּי; such vocalisation is not implausible.

[44] Sx is commonly used to express unreal situations (see WOC 30.5.4). That this is the case here is indicated by the fact that what follows implies that the poor man's wisdom is not heeded. In particular, v. 16, which offers the generalised moral of the story, would make little sense if the city had been saved by this man (cf. Crenshaw, 1988:166). Gordis (1955a:311) objects to such an understanding, claiming that זכר is not used in the sense to *think of*, but that is clearly the case in Qoh 11:8; 12:1. Fox's (1989:263) objection that זכר always refers to recalling a fact which is already known and cannot be used in the sense of paying attention to a new fact or advice is irrelevant here, because Qoheleth does not say that no-one remembered his advice, but that no-one remembered his person (cf. Qoh 12:1).

It is apparent that Qoheleth's paradigm is different than that of Proverbs; the unqualified proverbial '*better*' is replaced by '*better, but ...*'. In other words, Qoheleth is greatly concerned with the exceptions to the paradigmatic generalisations and with the external constraints which limit the validity of such a paradigm. This preoccupation with the imprecision brings his paradigmatic approach closer to an exact mode of knowing than is the case with Proverbs; there is a distinct sense in the book that Qoheleth operates within the inexact framework only out of necessity, being convinced that exact knowing is not within human capabilities.

The Reversibility of Qoheleth's Paradigm

The question of reversibility, so essential to the book of Proverbs, does not really apply to Qoheleth's paradigm. This is given by its nature. While the proverbial paradigm is based on the assumption that the world can be predicted with a reasonable degree of accuracy and the outcome can be influenced by choice of action, Qoheleth's model centres around the assumption that apart from the tendency toward equilibrium the world is stochastic. Qoheleth's paradigm is not about forecasting what will happen, but about making the most of the events that one cannot predict or control; the question of causality, i.e., why something that already happened took place, is not one that Qoheleth asks outside of the context of the positive-negative polarity.

Formal Expression of the Paradigm

The most notable formal feature of the book is the epilogue; the approach that will be taken here in this respect has already been outlined in the Introduction. What has been said earlier with reference to the proverbial forms, concerning the inherent performative nature of language, applies fully to Qoheleth; his observations tend to imply some kind of a personal judgment even when it is not explicitly stated. In fact, the framing inclusio of Qoh 1:2 and 12:8 indicates very clearly that Qoheleth is ultimately going to pass judgement on the entirety of human experience.

The book employs a number of different forms to get its reasoning across. Among these are the traditional wisdom saying and a pseudo-autobiographical narrative. While the text does not contain a singular smooth line of reasoning and the style is somewhat disjointed, it shows a significant formal uniformity both in terms of vocabulary and the way arguments are constructed. In the light of that it is not, in my view, likely that we should look in the core of the book for voices with different ideologies as a way to explain the internal tension. Rather, we should perceive these tensions as an expression of a life-experience in a real world.

It can be further observed that the formal nature of the material between the two halves of the book differs. The first six chapters are largely characterised by a first person discourse in an indicative mood, while the second half of the book employs a large number of second person verbal forms, mainly absent from the first half of the book, including a number of command forms (see the Appendix). This leads to the conclusion that the two sections have a different function. In the first half of the book Qoheleth develops his understanding of the world from his personal experience, while in the second half he relates his observations to the reader. Thus, in spite of the possible initial impression of chaos, the book has a certain definite flow of thought and intent, one which culminates in the final paragraphs, from which the persona of Qoheleth disappears entirely and the reader becomes the sole focus of the discourse. This shows quite clearly that in the final analysis Qoheleth is just as interested in making people behave in a certain manner, as the proverbial sages are.

Summary

I have shown so far that the basic approach of both Proverbs and Qoheleth is paradigmatic in the sense defined earlier in this chapter, i.e., the two books have primarily pragmatic concerns and offer a consciously simplified picture of reality. This conclusion is contrary to Golka's (1993:114–16) view that wisdom uses principally the same method as modern science. In fact, I am convinced that the very low esteem which wisdom, and particularly Proverbs, has in critical scholarship, is mainly due to the failure to appreciate that its aims and methods are not the same as those of modern science, and that the paradigms offered by the two books have to be treated as intentional simplifications intended for a specific purpose and meant to operate under limited conditions.[45]

---

[45] The paradigmatic nature of the wisdom enterprise should not be confused with the issue of the authority of wisdom. Namely, it should not be surmised that Proverbs or Qoheleth are not intended to be authoritative because they are paradigmatic. In

It is clear from the outline of the two perspectives presented above, that the two paradigms are quite different, and that the differences are not merely in minute details, but in matters of substance, as will emerge even more clearly in the following chapters. Yet, this should not obscure from us the fact that, in spite of the differences, behind both books lie quests that share a number of similarities. In most general terms, both books are driven by practical concerns, they revolve around an understanding of the world and the place that human beings have in it, and have the same basic aim, to foster successful life, conceiving of such a success in similar terms. Thus, in other words, the two books have identical points of departure, identical goals and similar overall approach to achieving these. The earlier suggested definition of the quest we find in Proverbs and Qoheleth can, therefore, be further narrowed as *the quest for self-understanding in terms of relationships with things, people and the Creator and self-realisation in the context of these relationships, based on a paradigmatic approach to understanding.*

---

fact, sometimes it is asserted that wisdom amounts to nothing more than a body of good advice that one may want to consider following. While wisdom is not a legal system with penalties applied externally for lack of compliance with it, obedience to the wisdom paradigm is nevertheless not portrayed as optional, nor do we gain the perception from our books that the paradigm can be applied selectively. While the authority of the paradigm is limited to it being applied within its intended working parameters, within that boundary its acceptance is assumed to be unconditional; the sages expected to be taken seriously. This is fully in line with the hints elsewhere in the OT that wisdom enjoyed a great degree of authority, e.g., the reputation of Ahithophel [2 Sam 16:23] at David's court.

CHAPTER 3

HOW DOES THE SAGE KNOW?

In the previous chapter I argued that the wisdom undertaking is pragmatic, with paradigm being its primary mode of thought. The paradigm is the conceptual end-product of the quest for practical understanding of the world pursued by the sages; its formulation is preceded
by a twofold undertaking, consisting of the collection of data followed
by its assessment. By *assessment* I do not mean here the process of drawing conclusions from the data, for in that sense I prefer to talk of formulation of the paradigm. Rather, by assessment I mean a process through
which a value is given to that which is observed; essentially a method
of sorting out bad data from good data, a method through which differences between separate observations are handled and through which
it is decided that a particular observation should be included in, or
may need to be excluded from, the formulation of the paradigm itself.
Both the methods used to collect and assess data are an essential part
of any epistemology, and while in our case the latter may not be overtly
explicit, it nevertheless constitutes a critical part of the sages' worldview.

The Epistemological Perspective of Proverbs

Direct Observation

The first method of collecting data found in the book is by personal
observation, although it should be noted immediately that in Proverbs
direct observation is presented as the source of the sages' knowledge
only on a limited number of occasions. Such observations are typically
marked by the presence of 1cs form of the verb ראה. A prime example
is found in Prov 7:

> Say to Wisdom: 'you are my sister,' and call understanding a relative—
> to keep you from an adulteress, from the foreign woman, who makes
> her words smooth. For through the window of my[1] house, through my

---

[1] $\mathfrak{G}$, $\mathfrak{S}$ have the whole of the following narrative in 3fs. The difference is probably
stylistic rather than textual, the $\mathfrak{M}$ version with the three narrative planes (that of the

shutters I was looking down, and I saw among the immature, I noticed among the sons, a boy who lacked sense. Crossing the street by her corner, and step by step heading[2] in the direction of her house ... And behold, the woman [comes] to meet him ... She seduced him by her persuasiveness, by the smoothness of her lips she beguiled him. He follows her in an instant,[3] like an ox to the slaughter he keeps on going,[4] ... for he does not know [that] with his life he [will pay]. And now sons, listen to me, and pay attention to the words of my mouth. Do not turn your mind in her direction, do not stagger by mistake onto her paths. For she caused the fall of many corpses, and those she killed are numerous. Paths to Sheol are her house, descending to the chambers of death. [Prov 7:4–27]

The father's insight into what happens to a youth who falls prey to a strange woman is based on his personal knowledge of a case of such a young man in the past. Here I disagree with Fox's (1987:146) view that the father's conclusions are not derived from observation, but are based on prior knowledge. While, due to the future frame of reference in v. 23, the father could be regarded as reporting the outcome without observing it and thus relying on prior knowledge, it is better to understand the shift from past to present (v. 22) and future (v. 23) as the result of a difference between the story time and the narrative time, the latter being delayed against the former. The narrative time is chosen so that the present, i.e., the most vivid, section appears at the critical moment of the narrative, when the point of no return is crossed. Instead of leaving the story with the primary focus on the consequences, the reader is left to contemplate mainly what led to the critical twist in the plot, which is what the narrator intends, as is clearly indicated by the imperatives of v. 25—the primary role of the story is preventative. Further, the father's claim that *she has caused the fall of many* [v. 26], indicates clearly that the whole paradigm relies on reoccurring experience, so that even if some prior knowledge is used here in evaluating the story, it is based on observation of the same type.

---

father, of the characters and of the addressees) is much more dynamic and preferable.

 [2] The Px has here a past iterative sense which creates a special dramatic effect; the observer hangs on each step of the youth with anticipation.

 [3] 𝔐 פִּתְאֹם; 𝔊 κεπφωθείς, *cajoled*, i.e., פתה. 𝔖 ܐ̣ܝܟ ܨܒܘܬ, i.e., reading כְּפֶתִי most likely on the analogy of the following כְּשׁוֹר; this is unlikely to be the correct reading since the character in the story *is* פֶּתִי not just *like* פֶּתִי.

 [4] 𝔐 יָבוֹא; 𝔊 ἄγεται, possibly reading Hophal, *is led*. I prefer the 𝔐 active voice to the 𝔊 passive, for the point being made here is that the boy fails to put up any resistance; the emphasis is on the boy's actions.

This particular case is generalised into a paradigm in which association with such a woman leads to destruction and death.

A similar type of observation is found in Prov 24:

> I crossed over a field of a lazy man, and over a vineyard of a person with no sense. And look: all over it weeds were coming up, chickweed covered its surface, and its stone wall was breached. And I observed [it] and I took [it] to my heart, I saw [it] and I learned a lesson: A little sleep, a little slumber, a little folding of hands to lie down, and your poverty comes like a tinker, and your need like a shielded warrior. [Prov 24:30–34][5]

The process through which the observation is turned into a paradigm is directly described in v. 33, with the paradigm expressed in v. 34: laziness, even in small doses, leads to impoverishment which, once it takes hold, is extremely difficult to overcome.

Sometimes the paradigm applicable to human behaviour is built from an observation that lies outside of human society. Consider the well known passage from Prov 6:

> Go to the ant, sluggard, see its ways and be wise. Although it does not have a leader, officer or ruler, it prepares its bread in the summer, it gathers its food in the harvest time. How long, sluggard, will you lie down, when will you get up from your sleep? Little sleep [here and there],[6] little rest [here and there], little folding of hands to lie down, and your poverty will come in like a tinker, and your need like a shielded warrior.[7] [Prov 6:6–11]

From our modern perspective, the world of the ant is not directly related to the world of humans, at least not to the extent that we would readily consider the behaviour of the ant as a suitable model for human conduct. Human intellect is almost invariably seen as the ultimate pinnacle of knowledge in today's world, and a certain epistemological leap is necessary to draw direct conclusions about humans from observations of other creatures; such observations might be used as secondary illustrations of a particular concept, but rarely would they be the source of the idea itself. While at first glance it might seem that the same is true in the case above, there are indications that the reference to the ant here is much more serious than a mere illustration. The proposed exercise in studying the behaviour of the ant is not some momentary

---

[5] For textual notes see p. 135.
[6] Note the extensive pl. שְׁנוֹת.
[7] See notes 20 and 21 on p. 135.

and superficial observation, but rather a long term study that spans several seasons and what is said indicates some significant insight into the behaviour of the ant collective; the speaking sage studied the ants systematically and in some detail. We find sayings with a similar thrust in Prov 30:

> These three things are hidden from me, and four I do not comprehend: the path of the vulture in the skies, the path of a snake on a rock, the path of a ship in the heart of the sea, and the path of a man with a marriageable woman. [Prov 30:18–19]

> These four are small earthly [creatures], and they are wiser[8] than sages. The ants are not a strong people, but they prepare their food in the summer. Rock badgers are not a numerous people, but they set their house in rock. Locusts have no king, but all of them come out in ranks. A gecko can be caught[9] with two hands, yet, it is [found] in royal palaces. [Prov 30:24–28]

> These three stroll elegantly and four walk well: the lion, the mightiest among animals, who does not turn back before anyone. Swaggering cock or he-goat, and king ??? among his people.[10] [Prov 30:29–31]

In all of these texts the understanding of the animal world is a serious business on a par with understanding the human world. In fact Prov 30:24 affirms explicitly that other creatures possess wisdom which is in no way inferior to that of the sages and can provide them with insight. In other words, these passages show that the world of the sages is a coherent and unified whole, of which human beings are a part, one of many. There is no deep dichotomy between the human sphere and the animal kingdom—the patterns and phenomena observed in nature are applied to human life without hesitation.[11]

---

[8] 𝔐 מְחֻכָּמִים; reading מְחֻכָּמִים with KBL-3, cf. 𝕲 σοφώτερα τῶν σοφῶν.

[9] 𝔐 תִּתְפֵּשׂ; reading passive with 𝕲.

[10] The Hebrew text of the verse is clearly corrupted. 𝕲 καὶ ἀλέκτωρ ἐμπεριπατῶν θηλείαις εὔψυχος καὶ τράγος ἡγούμενος αἰπολίου καὶ βασιλεὺς δημηγορῶν ἐν ἔθνει, *and a rooster walking courageously [among] hens and a he-goat leading a herd, and a king addressing a nation.* It is, however, likely that this is simply an interpretation of an obscure Hebrew text as preserved in 𝔐. Bewer (1948:61) proposed to emend on the grounds of 𝕲 מָתְנַיִם אַיִל to מְתֻנְשָׂא, מֶלֶךְ to מֹלֶךְ, אַלְקוּם to מְקֻדָּם, אַיִל מְקֻדָּם to אוֹ, rendering *the strutting cock and the leading he-goat, the leader marching in front of his people.* Although, in light of the extensive corruption of text, all reconstructions are tentative, that the reference is being made to animals is clear.

[11] See also Dell (1994a).

Collective Experience

Alongside direct observations as the source of knowledge, we find that the wise also gathered information indirectly from the experience of others. In fact, learning and teaching, rather than experiencing first hand, is the primary mode of data-acquisition in Proverbs. When stating that the book is intended to give knowledge [Prov 1:2], the introduction quite clearly implies that knowledge can be passed on. The father in the story of Prov 7, quoted earlier, does not exhort the listeners to go and watch a case of a youth involved with a strange woman in order to learn the same lesson he has learned; he assumes that his observation can serve as a reliable foundation for the young men to draw their own conclusions. A similar assumption lies behind all the other speeches of Prov 1–9 by the father, the grand-father and Wisdom herself. The distinction between personal and communicated experience may seem to be minute, but for the understanding of the overall epistemological perspective of the book it is crucial. From the sages' point of view, human experience is not subjective, but rather, it is perceived as an objective reality. What one person observes is applicable to other people. Consequently, the search for understanding in Proverbs is a collective undertaking; the simple are to learn from the wiser [e.g. Prov 12:15; 13:20] and the wise learn from each other [Prov 1:5].

Place of Revelation

While the experiential modes of data-acquisition are by far the most pronounced in the book, we come across a few statements that quite manifestly do not come from such human sources. The most striking example is the speech of Wisdom in Prov 8:22ff. The insights into the process of creation that this passage claims to offer are not acquired by human experience, but are being *revealed* to humans by the mysterious female figure. I will leave the question of her identity for the following chapter, and instead will focus at present solely on her function in the process of obtaining knowledge. She appears on three occasions in Prov 1–9 [Prov 1:20ff.; 8; 9], on all of which she addresses the listeners with more or less an identical message, captured in the following passage:

> Blessed is the person who listens to me, [who] keeps watch at my doors day after day, [who] guards the door-posts of my doorway. For who finds me, has found life, and received favour from Yahweh. But who

> sins against me does violence to his soul, and all who hate me love death.
> [Prov 8:34–36]

Essentially, she is admonishing the youths, whose identity was discussed in the previous chapter, to accept her instruction asserting that doing so will lead to prosperous life while ignoring her will mean sure destruction.

The role that Wisdom plays is indicated by the way Prov 8:22–36 is structured. There are two main sections, Prov 8:22–29 and 8:32–36; the former is dealing with Wisdom's presence during the process of creation, the latter is Wisdom's call for attention. These two sections are joined by janus verses 30 and 31, in which the thought progresses from Wisdom before Yahweh to humanity before Wisdom; just as Wisdom is Yahweh's delight at the close of the first section, so humanity is Wisdom's delight at the start of the second section. In other words, Wisdom functions as a mediatrix between Yahweh and humanity, linking the enigmatic divine world, which we get a glimpse of in vv. 22–29, with the tangible world the young men live in.[12] The relationship between humanity and Wisdom is in a sense an image of the relationship between Yahweh and herself; she wishes to find delight in humanity, just as Yahweh finds delight in her. Thus, following her means pleasing Yahweh with all the associated blessing necessary for life; rejecting her ultimately amounts to making an enemy of Yahweh with all the deadly repercussions.

Having concluded that she has a mediating function, what then is it that she mediates?

> 'To you men, I call, and to humanity my voice [is directed]. [You] imma-
> ture, understand prudence! And you fools, get sense! Listen, because
> I speak <important things>[13] and [when] I open my lips, [out comes]
> that which is right, because my palate utters truth and wickedness is an
> abomination to my lips.[14] All the words of my mouth are in righteous-
> ness, there is no twistedness, no crookedness among them. All of them
> are straight to the one who understands, and upright to those who seek
> knowledge. Accept my instruction in place of silver and knowledge in

---

[12] See also Yee (1982).

[13] Precise meaning uncertain. 𝔐 נְגִידִים, *rulers*, possibly used in a metaphorical manner; 𝔊 σεμνά, *holy things*; 𝔖 om ܪ̈ܫܝܬܐ, *what is true*. Oesterley (1929:57) proposes to emend to נְכֹחִים, which could be explained by an audible error in 𝔐.

[14] 𝔊 (preferred by Toy, 1899:162) ἐβδελυγμένα δὲ ἐναντίον ἐμοῦ χείλη ψευδῆ, *deceitful lip is an abomination to me*, but this is probably due to the translator's difficulties with the syntax. The parallel with 7a and 8a, where the concern is with Wisdom's utterances, speaks strongly for retaining 𝔐.

place of choice gold. ... I, Wisdom dwell [with][15] prudence, and I keep meeting knowledge of discretion.[16] Fear of Yahweh is to hate evil; I hate arrogance and pride and an evil way, and a perverse mouth. I have got advice and insight, I am[17] understanding, I have got strength. ... I love those who love me, and those who seek me do find me. Riches and glory are with me, splendid wealth and righteousness. My fruit is better than gold, and than chrysolite, and my produce [is better] than choice silver. I walk in the path of righteousness and in the middle of tracks of judgement. [I] make those who love me inherit property, and I fill their storehouses. [Prov 8:4–14, 17–21]

Essentially she provides *correct* understanding of the world, one needed to please God and succeed. It is, therefore, necessary to differentiate between Wisdom, the persona, and wisdom as knowledge or intellectual capacity, between the mediatrix and the mediated. The sages believed that God created the world intelligently, i.e., by wisdom and by understanding [Prov 3:19], and it is this intelligent design that Dame Wisdom discloses to humanity.[18] She is a source of knowledge and understanding, but she cannot be identified with it. If she is to be seen in terms of knowledge, then she is knowledge *par excellence*, ideal and absolute, unlimited and undiluted, and most importantly, existing independently of and outwith the creation. However, I will argue in the following chapter that she is more than this.[19]

---

[15] Delitzsch (1982a:177) understands *prudence* in sense of location, *I inhabit prudence*, but it is more likely that *prudence* and *knowledge of discretion* are personified here and presented as Dame Wisdom's companions.

[16] 𝔐 וְדַעַת מְזִמּוֹת אֶמְצָא. The Px has a habitual sense; 𝔊 ἐπεκαλεσάμην, *I call*, i.e., *I invite*; 𝔖 ܐܢܐ ܡܨܬ, *I acquired*, supports 𝔐 root, the choice of tense is more likely interpretative than textual. McKane (1970:222) translates *I find out the right procedures*, but in the light of 12a *knowledge of discretion* is best understood as a personification, and thus the verb is more likely to have the more personal sense *I meet*.

[17] Versions read *I have*, but that is most likely levelling of the text, although the difference could also be a result of an audible error confusing אֲנִי with עִמִּי.

[18] That *wisdom* in Prov 3:19 is not Dame Wisdom is implied by the fact that Dame Wisdom of Prov 8 plays no active role in the process of creation, the only assertion that the text makes is that she was present during it.

[19] The perception that Wisdom is in principle a mediatrix of divine knowledge is not new. From early on, the Jewish tradition understood Wisdom as the Torah; a well known instance of this identification is found in Ben Sira 24. The main problem with this identification lies in the fact that the proverbial material lacks the Israelite specificity associated with the Torah and that the book fails to make this identification explicit. At the same time it should not be dismissed simply as an attempt to reconcile Yahwistic traditions concerning salvation history with wisdom traditions in which salvation on a national level plays no role whatsoever, as does, for instance, von Rad (1972:164–66). In fact, Ben Sira's explanation shows a great degree of sensitivity to the

Within the narrative strategy of Proverbs, the knowledge which Dame Wisdom offers is to be identified with the contents of the book. This can be seen from the way the book is composed. It can be divided into four collections, which can be labelled as Solomon I (Prov 1–24), Solomon II (Prov 25–29), Agur (Prov 30) and Lemuel (Prov 31).[20] Solomon I contains a brief superscription [Prov 1:1–7] stating the purpose of the collection, an extensive introduction [Prov 1:8–9:18] meant to motivate the פֶּתִי, followed by three sub-collections of proverbial material [Prov 10–22:16; 22:17–24:22; 24:23–34]. The initial superscription indicates that wisdom is to be found in the מִשְׁלֵי שְׁלֹמֹה. Within this context it appears natural that when Dame Wisdom first emerges at Prov 1:20, the knowledge she offers to mediate should be identified with Solomon's wisdom, which, according to the biblical tradition, was of divine origin. While it is often argued that it is the status of Solomon as a divinely endowed sage that accounts for the attribution of the proverbial material to him, the direct link between this divinely imparted wisdom of 1 Kgs 3:10–12, and the infallible understanding mediated by Dame Wisdom frequently goes unnoticed.

I, therefore, wish to suggest that the speeches of Dame Wisdom in Proverbs are a poetic representation of the type of revelatory process through which Solomon was endowed by wisdom in the story from 1 Kgs 3. The qualification *type of* is important here, as there is no doubt that the reader of Proverbs is to think that Wisdom is speaking through the entire book, including the material which is not labelled as Solomonic.[21] Consequently, the activity of this female figure cannot be limited to revelation that Solomon alone received. Rather, this particular case of divine revelation and illumination appears to be a specific example *par excellence* of a more general process in which God imparts understanding. In other words, the sages believed that in their striving

---

issues involved. Torah, as the divine revelation and key to understanding the world and the place of humans in it, fits the profile of Dame Wisdom, which will be examined in the next chapter, rather well. (The tension that von Rad is sensing is to a large extent of his own making, being the direct result of his choice of national salvation as the central notion for formulating his OT theology.)

[20] For an extensive argument for such a division see Kitchen (1977).

[21] Here I am not concerned with the question to what extent these superscriptions are historical data. My sole concern is with the perception of the material as it was shaped into the present form of the book. It is clear that at least some of the material in Proverbs was understood to have originated outside Israel, e.g., the material ascribed to Agur and the mother of Lemuel.

for wisdom God provided them with a special insight, one that was deemed to reach beyond what the human mind alone was able to grasp through its natural abilities, and essentially allowed the sages to see things from the divine perspective. To the young addressees of Proverbs this type of divine revelation is presented in the poetic terms of intimate relationship with a female companion, Dame Wisdom. It is quite clear that this revelation is of a different kind than is found in other OT traditions, for it does not revolve around dreams, visions and auditions, but rather, it is implied that God uses the normal intellectual processes to indirectly speak to those who revere him. Thus, it is justified to speak of *indirect revelation*, since the ability to understand the world is conditioned by person's piety, and this view is occasionally made explicit:

> Evil men do not understand justice, but those who seek the Yahweh understand all [of it].[22] [Prov 28:5]

Having established that divine revelation plays a part in the proverbial epistemology, it is necessary to consider the mechanics of the revelatory process. At first it might seem that this revelation is not tied to any particular locality. Wisdom is speaking at a variety of public places: squares, open spaces, near paths, crossroads, at city gates. It should, however, be noted that on none of these occasions she actually offers the insight she promises. Rather, on all of these occasions she gives out invitations to come and receive such an insight, i.e., the insight is not found at the public places where she speaks, it is located elsewhere. This is most blatant in the third appearance of Wisdom found in Prov 9. Here, she sends out her maids to distribute invitations in a public manner that resembles what we find in Prov 1 and 8, but the actual revelation, represented here by the image of food and drink at the banquet she prepared, is going to happen inside the house she built; it requires that the invitees follow her to the place of her choice and design. Thus, what really emerges from these calls is far from a universal and unconditional revelation of truth to the human race for which they are sometimes taken. Rather, the relationship to which Wisdom invites her listeners bares an uncanny resemblance to the concept of discipleship as it appears with reference to the prophets in the OT or John the Baptist and Jesus in the NT; the address is public but only the initiates have access to the full teaching.

---

[22] Toy (1899:497) is in my view correct seeing *justice* gapped from the previous colon.

Can more details about the character of the wisdom discipleship be derived from our text? Some insight into the nature of Wisdom's house and her banquet is found in the second half of Wisdom's speech in Prov 9:

> Who corrects a mocker receives an insult and who rebukes the wicked [receives] harm.[23] Do not rebuke a mocker, so that he does not hate you, rebuke a wise person and he will love you. Give to the wise and he will be even wiser, teach the righteous and he will add to his learning. The beginning of wisdom is the fear of Yahweh, and the knowledge of the Holy One[24] is understanding. For with me[25] your days will multiply and years of life will be added to you. [Prov 9:7–11]

It has been argued that Prov 9:7–11 represents a later addition to the material, or that it originally belonged to a different part of the book.[26] While this is possible and even likely, I am inclined to think that the material has been placed at its present location intentionally, in order to elucidate the nature of the banquet. The feast is envisaged as an opportunity for the wise and righteous to withdraw from the company of the incorrigible mockers and to mutually correct and educate each other. It is difficult to avoid the impression that the house of wisdom is an image for a more formal educational gathering.

There is a further aspect of the picture of wisdom painted in the opening nine chapters, as well as in the following sayings, which is directly relevant to the considerations about the significance of the house of Wisdom. The son is encouraged repeatedly to acquire wisdom at all costs. Consider the following texts:

> Acquire wisdom, acquire understanding,[27] do not forget and do not turn away from the words of my mouth. Do not abandon her, and she will keep you, love her, and she will guard you. [28]Wisdom is the best—acquire wisdom, and for all your possessions acquire understanding. [Prov 4:5–7]

---

[23] The parallelism between the colons suggests that מוּמוֹ is equivalent to לָקַח לוֹ קָלוֹן, the verb being gapped and the preposition with suffix replaced by nominal suffix alone.

[24] The parallelism suggests this is a plural of majesty, but see also the discussion in the next chapter on p. 88ff.

[25] Versions seem to have read *with her*, but this is still part of the direct speech by wisdom.

[26] See the discussion in Whybray (1994a:43–48).

[27] The beginning of the verse is missing in some 𝕲 manuscripts, however, it is required by the 3fs sfx in v. 6.

[28] The entire v. 7 is missing in 𝕲, possibly omitted due to the syntactical difficulties it presents.

Blessed is a person who has found wisdom, and a man who meets[29] [with] understanding. For her gain is better than the gain of silver and her [produce] is better than produce of pure gold. She is more precious than corals, nothing you may desire can equal her. [Prov 3:13–15].

What are finances for in the hand of a fool—to get wisdom? But he has no sense! [Prov 17:16]

Wisdom is quite clearly perceived in these passages as a commodity, which on the one hand has a value that cannot be expressed in material terms, yet, at the same time, can be acquired for money. Since knowledge is a thoroughly abstract concept, in order to become a commodity it has to be materialised in some fashion. There are only two ways in which this can occur, either through an object, such as a written text, or through a person. In these two forms it becomes a commodity, in terms of the cost necessary to pay for the object or to the person. In societies such as ancient Israel, where production of written records is labour-intensive, slow and ultimately expensive, the teacher remains the primary source of knowledge. Consequently, the present references to purchasing wisdom can hardly be understood otherwise than largely as allusions to learning from a person for a tuition fee. In other words, the book is aware of education with a commercial basis. The similarities between the wisdom banquet and the passages to do with purchasing wisdom on the one hand and Sir 51:23–28 on the other are noteworthy. Within this context it appears reasonable to understand the house of wisdom, and the seclusion it provides to those, and only those, who choose to join in, as referring to a school.

The existence of schools in ancient Israel has been widely debated for some time now, but as this discussion is of a marginal interest to the present study, only a very brief sketch is going to be presented here.[30] The already mentioned similarities between Prov 22:17ff. and the *Instruction of Amenemopet* had a far-reaching impact on the study of biblical wisdom, leading to the tradition being seen and studied as a common ANE phenomenon. One of the consequences of this comparative approach was the conclusion that OT wisdom material must have originated in a similar setting as the wisdom texts of other ANE cultures, and in particular, in a similar setting as the Egyptian didactic writings. As these would appear to have been used in scribal

---

[29] Note the shift from the Sx in the A colon to the habitual Px in B colon.

[30] A recent survey and evaluation of the arguments can be found in Davies (1995), whose conclusions the present author shares.

schools associated with the royal court, the view that the OT wisdom was also used for the purposes of training scribes came to be adopted by a number of scholars.[31]

However, such an understanding of the nature of the wisdom tradition has its weaknesses and came to be criticised fiercely by others in the field; Golka (1983) went so far as to compare the whole school theory to the tail of Caesar's new clothes. There are three principal objections that can be levelled against the school origins of OT wisdom: (1) there is no mention of schools in the OT prior to Ben Sira; (2) there is no unequivocal archaeological evidence for the existence of schools in ancient Israel; (3) the internal evidence for the origins of OT wisdom material in formal educational setting associated with the royal court is weak.

While the criticism of over-enthusiastic acceptance of the comparative evidence is justified, the whole issue is far from black and white. Regarding the archaeological evidence, Lemaire (1981) collected a significant amount of epigraphic material that led him to conclude that the writing skills reflected in it require the postulation of a formal school system in ancient Israel, and as Davies (1995:209–10) pointed out, some discoveries made since the original work give extra weight to this conclusion. In addition to the technical skills reflected in the epigraphic evidence, the literary quality of material found in the Hebrew bible must also be taken into account. It is one thing to say that a 22 letter alphabet could be learned easily and without formal schooling, and another matter entirely to claim that high poetic and literary skills could have evolved without any co-ordinated effort and become widespread; a high level of literary skills can only be obtained by extensive first-hand experience, which is something that is unlikely to have been readily available in a society whose life was centred around labour-intensive and low-return agriculture and farming.[32] Further, the royal court would have a need for literate clerks, in the running of both its domestic and international affairs, and scribes do appear on the lists associated with royal

---

[31] See, for instance, note 7 on p. 24.

[32] Even the argument about literacy being easily acquired due to the simplicity of the alphabet, made originally by Albright and recently restated by Weeks (1995:151), is questionable. Modern-day experience shows that in societies that do not have sufficient formal schooling the proportion of literacy in the population is low. This is in spite of the fact that the wide availability of written materials in printed form creates conditions for literacy that are greatly superior to that of ancient pre-press societies.

administration;[33] in is unlikely that the court would not make formal provisions for training of these.

In addition, the argument about the lack of internal evidence in the wisdom material for its school origins is only of a limited value in the overall debate, since at best it proves that the wisdom texts are not school texts *per se*; it proves nothing about the actual existence of schools and the nature of their relationship, if any, with the wisdom enterprise. Very much the same is true concerning the overall silence of the OT on the subject of schools. It merely suggests that the OT is not to be viewed as principally a school-text, and further, that existence of extensive and all-pervasive system of education in ancient Israel is improbable. However, to argue from this silence on its own that there was no formal schooling in ancient Israel would be unwise.

When all the evidence is considered, it suggests that although there must have been some formal schooling available in ancient Israel to account for the attested technical and literary skills, such an education would have been provided on a limited scale, most likely in the proximity of the royal administration. Such an assessment of the available data fits well with the picture we find in the book of Proverbs, for even though the house of seven pillars would appear to be some kind of a school, this is not to say Proverbs *per se* is a school text; to the contrary. There are clear indications that the centre of the instruction in Proverbs is in the family, as I will argue in chapter 6. The overall picture is of a young man under the instruction of both of his parents but primarily of his father, who is being presented with an invitation to come to a wisdom banquet in the house of seven pillars. In other words, we meet here a young man at a significant milestone in his life. He has been informally trained within the context of his family but is now encouraged to pursue wisdom in a more intensive manner, outside of the family circle, possibly in a school. Such an understanding makes good sense both of the repeated exhortations not to abandon the basic instruction of the parents, and of the stress on the necessity to purchase wisdom and the numerous references to the desirability of association with the wise.

The real epistemological significance of the banquet in the house of seven pillars is not so much in the fact that it points to a probable link between the wisdom undertaking and formal education, but that it shows very clearly that the revelatory element of the process of gaining

---

[33] For instance 2 Sam 8:16–18; 20:24–25; 1 Kgs 4:3; 2 Kgs 18:18.

wisdom does not happen on an individual level, but in the context of a community, through dialogue of the wise. As this communal aspect of the wisdom quest is also predominant in the non-revelatory data acquisition of the sages, it prevents us from understanding the proverbial quest for wisdom as an individualistic and self-centred search for knowledge and success; the epistemology of proverbial wisdom is characterised by community orientation.

While dealing with the place of divine revelation in Proverbs, a brief note concerning the cult is needed. There are at least a couple of occasions in the book where reference to revelation of cultic nature is made:

> He who turns[34] his ear from listening to the Law—even his prayer is an abomination. [Prov 28:9]

> When there is no vision,[35] people go loose, but he who keeps the Law is blessed. [Prov 29:18]

It is generally difficult to determine whether the term תּוֹרָה is used in the book with reference to human instruction or whether it is used with the religious significance the term often has in other parts of the OT. However, the context suggests that on these two occasions it is likely the latter. While it would be possible to understand the word in the former sense in the first of the passages, the resulting link between the two colons is loose and weak. The rendering adopted here creates much stronger parallelism, picturing two way communication between a person and God. In the second passage quoted, תּוֹרָה is paralleled to חָזוֹן, which is a term for prophetic revelation. In that context it is unlikely that תּוֹרָה was intended otherwise than as a reference to divine instruction. Overall, though, the cult plays no significant role in the proverbial epistemology; we shall see the reasons for this in the following chapter.

Evaluating Experience

Having looked at the means through which the sages gathered their data, it remains to add a note on the way they assessed their observations. As has been pointed out earlier, one can discern in the book a

---

[34] 𝔖 ܢܬܡܣܟܢ, the root ܣܟܢ means *to refrain, restrain*, and so there is no reason to assume, *pace* BHS, that 𝔖 was reading anything else than 𝔐.

[35] 𝔐 חָזוֹן; 𝔊 understood this personally rendering ἐξηγητές, however, the parallelism favours an impersonal interpretation.

conviction about the objective value of human experience. This objectivity is quite clearly understood not only in synchronic terms, but also diachronically. While there is the awareness that what is being presented is a simplified portrayal of reality, there is a strong and unmistakable conviction that on the larger scale the paradigm ultimately works and no indication is given that at any future date it might need serious reconsidering. The world is seen ultimately as static, operating within a fixed framework that was put in place at creation and does not change. Consequently, experience that has been collectively accumulated through many generations has to take priority over the immediate experience of an individual; the present is to be evaluated in the terms of the past, the narrower picture in terms of the large one.

In other words the basic principle of the sages' data assessment is that good data conforms to the existing paradigm and lends it further support, while behind that which appears to contradict it must be some additional reasons that cause the apparent discrepancy. The following text can serve as an example of this attitude:

> Trust in Yahweh with all your heart, and do not lean on your understanding, know him in all your ways, and he will straighten your paths. Do not be wise in your own eyes—fear Yahweh and turn away from evil. There will be healing to your body[36] and refreshment to your bones. Honour Yahweh from your wealth and from the choicest [part] of all your produce—and your stores will be filled abundantly, and your presses will burst with new wine. As for Yahweh's discipline, my son, do not reject [it] and do not loathe [it] when he rebukes you. For whom Yahweh loves he rebukes,[37] but like a father[38] he delights in his son. [Prov 3:5–12]

Verses 5–10 outline the basic proverbial perspective: fear God and all will be well. The final two verses are of a greater interest to us, for they clearly suggest that in fact what has just been said is not always

---

[36] Reading לִשְׁאֵרֶךָ with 𝕲 and 𝕾; 𝔐 לְשָׁרֶּךָ, *to your naval string*. Driver (1951b:175) argues from the cognate languages for existence of root שׁהר, *healing*, but in the light of the fact that in our passage the word is parallel עַצְמוֹתֶיךָ and not שִׁקּוּי, such an explanation is implausible.

[37] Note the habitual use of the Px conjugations here; Yahweh's rebuking is not portrayed here as an isolated, one-off act, but as a continuous unfolding process.

[38] 𝔐 וּכְאָב; 𝕲 μαστιγοῖ, reading כאב as a verb, *and he whips every son he likes*. Toy (1899:65) follows 𝕲 because of the similarities with Job 5:17–18, but while those two texts share some features, they are sufficiently distinct to invalidate the argument. Further, it is quite possible that 𝕲 adopted its reading because it found the reference to God as father irreverent. On the other hand, 𝔐 pointing could have been influenced by the following reference to son. The evidence is inconclusive.

true. Experience that diverges from the paradigm is in this particular instance seen through theological glasses; the unpleasant is understood as disciplining that is part of divine love, and ultimately, approval.

It is obvious that the proverbial epistemology is flawed due to the apparent circularity; the paradigm is based on experience, but only the experience that conforms to the existing paradigm is accepted as valid. Yet, we need to appreciate the causes of this circularity. The problematic belief in diachronic objectivity of human experience is closely linked to the conviction that the search for wisdom is divinely inspired. Within the proverbial paradigm God is firmly on the side of those who pursue wisdom, and it is, therefore, virtually impossible that those genuinely engaged in this search (which in Proverbs are only those who fear God) would not find the truth; they may not know everything, but they are more or less right about that which they do know. In other words, the paradigm presented by the book needs not to be questioned. Indeed, it is the fools, say the sages, who question and reject the kind of wisdom that we find in Proverbs; the proverbial instruction is authoritative, it is to be heeded, rather than scrutinised.

It is here, at the heart of the proverbial epistemology, that the serious problems that wisdom encounters later, and to which Job and Qoheleth respond, begin; the conviction that experience is in fact a source of divine revelation, coupled with the view that the world is static, allows very little space for manoeuvre should the external circumstance change, and further, creates a vicious circle. On the one hand the sages need the claim of divine inspiration to give authority to their teaching, but at the same time, they need the common experience to affirm this teaching in order to maintain the claim of divine inspiration. Consequently, any discrepancies between the teaching and the experience are impossible to reconcile—they undermine the cornerstone of the proverbial authority, the assertion about divine inspiration. And yet, it would appear that the proverbial sages were blissfully unaware of this basic flaw of their outlook, i.e., they seem to have lived in a world that was relatively static and conformed to their teaching. It was left to later generations of the wise men to tackle this problem, one that does not lie in what the sages it claimed about the world, but in what they believed about the nature of their claims. And so we can now turn to the epistemology of Qoheleth, to see how he dealt with the issues which by his time were impossible to ignore.

The Epistemological Perspective of Qoheleth

Individual Observation and Collective Experience

Even a fairly casual reader of Qoheleth will realise that experience is at the heart of Qoheleth's epistemology. Thus, as we turn our attention to the book, we will start by looking at the details of the role experience plays in it, and more specifically, at the relationship between the individual and collective experience within Qoheleth's epistemology. A passage that throws a significant light on the role of observation in the book is the opening poem [Qoh 1:4–11]. Since the most important contribution of this material is to our understanding of Qoheleth's cosmology, its detailed treatment will be left for the following chapter. At this stage I will anticipate some of the conclusions that will be reached there focusing on the epistemological implications of the text. These are twofold. First, the poem shows that Qoheleth's world is coherent; the human and the natural are fully integrated with each other. It is, therefore, possible to study the larger phenomenal patterns, such as the movement of the sun, apply them to humanity, and to draw from them conclusions about the nature of human existence. So even though we do not find in the book observations of creatures comparable to those found in Proverbs as discussed earlier,[39] this poem shows that Qoheleth's world has the same overall integrity as the world of the proverbial sages.

The second epistemological implication of the opening poem has to do with Qoheleth's claim that existence is cyclic, yet constant. As a result of it, Qoheleth is convinced that his personal observations have an objective value, that they can be generalised and applied universally. The implicit belief in objectivity of personal experience surfaces in the frequent occurrences of command forms in the book, and is picked upon by the epilogist when he describes Qoheleth as a teacher [Qoh 12:9]. Thus, we see here a significant point of contact with the epistemology of the proverbial sages.

However, while in Proverbs direct observation is only occasionally presented as the source of knowledge, in Qoheleth the personal experience is the primary *modus operandi*, as is shown by the frequent appearances of the 1cs forms of ראה, ידע, and מצא.[40] This, though, does not

---

[39] With the possible exception of Qoh 12:5ab, but considering the obscurity of the imagery of Qoh 12:3–7, it is not possible to draw any firm conclusions from these verses.

[40] There are some 30 occurrences of these verbs in total.

mean, as it is sometimes implied, that Qoheleth does not, at least to some extent, build on the experience of others (*pace* Fox, 1987:142). This can be shown in the following two examples. The first case in point is found in the already mentioned opening poem [Qoh 1:4–11]. Qoheleth assumes here that the natural phenomena he speaks about behave in an identical manner from one generation to another; this is something that he cannot, quite obviously, verify by his own observation. Instead, he is implicitly relying on the collective human memory, believing that it provides sufficient and firm grounds to make definitive statements about the nature of these phenomena. In reality, this assumption means that in the final analysis Qoheleth is begging the question, for he uses these phenomena to justify his belief that the world is in principle static and unchanging. This particular assumption, which rests on prior and collective knowledge, rather than his personal observation, cannot be dismissed as trivial, as one may be tempted to do at first; as we will see in the following chapter, Qoheleth's entire understanding of the world hinges on the premise of constancy.

The second example of Qoheleth using second-hand experience is found in the Solomonic experiment [Qoh 1:12–2:26]. In this section of the book Qoheleth takes the experience of Solomon, identifies with it and draws his own conclusions from it.[41] This material shows that sometimes Qoheleth relies on another person's experience not purely out of necessity but by choice. There could be numerous reasons for Qoheleth using Solomon in this way, in particular, within the biblical tradition Solomon is the wise and successful man *par excellence*, and if anyone could possibly achieve anything substantial in life, it would have been him. However, we are at present less interested in the reasons for this approach, and more in its epistemological significance. It shows, just as the former example does, that similarly to the proverbial sages,

---

[41] There is little doubt that the king in Qoh 1:12 is to be identified as Solomon, especially in light of the king's exceeding wisdom [Qoh 1:16] and achievement [Qoh 2:4–11]. While it is true that the superscription [Qoh 1:1] extends this identification to the entire book, so that from the canonical perspective it is to be seen as a story about Solomon, I agree with the majority of scholars that within the core of the book, Qoheleth assumes Solomon's identity only temporarily. That Qoheleth cannot be identified with Solomon in real terms is clearly indicated by the linguistic evidence, for the book contains a large number of Aramaisms, two Persian words, and a number of grammatical peculiarities, all pointing to a late date. On the overwhelming cumulative weight of the evidence, there is a general agreement that the book should be dated in the 3rd century BC. Attempts to establish a pre-exilic date (Fredericks, 1988) or a later 2nd century date (Whitley, 1979) have proven to be unconvincing.

Qoheleth's epistemology is not purely individualistic. Yet, admittedly, Qoheleth does not draw on other people's knowledge very often and this fact leads us to the question of how Qoheleth assesses different experience and how he decides what to include and what to exclude when forming his outlook on the world around him.

Evaluating Experience

In spite of the aforementioned collective element to Qoheleth's epistemology, there is a significant divergence between Qoheleth and Proverbs in this respect, one that goes far beyond merely a difference in emphasis. In Proverbs the diachronic collective experience is treated synchronically and takes precedence over the immediate individual one; it is the knowledge accumulated by the subsequent generations that represents the standard against which everything else is measured. In contrast, for Qoheleth his immediate experience is the norm by which any past experience is judged, and if the two contradict each other, it is the personal experience that is upheld. The following passage offers an excellent example:

> Since the sentence of[42] the evil deed is not carried out quickly, therefore, the heart of human beings which is within them is full to do evil —because a sinner does evil a hundred[43] [times], yet, his [life] is prolonged[44]—although I know that it should[45] be well with the fearers of God, those[46] who continue to fear[47] him, and it should not be well with

[42] Reading with 𝕲 and few manuscripts פִּתְגָם as a construct, *pace* the 𝔐 accents.

[43] 𝔐 מֵאַת; 𝕲 ἀπὸ τότε possibly reading מֵאָז; α', σ', ϑ' ἀπέϑανεν, i.e., מֵת. The 𝔐 form is a construct which would seem to indicate a word (such as פָּנִים) has dropped out (Ogden, 1987b:137), or, it could be repointed to the feminine pl. מֵאת. Gordis (1955a:297) asserts that מאה always modifies a singular noun, but that is not the case, cf. מֵאָה פְעָמִים in 2 Sam 24:3 (although, this phrase uses the absolute). Barton (1908:156) proposes to read מֵאַד, which could be accounted for by an audible error.

[44] 𝔐 וּמַאֲרִיך, 𝕲 ἀπο μακρότητος, i.e., מִן + ארך. While this fits reasonably well with the delayed execution of the sentence in the previous verse, it would be a mere restatement of what that verse already said, and so it is most likely the translator's attempt to make sense of the Hebrew. Gordis (1955a:298) understands מאריך as shortened for מאריך אף לו, but that is unlikely in the light of Qoh 8:12–13 which shows that the idiom is מַאֲרִיך יָמִים.

[45] Modal use of Px; the statements of the following verses, declaring that things are not like this in the real world, preclude this and the following two Px forms to be interpreted as denoting a simple future.

[46] Possibly, *because they fear him*, but that is a somewhat self-evident statement. It is therefore more likely that this clause is epexegetical, refining the phrase *fearers of God*.

[47] Habitual use of Px, parallel to the sinner committing evil a hundred times.

the wicked, and [his] days should not be prolonged like[48] a shadow, because he did not fear God. There is absurdity which happens[49] upon the earth, that there are righteous men to whom it happens as if they were wicked and there are wicked men, to whom it happens as if they were righteous. I said that also this is absurd. [Qoh 8:11–14]

Here Qoheleth quite openly questions the perspective we have seen in Proverbs, namely, that the wicked suffer and the righteous prosper. He acknowledges that things should be like that, but is unable to reconcile his own experience with such a view.

What needs to be stressed, is that in dealing with the problem created by the assertions about appropriate consequences for both the righteous and the wicked, Qoheleth does not really get to the heart of the matter. Even though his epistemology is different than that found in Proverbs, he does not relinquish either of the two problematic tenets on which the proverbial epistemology was built, namely, that the world is basically immutable, and that human experience is objective in a timeless manner. His basic approach to the issue is that since his observations are different from observations similar to those made by the proverbial sages, the other observers must have been mistaken. This ultimately means that his basic perspective is no more capable of adapting to changes in external circumstances, than was the case with the proverbial sages.

Place of Revelation

In the case of Proverbs, it has been observed that alongside the empirical modes of learning, there is some place for divine revelation, even though the mode of the revelation does not have rigidly defined contours. I wish to suggest that revelation also has its place in Qoheleth's quest for understanding. Consider the following passage:

---

[48] 𝔐 כְּ; 𝔊 בְּ. The long shadow in the 𝔐 symbolises a late hour of a day, the 𝔊 text makes poor sense.

[49] I follow Fox (1989:173) in rendering Niphal of עשׂה in this manner. The Sx form that Qoheleth uses with this expression throughout the book denotes a static point of view similar to the proverbial gnomic perspective. Qoheleth is not referring to what is being done presently, nor what has been done, but essentially to what is universally true of the human world.

There is nothing better for a person than[50] that he should[51] eat and drink, and make his soul to enjoy[52] his achievement. Yet,[53] this, I saw, is from the hand of God. For who can eat and who can amass[54] apart from him?[55] For to the person who is pleasing to him he gives wisdom and knowledge and joy, and to the sinner he gives affliction to gather and to amass [in the end] to give it to one who is pleasing to God. Also this is absurd and striving after wind. [Qoh 2:24–26]

Again, it is apparent that Qoheleth severed the link between wisdom and material success, since both the person who is pleasing to God and the sinner are in a similar position to start with; neither of them is lacking in material terms. In the case of the one who is pleasing to God, this is clearly implied by the fact that he has joy which in v. 24 is conceived in terms of eating and drinking. In the case of the sinner, this is made explicit, he is hoarding possessions. Therefore, the distinction between the two is not that one receives material success and the other does not. The difference is that one is endowed by God with wisdom, knowledge and joy and the other is not. It is the link between wisdom and joy as divine gifts that deserves further consideration in our attempt to understand Qoheleth's epistemology.[56]

It can be observed that the link between the ability to enjoy and divine approval is not limited to the passage above. Consider for instance the following text:

---

[50] Reading with 𝔖, 𝔗. ם probably missing due to haplography with בָּאָדָם. What follows requires that the clause has a positive sense, and so cannot be rendered *that it is not good* (*pace* Loader, 1986:31).

[51] Modal use of Px, this sense is made even clearer in some manuscripts and 𝔖 reading לאכל.

[52] Lit. *to make his soul to see good*.

[53] גַּם means *yet* when linking clauses that are in a disjunctive relationship. While there is no explicit negative present here, it is, in my opinion, implied, for v. 24a states that the only thing one can get out of one's labour is the short-term satisfaction, while vv. 24b-26 assert that *not* all people can derive this type of satisfaction from their achievement, but only those favoured by God.

[54] 𝔐 יָחוּשׁ; 𝔊, θ', 𝔖 read ישתה but the following verse, linked by כִּי, continues the thought and it is, therefore, most likely that יָחוּשׁ is antithetical to אכל (Gordis, 1955a:216–17). 𝔊ᴼ, α', σ' φείσεται, *to refrain*, also seemed to have understood the two as antithetical. Fox (1989:188) renders *wonder, fret*, while Ellermeier (1963:197–217) argued for the meaning *to worry* from comparative evidence, and Ogden (1987b:48) makes an otherwise unsubstantiated claim that חוש means *to enjoy*. The best solution appears to be that of Seow (1997:139–40) who argues for the sense *to gather* based on the Arabic *ḥâša*, which is supported by the contrast between enjoyment and amassing of property in v. 26.

[55] 𝔐 מִמֶּנִּי; reading מִמֶּנּוּ with 𝔊 and 𝔖.

[56] See also Lohfink (1990).

> Go! Eat your bread with joy, and drink your wine in enjoyment of heart, for God already paid off your deeds. [Qoh 9:7][57]

Eventually, all of the repeated calls for enjoyment culminate in Qoheleth's final advice:

> The light is sweet and it is pleasant for the eyes to see the sun. Indeed, if a person lives many years, let him rejoice in all of them, but let him remember the dark days, for they could be many, all that comes is absurd. Young man, rejoice in your youth, and let your heart make you happy in your young days, and walk in the ways of your heart, and visions of your eyes, but know that concerning all of these God will bring you into judgement. [Qoh 11:7–9][58]

The reiterated claims that there is nothing better than to enjoy one's accomplishments point in the same direction, one explicitly stated in Qoh 2:24: true wisdom encompasses the sense to enjoy in the present that which can be enjoyed. However, Qoheleth believes that this sense is gained not by some rational deliberation, but is ultimately God-given; the sinner in Qoh 2:26 lacks this divine endowment and continues to hoard possessions which someone else will end up enjoying. Thus wisdom, in the fullest sense Qoheleth uses the word, can only be obtained through divine revelation. It would appear that the mode of the revelation we find here is quite similar to the divine insight that the proverbial sages believed to be receiving from God in their earnest pursuit of wisdom; it comes from divine benevolence outside of the confines of the formal boundaries of the cult.

However, even though both Qoheleth and the proverbial sages believe that God plays an active role in the human search for understanding, the two perceptions of this divine involvement differ significantly:

> And I saw the occupation which God gave to human beings to occupy/afflict[59] [themselves] with. He makes everything beautiful[60] in its[61] time;

---

[57] For textual notes see p. 191.

[58] For textual notes see p. 192.

[59] The meaning of the verb ענה is ambiguous here; I am inclined to think that this ambiguity is intentional (see also note 53 on p. 151 with reference to Qoh 1:13).

[60] This is the sense of יָפֶה in BH. The sense in later Hebrew is *good, appropriate* (see Jas and the discussion in Barton, 1908:105), which might be more appropriate here. It refers to the equilibrium of things stated in the preceding poem, which will be discussed in detail in the following chapter.

[61] The main concern of this section of material is with the time of things. This suggests that the time rather than God is the referent of the 3ms sfx.

also, he put ignorance[62] in their hearts, because of which[63] a person is not able to find[64] out [about] the things which God does—from the beginning to the end. I came to know that there is nothing better for them[65] but to rejoice and to do well in one's life. But also any person who can eat and drink and enjoy the fruit of his labour—it is a gift of God. I came to know that whatever God may do, will be forever[66]—it is

---

[62] Reading הָעֹלֶם, *ignorance* as first suggested by Joseph Karo (see Perry, 1993:185). This makes best sense in the context and the defective spelling serves here as a clue (the only other time עוֹלָם is spelled defectively in Qoheleth is the plural form in Qoh 1:10, cf. the full spelling Qoh 3:14). The verbal root עלם with the sense *to conceal* appears in Qoh 12:14 (Crenshaw, 1988:99). The use of *nota accusativi* with a non-determined noun is found elsewhere in the book (e.g. Qoh 3:15; 7:7). Gordis (1955a:221–22) prefers to read עוֹלָם as *world*, but this, in BH unattested, sense has no special merit in our passage. Ogden (1987b:55) accepts 𝔐, arguing that the temporal expression fits the context, offering a new dimension alongside of עֵת and זְמָן, but considering that this reality is not external, but rather internal to humanity it is hard to understand it as a 'dimension' of the world, which is what the preceding temporal references have in mind. Even if one wishes to read *eternity* with 𝔐 and the versions, or *world* with Gordis, the meaning of the whole verse is not significantly impacted—whatever God put into the human mind, it prevents humanity from intellectually catching up with him (see note 63 below). Fox (1989:194) emends to עמל but there is no textual evidence or need for such an emendation, and the resulting sentence is awkward.

[63] מִבְּלִי can be used as a substantive meaning *nothing* (only once in the OT in Job 18:15), a preposition or a conjunction. As a preposition מִבְּלִי means *without*, a use also attested in MH. As a conjunction it normally introduces a nominal clause and means *because of no ...*, e.g. Exod 14:11 (BDB suggests *so that there is no...*, but this rendering is misleading as in English this construction can be both final and causal, while this use is never final in the OT, but rather causal-epexegetical - see Jer 2:15; 9:9–11; Ezek 14:15; Zeph 3:6; Job 6:6). Only once is it followed by a finite verb (Deut 28:55) with the same meaning. The nominal use is clearly ruled out for Qoh 3:11 and the prepositional sense *without* does not suit the context because the main clause is concerned with presence, not absence (*pace* KBL-3). Thus מִבְּלִי must function in Qoh 3:11 as a conjunction, and as the OT use is uniform, it needs to be rendered as causal. It fits the standard construction when it is followed by a nominal expression, here the relative pronoun אֲשֶׁר, i.e., *because of which*. The negative לֹא is pleonastic (cf. מִבְּלִי אֵין Exod 14:11; 2 Kgs 1:3, 6, 16). The common renderings *yet*, *so that* (KBL-2) and *so that not* (BDB) are unjustified in the light of the evidence.

[64] In the context of God imposing limits on human capabilities, modal understanding of the Px is preferable to simple future.

[65] 𝔐 בָּם. Gordis (1955a:222) considers this a dittography from טוֹב כִּי (כ and ם being very similar in the script from the Maccabean period), but 𝔐 is supported by both 𝔊 and 𝔖 and makes a reasonably good sense.

[66] Fox (1989:194–95) suggests that the sense here is not *it will last forever*, but rather *it will always happen*. Yet, Qoheleth does not think in the poem of individual and isolated actions, but rather in terms of the broader phenomenal framework within which everything happens, and this framework is fixed and unchangeable, i.e., eternal (see the discussion of the poem on p. 119).

impossible to add to it and it is impossible to subtract from it. And God
does this so that they would fear[67] him. [Qoh 3:10–14]

This passage is in some respects similar to Qoh 2:24–26 considered
earlier; here we meet again the statement that there is nothing better
than to enjoy life, with the enjoyment conditioned by divine approval.
However, this passage offers a greater insight into nature of the human
search for wisdom. In Proverbs, Yahweh is the ultimate patron of the
wisdom quest and Dame Wisdom, acting on God's behalf, is keen to
share understanding of the world's deepest secrets with those wishing to learn on her terms. However, in the passage above Qoheleth
paints God in an entirely different light. Qoheleth's God is much more
reserved in disclosing any secrets to humanity. In fact, he has intentionally limited human ability to understand the world and the ways
in which he operates; the imposed limitations are a means for keeping humanity in proper relationship with him. Thus, while in Proverbs
ignorance was a sign of rejection of the divinely sanctioned search to
understand the world, for Qoheleth ignorance is ultimately something
that God desires, for he ensures through it that human beings will not
succeed in disrupting the overall equilibrium he imposed on the world,
the equilibrium at the heart of Qoheleth's paradigm.

Alongside the indirect revelatory processes, Qoheleth accepts the
possibility of revelation through the cult. This can be seen in his following advice to the reader:

> Watch your step when you go to the house of God, and approach more
> to obey than to offer a sacrifice, … do not be hasty with your mouth and
> do not let your heart to utter a word before God rashly … let your words
> be few. [Qoh 4:17–5:1][68]

Whether שמע in Qoh 4:17 should be rendered into English as *obey* or
listen can be debated, but irrespective of the decision an interpreter may
make in this matter, the surrounding text shows that Qoheleth has in
mind two way communication between the worshipper and the deity;
on the one hand the worshipper is cautioned to speak little, on the
other hand listening is encouraged. Since it is quite clear that when

---

[67] Ogden's (1987b:57) proposal to read ראה instead of ירא is unconvincing. The
appearance of ראה in v. 10 has little bearing on the decision and the resulting use of
מלפניו with ראה is awkward, while Qoheleth uses the preposition with ירא elsewhere
[Qoh 8:12].
[68] For textual notes see p. 109.

advising against excessive talk Qoheleth has in mind speech directed toward God [Qoh 5:1], the listening also needs to be understood as listening to the deity. However, this does not necessarily mean direct revelation is in view, for the *messenger* in Qoh 5:5 is most likely a temple servant (or a human official of some kind), making it probable that Qoheleth conceives of the revelation as mediated. In any case, the precise mechanics of the revelatory process are not as important here as the fact that by encouraging the reader to listen, Qoheleth implicitly acknowledges that any information gained via the cultic channel is of importance, i.e., revelation plays some role in Qoheleth's epistemology.

The assertions found in the two passages quoted above seemingly present radically different perspectives. The latter shows that Qoheleth accepts that divine revelation is channelled through the cult and further that he even considers such revelation as authoritative, yet, in the former text Qoheleth is adamant that God severely limited the human ability to understand him and what he is up to. However, these two assertions are not mutually exclusive, since they refer to a different type of knowing. One flows downwards from God to humans, and the other upwards from humans to God—Qoheleth's God can be only understood from what he himself chooses to reveal about himself.

The divine involvement in the process of knowing has two cascading ramifications for the wisdom enterprise. First, somewhat obviously, the sage cannot claim that he knows what God is up to, if he does, he is a liar [Qoh 8:17]. This stands in contrast to the proverbial view, for the proverbial sage believes that he more or less knows what God is doing. Second, a necessary implication of the first, the value of wisdom is diminished. There is a limit to what wisdom can achieve and, therefore, there must be a limit to which one pursues wisdom. When wisdom is sought after excessively, the outcome will not justify the investment. While this does not mean that wisdom does not have value and is not worth pursuing in principle, it does stand in a stark contrast to the emphatic admonitions of Proverbs to acquire wisdom at all costs.

Further, it is not only that Qoheleth considers unrestrained search for understanding to be a loss-making business, but there seems to be some indication that he may even consider it harmful:

> 'Look! This is what I found,' said Qoheleth, [adding] one to one to get [the] answer. 'My soul sought again—and [again] I did not find: one man out of a thousand I found, but a woman among all of these I did not find. Only, look at what I found, that God made mankind straight, but they sought many answers.' [Qoh 7:27–29][69]

We shall return to this passage in some detail in the following chapter. What should be noted at this point is that Qoheleth blames the demise of the initial human uprightness on search for חֶשְׁבּוֹן. This term has clear intellectual connotations, and, as I will argue in the following chapter (p. 156), the whole verse most likely refers to a search for black and white solutions to difficult, if not insoluble problems, to the perpetual human desire to understand, and thus control, the surrounding world. Such endeavour in Qoheleth's view can only lead to frustration and loss of intellectual clarity.[70]

One final issue needs to be considered—whether there is any discernible difference in the epistemological perspective of the core of Qoheleth and of the editorial frame, specifically of the epilogue. I am inclined to agree with Sheppard's (1977) analysis, that the ideas contained in the epilogue can all be traced to the core of the book. Yet, while the epilogist builds on Qoheleth's own claims, he treats them selectively, placing emphasis on certain notions:

> The words of the wise are like spikes and like nails set in place [by] collectors,[71] given by one shepherd. Above these,[72] my son, be warned:

---

[69] For textual notes see p. 157, where the whole passage Qoh 7:23–29 is discussed in a greater detail.

[70] It is worth noting that the theme of the corrupting impact of wisdom and knowledge is not unique to Qoheleth. The simplicity of life in the garden of Eden is ruined by the human desire to know more than God intended in Gen 2–3, and again, wisdom is at the heart of shattering of the initial idyllic state of affairs in the garden of Eden in Ezek 28:11–19.

[71] Assuming haplography and reading מִבַּעֲלֵי, cf. ᴳ οἴ παρὰ τῶν συναγμάτων. Another possibility is that בְּ, used alongside לְ to express an agent of a passive Niphal (WOC 23.2.2f), could be assimilated in בַּעֲלֵי, cf. a comparable phenomenon attested in the OT in case of בֵּת. Driver (1954:234–35) is of the view that ᴹ division of the verse is incorrect and בַּעֲלֵי אֲסֻפּוֹת should start the next line, i.e., it is the collectors rather than the sayings that are given by one shepherd. He further understands the phrase as referring to gathering people. However, the principal subject of vv. 11–12 is quite clearly *words of the wise* and their usefulness, and this makes ᴹ division of the line preferable to Driver's. Wilson's (1984:176) suggestion that בַּעֲלֵי is a reference to the collected material has to be rejected since בַּעַל is always personal.

[72] Fox (1989:326–7) proposes to set the pause between וְיֹתֵר and מֵהֵמָּה (*pace* ᴹ), but this produces awkward word order in the resulting clause.

there is no end to producing many books, and much reading[73] tires the
body. End of [the] matter, [of] everything heard, fear God and keep his
commandments, for this perfects[74] a human being. [Qoh 12:11–13]

The epilogist seized the logical implications of Qoheleth's epistemology
for the value of wisdom, taking them much further than Qoheleth
was prepared to do. He asserts plainly that the upward search for
knowledge is endless and produces very little and, therefore, one has
to order one's life according to the downward stream of wisdom, the
revealed divine command. Significantly, the epilogist's concept of divine
revelation is more clearly defined than either that of Proverbs or the
Qoheleth proper. Verse 11 seems to have in mind the vague and indirect
revelation that both books seems to consider, where the sages in their
search for understanding receive illumination from God. However, the
following reference to God's commandments indicates that alongside it
the writer has in mind a more clearly defined revelation, which involves
direct divine speech. This is something that traditionally belongs to
the sphere of the cult rather than wisdom and the epilogist appears
not only to be concerned that these two modes of revelation should
not be separated from each other, but quite clearly perceives the cultic
revelation as taking precedence over the wisdom quest.

The seemingly positive reference to the wise men and their work
should not obscure from us what is really happening in the epilogue;
the endlessness of the wisdom quest is purely rhetorical. From the
epilogist's point of view it does not reside in the fact that the complete
knowledge cannot be obtained by humans, as it did for Qoheleth,
but rather that all that is to be known is already known and written
down; the endlessness of any further search resides in the fact that such

---

[73] Reading infc. of הגה with the final ת lost due to haplography (see Qoheleth
Rabbah 12:12), which in the context is preferable to ᴳ μελέτη, *care, anxiety*.

[74] The meaning of כָּל־הָאָדָם is uncertain and the versions appear to struggle with
the same text. Gordis (1955a:355) gives examples of construction of the type אֲנִי תְפִלָּה in
support of rendering *this is the whole duty of man*, but it should be noted that all of these
examples are in poetry, while our passage is prosaic. Fox (1989:329) pointed out that
כָּל־הָאָדָם normally means either *every man* or *all men*, but never *the whole man*; elsewhere
in Qoheleth this construction is used only in the former sense [Qoh 3:13; 5:18; 7:2].
A number of very attractive options open when the possibility of כָּל being a verb is
considered: (a) כול, *for this a human being comprehends*; (b) כלא (loss of א via scribal error
due to the proximity of הָאָדָם) *for this restrains a human being*; (c) כלה (loss of ה due to
haplography) *for this is the end of a human being*; (d) כלל *this perfects a human being*. All of
these fit either the epilogist's attitude toward striving for wisdom and progress (a) or the
immediate context of judgement (b-c) or both (d).

a search is carried out in a vacuum of new facts. This represents a significant epistemological shift from both Proverbs and Qoheleth, for it essentially implies that the principal source of human knowledge is not found in experience and the ability to evaluate it and learn from it, but rather that it is located in the cult. In other words, the epilogist does not stand in the same tradition of thought from which both Proverbs and Qoheleth stem; he is not a sage, but a theologian.[75]

Summary

To summarise the examination of the epistemological perspectives of the two books, there are some similarities and some differences. For the two main voices of these books, observation and experience are the decisive sources of knowledge and in both cases human experience is perceived as objective,[76] thus allowing for generalisation as well as co-operation in the quest for understanding of the world and the human place in it. In other words, the epistemology of both books is primarily empirical, and we can, therefore, further narrow the definition of their quest to *the quest for self-understanding in terms of relationships with things, people and the Creator, and self-realisation in the context of these relationships, based on a primarily empirical epistemology and a paradigmatic approach to understanding.*

However, the two epistemologies are not identical. In Proverbs the cumulative collective experience is the standard against which every new experience is measured and by which, if necessary, it is overruled. Qoheleth's attitude toward secondary information is much more critical, for him the immediate personal experience is the criterion, and only secondary experience which conforms to this measure is considered any further. This principal difference impacts the nature of the two books. Qoheleth is much more contemplative than Proverbs, and his reader is let into 'the workshop'; the rules are made here and now and the conclusions stem from an argument that the reader is invited to examine. In contrast, in the proverbial world the rules are already there, they are inherited, passed on from one generation to the next.

While quite clearly both epistemologies are principally empirical, in both Proverbs and Qoheleth the success with which one may penetrate

---

[75] *Pace* Fox (1977). The link between the epilogue and the cult was noted by others, e.g., Dell (1994b:311–13) concluded that the epilogue's function is to establish a link between wisdom and Torah.

[76] Cf. Fox (1987:151).

the inner workings of the world is not entirely up to human capabilities; it is only at the will of God that the sage is able to understand. The main distinction between the two books in this respect is in the extent to which God is prepared to grant such an understanding to those who seek it. In Proverbs, there seem to be few limits to what the sage can achieve; the search for wisdom is divinely sanctioned, indeed it is a divine demand. In contrast, Qoheleth's God is prepared to provide only limited insight to humanity in order to preserve his superior position, and this leads to depreciation of the entire wisdom quest. The limits of wisdom and its value are in this respect taken a step further by the epilogist who advocates a dependency and subjection of the wisdom quest to a direct, cultic, revelation.

While the epistemological differences between the two primary voices cannot be marginalised, conceptually they have much in common, both being built on assumptions about immutable world and objectivity of human experience. Thus, it is not possible to see the two perspectives as entirely rival and antagonistic.[77] The principal difference between the two epistemologies lies in *how much* a sage can understand the world, and how much impact can such understanding make. In considering this difference we have to appreciate that to some extent the two epistemologies reflect the distinct working confines of the books, namely, the explicit focus of Proverbs on the beginner in the field of wisdom. From the point of view of the immature youth, the difference that knowledge can make is enormous, and can be easily perceived as, and therefore also presented as, endless. On the other hand, when Qoheleth assesses the relative value of wisdom, he is not taking as his reference point the possibilities that learning opens to the immature, but rather how much the sage is unable to achieve in spite of his learning. However, while the different working confines of the two books clearly influence their perspective, it has to be acknowledged that the epistemological differences cannot be reconciled entirely on these grounds, just as I have pointed out in the preceding chapter that the principal difference in the two paradigms cannot be explained satisfactorily along these lines. The proverbial world is genuinely open to examination while Qoheleth's world is not. This is not so much in the sense that one could not, or was not supposed to, strive to understand the world, but rather Qoheleth's God is actively frustrating any human

---

[77] Cf. Fox's (1987:154) understanding that Qoheleth does not attack traditional wisdom, but rather appropriates and extends it.

effort to comprehend it, and so to gain control over it. In other words, the epistemological role played by God is qualitatively different, and we will have to look for an adequate explanation of this epistemological shift somewhere else than in the different audiences which the books address.

Finally, it was observed that the epistemological perspective presented in the epilogue of Qoheleth differs radically from both Proverbs and Qoheleth proper. The epilogist is a theologian rather than a sage, who in fact believes not only that human ability to know is limited, but that it has ultimately reached its limits; any genuine insight from now on must originate in the cultic context. Thus, while from the epistemological point of view Proverbs and Qoheleth proper can be seen as a record of an internal debate and evolution of the wisdom quest, two entirely different worlds meet at the boundary between Qoheleth proper and the epilogue of the book.

CHAPTER 4

THE SAGES, GOD AND THE WORLD

In the previous chapter I touched several times on issues pertaining to the cosmology and theology of the two books. Now, I am going to focus on these two aspects of the sages' worldview. It must be pointed out from the outset that the theological and cosmological elements in Proverbs and Qoheleth are difficult to separate from each other, and doing so would prevent us from understanding the very nature of the world as the sages perceived it. Boström (1990:83) makes the following observation:

> ... the world theme is employed to enhance the status of wisdom by portraying is [*sic*] as closely associated with the Lord as an instrument in, or a unique witness of, his creation. In this fashion the creation motif itself turns out to be secondary, though at the same time it conveys a number of ideas and views of creation which were part of the theology cherished within the wisdom traditions.

God is a critical ingredient of the world the sages saw themselves as a part of, for their world is ultimately God's world. He is inseparable from the world through which he is known, and consequently neither can the cosmos be separated from, and therefore understood apart from, him. Any statements the sages make about the world are necessarily also statements about God; their cosmological deliberation has immediate theological implications. Yet, no attempt is made to examine or discuss God apart from the cosmos; the theological perspective of these books runs purely on the level of the interaction between God and the cosmos. We find here no ontological statements about God, nor direct and abstract statements about the divine character; God is always a factor in, and yet, never the true subject of, the sages' deliberation. Thus, it is apparent that theology is not what the sages were primarily interested in; their approach to theological issues is from a perspective which we would nowadays call interdisciplinary. Therefore, in contrast to Boström, I wish to suggest that in the relationship between cosmology and theology the theological perspective is secondary and depended on the cosmological outlook. In the rest of this chapter I am going to consider the sages' understanding of the world they lived in, the key principles they perceived to have operated within it and the role played by God in it.

The Makeup of the Proverbial Cosmos

The Divine Sphere and Its God

The world of the proverbial sages, in line with the widespread ANE view, is tripartite: it is made up of a divine sphere, a sphere that belongs to the living and a sphere that belongs to the dead. I will start with the examination of the first, the divine domain, in which the sages show only limited interest. The main reason for this lies in the fact that in the proverbial view this sphere is inaccessible to humans:

> Words of Agur, son of Jake, the Massaite.[1] Statement of the man: 'I am weary, O God, I am weary, O God, and consumed,[2] for indeed I am more stupid than [any other] man, and do not have human understanding. And I did not learn wisdom[3] and cannot have divine

---

[1] I follow McKane (1970:644) emending הַמַּשָּׂא to הַמַּשָּׂאִי.

[2] 𝔐 לְאִיתִיאֵל לְאִיתִיאֵל וְאֻכָל cannot be correct on syntactical grounds; the following clause opened by כִּי requires an antecedent statement, which the 𝔐 superscription does not provide. It has been suggested that כִּי is emphatic here (Schoors, 1981:245), but the particle is never purely emphatic always retaining some of its logical value just as the English emphatic *surely* or *indeed* do (the emphatic use can be thought of as a special case where an explicit idea that follows is linked to an implied context). In my view it is implausible that the particle would open the entire discourse. Further, the repetition of a personal name is inappropriate if the whole v. 1 is a superscription. I am, therefore, reading לאיתי אל לאיתי אל ואכל (see also Franklyn, 1983:242–44, who derives אכל from כלה understanding it as a reference to Agur's dying). An alternative attractive emendation was proposed by Strömberg-Krantz (1996), suggesting to read לא אתו אל לאיתי אל ואכל, and rendering a whole line *the word of a man not supported by God*: 'I am weary, O God, and exhausted.' Torrey's (1954) suggestion, that original text read לא אָנֹכִי אֵל לא אֲנִי אֵל וְאוּכָל, which was offensive to some later editor who translated it to Aramaic and then revocalised it to obscure the sense, is far fetched and does not have any particular merit. Equally the objection that אֵל cannot be a vocative, which would have to be הָאֵל, is moot in light of Num 12:13; Ps 10:11; 83:2 as pointed out by Franklyn.

[3] 𝔐 וְלֹא־לָמַדְתִּי; 𝔊 θεὸς δεδίδαχέν με, i.e., אֵל למד אתי. While some support for 𝔊 could be found in the absence of the negative in the B colon, the larger context speaks strongly in favour of 𝔐.

knowledge.[4] Who went up to the heavens and came down? Who gathered wind in his hands?[5] Who restricted waters in a mantle? Who established all the ends of the earth? What is his name? What is the name of his son? Surely, you know! Every word of God is refined, he is a shield to those who seek refuge in him. Do not add to his words, lest he rebukes you and you are shown to be a liar.' [Prov 30:1–6]

A sarcastic tone is quite clearly detectable in this passage, culminating in v. 4. This ironical statement is an acknowledgement that the divine and human worlds do not overlap and human beings are incapable of entering heaven. Agur's intention is to place wisdom within proper boundaries; there are limits to what it can achieve. While this is the only place in Proverbs where the inaccessibility of the divine sphere is explicitly asserted, the striking lack of interest in it throughout the book, and the need for a mediator between humans and the deity discussed in the previous chapter, suggest that this view is not limited to Agur, but was widespread among the proverbial sages; proverbial wisdom is an earthly exercise with earthly concerns, it has no mystical elements.

In spite of the sages' lack of interest some information about the divine domain can be gathered from the speech of Dame Wisdom in Prov 8:22ff:

---

[4] Note the shift from the nominal clause in v. 2b to the use of Sx in 3a and Px in 3b, which corresponds to the references to progressively better type of knowledge in vv. 2–3, starting with natural intelligence, followed by the learned חָכְמָה, and ending with the final דַּעַת קְדֹשִׁים. In this context, the Px is best understood as modal: while Agur lacks the former two types of knowledge, of the third type he is not even capable. 𝔐 דַּעַת קְדֹשִׁים is ambiguous. The genitive function can be understood in three ways: objective, i.e., knowledge about gods, subjective, i.e., knowledge that gods possess, or attributive, i.e., sacred cultic knowledge. The general thrust of the passage suggest the subjective genitive as the most likely option, creating a hierarchy of intelligence: ordinary man, the sage, and gods. Toy (1899:521) renders קְדֹשִׁים as *Holy One*, referring to Prov 9:10, which is almost certainly how the phrase would have been understood when the 𝔐 text was finalised, but the expression has unmistakable polytheistic overtones. The negative is carried over from the A colon.

[5] 𝔐 בְּחָפְנָיו; 𝔊 ἐν κόλπῳ, i.e., בְּחֵצְנוֹ, but the imagery of gathering speaks in favour of 𝔐. Cathcart (1970) proposes rendering *in his garments* on the basis of Ugaritic, which makes a good parallel to the following בְּשִׂמְלָה.

Yahweh brought me into being,[6] [7]the beginning of his way,[8] before his deeds of old. From eternity[9] I was formed,[10] from[11] the beginning, prior to the earth's existence. When there were no primeval oceans, I was born,[12] when there were no springs rich in water.[13] Before the mountains were settled, prior to the hills I was born. While there was still no earth and open space,[14] and ahead[15] of the dust of the world. When he established the heavens, I was there, when he engraved[16] the horizon

---

[6] The question whether קנה should be translated here *to acquire, to create* or *to beget* has not been satisfactorily resolved. In a detailed study Burney (1926) presents a convincing case that קנה has the primary sense *to acquire by buying/creating/begetting*. He argues for the sense *to beget* in our passage, on the grounds that חלל and נסכתי (see below note 10) imply the context of birth. In contrast, Fox (1997:163) prefers *acquired, by creating* and similarly Delitzsch (1982a:184) argues for *created*, asserting, however, that קנה, contrary to ברא, does not imply the beginning of existence, yet, little is offered to substantiate the argument. Irwin (1961) then denies the sense of creating in favour of begetting altogether, while Vawter (1980) repudiates any other meaning than *to acquire*, but his arguments concerning the use in Gen 4:1 and Ps 139:13 are not fully convincing. McKane (1970:352) objects to rendering *acquired*, pointing out that within the context of Prov 8 we expect some statement about the origins of Wisdom, with which view I am inclined to agree. Considering that קנה can be applied to origins of both humans and material objects, it is questionable whether significant distinction between *create/beget* is inherent to the verb, and, therefore, I have chosen a more neutral rendering.

[7] 𝕸 has no preposition, 𝕾, 𝕿, and some 𝖁 manuscripts read בְּ, probably under the influence of Gen 1:1. The difference is not negligible, for in 𝕸 Wisdom is not simply the first of the created things, but the very starting point of God's activity, she stands apart from that which is later created (cf. Delitzsch, 1982a:184).

[8] Dahood's (1968a) Ugaritic-based proposal to read 𝕸 דְּרְכּוֹ as a verb meaning *to control* is not convincing.

[9] Dahood's (1968a) suggestion that עוֹלָם and the preceding and following קֶדֶם are references to deities is hardly correct, since the focus of the text is temporal at this point, as vv. 24–29 show.

[10] 𝕸 נִסַּכְתִּי, i.e., Niphal of נסך, *I was consecrated*. I follow Burney (1926:165–66) and read Niphal of סכך, *to interweave*, which is applied to the formation of an embryo in Job 10:11 and Ps 139:13.

[11] 𝕸 מִן, 𝕲 reads בְּ which reflects the use of the preposition by the version in v. 22 (see note 7).

[12] For this sense of חלל see Job 15:7.

[13] 𝕸 מַעְיָנוֹת נִכְבַּדֵּי־מָיִם; Albright (1955) argues for emendation of נִכְבַּדֵּי to נבכי on the basis of Ugaritic. However, the root is not attested in Hebrew, and the Ugaritic meaning *source* does not fit the context, being semantically redundant and syntactically awkward.

[14] 𝕸 חוצות; 𝕾, 𝕿, 𝖁 read *rivers*. Thomas (1965) suggested that there could have been, based on Arabic, a Hebrew root חוץ referring to water, but the evidence is not sufficient. Further, the discussion has moved in vv. 25–26 from water to dry land.

[15] McKane (1970:355) following KBL-2 רֹאשׁ עַפְרוֹת תֵּבֵל *mass of the earth's soil*, but the parallelism with 26A and the surrounding context favour temporal understanding.

[16] 𝕸 בְּחֻקוֹ. 𝕲 ἡτοίμαζεν, *prepared*, is possibly a generic rendering of an unfamiliar verbal root חקק, although considering the rest of the verse, a difference in the 𝕲 Vorlage is more likely here. An emendation to בְּחֻזְקוֹ (KBL-2) is not implausible (cf.

upon the surface of the primeval ocean,[17] when he made the sky[18] above firm, when he overpowered[19] the springs of the primeval ocean, when he set for the sea its limit (so that water would not cross its edge[20]), when he hollowed out[21] the foundations of the earth. And I was growing up[22] by his side and I was [his] delight day by day,[23] laughing before him all the time. Laughing in the world, his earth, and my delight was humanity.[24] [Prov 8:22–31]

This passage shows that the divine sphere has an existence which is entirely independent of the human world, for God is active before the human world is brought into being by his creative work. The above account of divine actions starts with Yahweh bringing into being the

---

note 21).

[17] 𝔊 καὶ ὅτε ἀφώριζεν τὸν ἑαυτοῦ θρόνον ἐπ' ἀνέμων, *and when he set apart his throne upon winds*; this is most likely an improvisation by the translator.

[18] The Hebrew שְׁחָקִים is frequently rendered *clouds*, but the OT usage indicates that it is more akin to שָׁמַיִם than to עָבִים (see for instance Ps 18:2; 89:38). The reference here is to a solid layer that separates the waters above and below, also called רָקִיעַ (see in particular Job 37:18).

[19] See Dan 11:12 for a similar use of עזז.

[20] This rendering of פִּיו is preferable to *his command* (e.g. Toy 1899:173) in the light of the preceding חֹק.

[21] 𝔐 בְּחוּקוֹ; 𝔊 בְּחֶזְקוֹ. Both readings are feasible, I follow 𝔐.

[22] The versions understood 𝔐 אָמוֹן as a verb: 𝔊 ἁρμόζουσα, *preparing, fitting together, setting in order*, α' τιθηνουμένη, *nursing, maintaining*, 𝔖 ܟܝܢܐ ܗܘܝܬ ܠܘܬܗ, *I was working with him*. Delitzsch (1982a:190–2) renders *director of works* (cf. Can 7:2); he argues that אמן with reference to children denotes the notion of fostering, which is quite inappropriate in the context, for Wisdom is God's real child, if anything, and asserts that the activities in which Wisdom is involved in this chapter hardly fit child-like imagery. However, it should be noted that Wisdom is merely present, but otherwise uninvolved up to v. 30 and, as Scott (1960) observed, nothing is said of Wisdom's creative activity. Yet, somewhat self-contradictory, Scott advocates rendering along the lines of *binding, uniting, fashioning* which in his view allows for Wisdom's participation in creation without requiring hypostatic interpretation. Unfortunately, Scott's methodology cannot be applied to an unpointed text, and must, therefore, be rejected. Rogers (1997) defends the meaning *master workman* but argues that it has Yahweh, not Wisdom as the referent, based on the gender of the noun (see also Dahood, 1968a). However, the masculine gender in BH is unmarked and the entire verse is concerned with Wisdom's activity. Fox (1996a), following Qimhi, pointed out that the infa. of אמן can be used in the sense of growing up, being raised (e.g. Esth 2:20), and such understanding makes good sense in the context, where the previous verses speak of the birth of Wisdom. I am, therefore, inclined to read infa. along these lines.

[23] Cf. 𝔊 ἐγὼ ἤμην ᾗ προσέχαιρεν, *I was in whom he rejoiced*, which in my view is the correct understanding of the Hebrew, Wisdom is Yahweh's delight here, cf. v. 31b.

[24] Dahood (1968a) wishes to read אֶת בֹּנֶה אָדָם, *with the Builder of Earth*, based on the Ugaritic use of ptc. *bnh* as an epithet for El. However, 𝔐 flows very naturally from Wisdom in the presence of God, to Wisdom in the world, to Wisdom with humanity, preparing the ground for the admonition of the next stanza, and should be retained.

enigmatic figure of Wisdom. The birth of Wisdom is then followed by
the creative activity proper out of which the human world emerges.

However, there is an informational vacuum between these two
phases, one which in my opinion offers a significant insight into the
nature of the divine domain. In between Yahweh bringing forth Wisdom and creating the world, the forces of chaos, תְּהוֹם, quietly and
without explanation enter the scene. The sudden appearance of תְּהוֹם
creates a tension in the text. On the one hand Wisdom, and therefore
also Yahweh, are clearly pre-existent to תְּהוֹם, but on the other hand,
nothing is said of Yahweh creating תְּהוֹם, on the contrary, as we will
see in a moment, the creative activity is about defeating it. Is Yahweh
responsible for the appearance of תְּהוֹם, or if not, does it mean that he
is not fully in charge of the divine domain? The proverbial sages do not
provide a straight answer to this dilemma. This is not an oversight on
their part, but rather it is conditioned by the nature of the proverbial
paradigm. They are faced by the same problem that is encountered
within any ethical-monotheistic theology,[25] for if the sovereignty of God
is emphasised, it raises questions about the divine character, and vice
versa, if the moral uprightness is emphasised, the sovereignty of the
deity over the world is in question. For the proverbial sages neither
can be weakened on the expense of the other. If the basic tenet of the
proverbial understanding of the world is to be maintained, namely that
both the wicked and righteous always get what they deserve, the proverbial God must be both righteous and sovereign. Consequently, in the
proverbial understanding there cannot be any connection between God
and the forces of chaos, and further, God must be always seen as in control of the chaos. Not having a satisfactory answer to the question about
the origins of תְּהוֹם, the sages simply ignore it,[26] but, as we will see in a
moment, they do come up with a theo-cosmological framework which
allows them to maintain both divine sovereignty and righteousness.

It is worth noting that even though the proverbial cosmology builds
on a common ANE myth about the battle between the forces of order
and chaos, the sages' understanding of the divine avoids any overt poly-

---

[25] I will deal with the suitability of the term monotheism as a depiction of the
proverbial perspective shortly.

[26] This manner of dealing with the problem is not unique to Prov 8:22ff. Very much
the same approach can be found in the opening chapters of Genesis, for instance,
where on the one hand God declares the whole of creation as good, and on the
other hand the shrewd snake, that does not fit that evaluation, emerges without an
explanation.

theism. While there are two places where the word קְדֹשִׁים, with its clear polytheistic connotations, is used with reference to the divine [Prov 9:10; 30:3], the book almost exclusively uses the personal name יהוה when talking about God. Only exceptionally is אֱלֹהִים employed, but with respect to this designation it can be observed that the choice is mainly poetic and on only one occasion it appears entirely arbitrary.[27] The systematic use of the personal name יהוה indicates a clear effort at some stage in the development of the tradition to identify emphatically with the Yahwistic religion. However, we should not immediately conclude from this that the religious outlook that hides in the background is identical to that found elsewhere in the Yahwistic traditions of the OT. The fact that Proverbs shows little contact with, and interest in, any other OT traditions demands that we look to the book alone when trying to define the nature of the Yahwistic perspective it preserves.

The use of the tetragrammaton in the book has one peculiar feature: it appears even in those sections of the material that are of foreign provenance. These include Prov 22:17ff.,[28] 30,[29] 31:1–9 and possibly also 31:10ff., if the entire chapter is understood as words of Lemuel's mother. It is not particularly important whether the exo-Israelite origins are so in real terms or purely on a literary level. In either case, the personal name יהוה was at some point applied to God in material which was

---

[27] The personal name יהוה is used on 87 occasions in the book, while אֱלֹהִים is found only in Prov 2:5, 17; 3:4; 25:2; 30:9. On two of these occasions [Prov 2:5; 30:9] the word is used as a B colon parallel to יהוה. The same is most likely the case in Prov 3:4 with the parallel in 3:5. In Prov 2:17 the term is used with respect to אִשָּׁה זָרָה, and so it is possible that foreign gods are referred to. Only in Prov 25:2 no special reasons for the choice of אֱלֹהִים as the designation for God are apparent.

[28] This section of the book is based on the Egyptian *Instruction of Amenemopet*, although it must be acknowledged that the relationship between the two texts is not entirely simple. On the one hand there is a significant amount of material in the two collections which resembles each other, and occasionally the parallels are close to verbatim. At the same time, the clear thirty-chapter structure of the Egyptian text is lacking and on a number of occasions the Hebrew thought develops in a different direction. My view is that Amenemopet lies in the background of the proverbial material, but that the Hebrew author took such a degree of liberty with respect to both form and content, that the value of the Egyptian text for any text-critical work is virtually nil. For an overview of the discussion see McKane (1970:371–74) and more recently Whybray (1994b).

[29] The names Agur and Jaqeh are attested on 8th century BC ostraca from Arabia and are likely to be of Arabic origin. References to Massah are made in 1 Chr 1:30, and in Assyrian texts (Gottlieb, 1991:280). For translation of Prov 30:1 with textual notes see p. 84.

known, or perceived, as to have originated in a non-Yahwistic milieu.[30] It follows from this that in the proverbial perspective the personal name יהוה is not defining, only descriptive. The use of יהוה here denotes not so much that Yahweh, the God revealed in the Israelite cult, is the sages' God, but rather that the sages' God, witnessed in the world, is Yahweh, who also revealed himself in the cult. It shows that Yahweh was not considered by the sages to a be a local deity, but rather as having a universal sphere of influence; his activity could be seen in different environments and by different peoples, even those not partaking in Israel's cult, and what is more, such people could also be pleasing to him. This stands in contrast to the Yahwism of the prophetic and legal traditions, which tends to have a negative attitude toward foreigners and foreign imports.

Yet, if the sages believed in Yahweh being the God of all peoples, why do they make such a systematic use of the tetragrammaton which is so Israel-specific? The most plausible explanation is that this methodical and virtually exclusive use of יהוה is meant to assert emphatically that the two, the broadly understood proverbial God of the entire world, and the deity of the name יהוה, are one and the same; the use of the divine name in Proverbs is *de facto* apologetic. It suggests strongly that such a perspective was not a commonplace at the time when the theologically explicit material in the book was being formed, but rather that the common Yahwism was of a different kind, probably with Yahweh being seen as a tribal God. Thus, it is probable that what we see in Proverbs are early stages of a major theological shift that eventually makes its way into other biblical traditions; the sages stood at the sharp end of the theological enterprise of their day.

It is possible, therefore, to conclude from the handling of the appearance of תְּהוֹם on the scene in Prov 8:22ff. and from the way the personal name יהוה is used, that in spite of the underlying polytheistic roots, the tradition as it is captured in the book in fact reflects a religion of a single God. Yet, at the same time, the term monotheism may not adequately capture the book's perspective, as the theo-cosmological picture in Proverbs is rather complex.[31] First of all, we have to consider what or who is the enigmatic figure of Wisdom.

---

[30] It is worth noting that the same is true of the book of Job, where in particular the frame of the book uses יהוה repeatedly.

[31] The difficulties in describing the theological perspective here are symptomatic of a larger terminological problem. For a wider discussion of the suitability of the

She has been interpreted in a number of different ways, yet, it is my view that if we limit her identification to what the text itself has to say (rather than trying to make it conform to some external concept), the way in which she can be understood is fairly limited. First of all, while it is possible that the figure of Wisdom originated in a polytheistic myth (see Lang, 1986), in the present shape of the text she is not portrayed as a goddess, for there is no indication that she should be worshipped and further, she does not directly interfere with humanity's destiny.[32] Her sole role, as we saw in the preceding chapter, is to mediate true understanding but the consequences of accepting or rejecting it are not brought about by her. This is most clearly seen in Prov 1:24ff. where she is a mere observer of the calamity that befalls the fools, and in Prov 8:35 which shows that it is Yahweh who is responsible for the blessing that comes from accepting Wisdom.

Not only is Wisdom not a goddess, but interpreting her as a hypostasis of Yahweh (e.g. Ringgren 1947:95–106) is also implausible. Such an understanding is precluded by the fact that she is not a divine attribute, but rather her origins postdate those of Yahweh, i.e., there was time when God was without Wisdom. She is something that God brought into being, his child, and the child-parent imagery of Prov 8:22ff. shows clearly that she has an existence entirely independent of Yahweh.

Yet, although she is not a deity or hypostasis, the fact that Wisdom functions as a mediatrix between Yahweh and humanity precludes understanding her as a mere personification of an impersonal order, for the way in which the mediatory role is depicted, particularly the parallel between Yahweh rejoicing in Wisdom and Wisdom rejoicing in humanity [Prov 8:30–31], requires that the underlying reality for which she stands is understood in personal terms (*pace* von Rad, 1972:144–76). Further, the proverbial material indicates quite clearly that the persona of Wisdom is not a subjective concept that could be broadly summarised under the categories of knowledge and intellectual faculties, or

---

term *monotheism* as applied to Jewish theological thought prior to the Middle Ages see Hayman (1991b).

[32] Kayatz (1966:93–119) brought attention to a number of similarities between Wisdom and the Egyptian goddess of order and justice, Maat. However, simple identification of Wisdom with Maat is problematic (von Rad, 1972:153–54, Shupak, 1993:345). The main difference in my view is the fact that Maat *is* the order, i.e., 'one speaks *maat*, does *maat* and follows *maat* ... [even] the gods [live] by *maat*' (Whybray, 1965a:55), while Wisdom merely *reveals* the order, i.e., she speaks truth and her lips dislike wickedness [Prov 8:6–9].

lack of them (*pace* Fox, 1997), for Wisdom not only pre-dates the creation of humanity but she retains her autonomy from humans, just as
she exists independently of God. This independence of human intellect
and wishes is most clearly seen in the incident of Prov 1:24ff. where she
mocks the fools who turn to her for help in time of trouble. The point
here is that it is wisdom that decides who to assist and who to abandon;
the access to her is not controlled by humans. Thus, the text leaves
us with a personal understanding of Wisdom, who, while not strictly
speaking divine, enjoys a very close association with יהוה, portrayed in
the terms of a relationship between father and a child, and, as Boström
(1990:83) puts it, '[she] is nearly identical with the Lord in the terms of
authority.'

An additional insight is offered by the extremely important, yet,
sometimes overlooked fact that Wisdom exists in a permanent oppo-
sition to the other female person of those chapters, Folly.[33] In contrast
to Wisdom, nothing is specifically said about the origins and the source
of Folly, but throughout the book fools create havoc and destruction,
and so it can be surmised that Folly is a representation of the forces
of chaos, the primeval תְּהוֹם, and the silence about the origins of Folly
has similar causes as that concerning the origins of תְּהוֹם. When considering the relationship between the two women, we should observe
that they are on an identical mission, both actively pursuing humanity,
trying to gain followers. In fact, the invitations that each gives to the
passers-by are in principle similar, and even open with exactly the same
formulae; they both claim to know what is beneficial to human beings
and furthermore, both of them focus especially on the impressionable
פֶּתִי. Thus, any conclusions that are drawn about the nature of Wisdom, have to be equally applied to Folly; she needs to be understood
in personal terms. The difference between the two women is mainly in
their approach to life; Wisdom advocates ethical behaviour as a route
to success, while Folly rejects ethics as irrelevant [Prov 9:17].

The cosmos that hides behind the two figures is that of a persistent
battle between Wisdom and Folly, order and chaos, good and evil. This
persistent war is an extension of Yahweh's taming of תְּהוֹם in the process

---

[33] Blenkinsopp (1991) attempted to argue that the figure of Wisdom is only secondary
in origin to the strange woman of Prov 1–9, but that is in my view unlikely. Strictly
speaking the figure of Wisdom does not stand in antithesis to the strange woman, but
to the personified Folly in Prov 9. The strange woman is one of flesh and blood, and
although I am inclined to think that a secondary contrast between her and Wisdom is
intended in Prov 7, her real antithesis is the flesh and blood wife of Prov 5.

of creation, yet, it is important to grasp that in Proverbs this conflict is waged on the earthly battlefield, with human beings being part of the battle. Wisdom is a mediatrix between God and humanity, conveying the nature of the divine order to human beings and leading them to follow it. It is the human followers of Wisdom, not Wisdom herself, who effectively create the order and defeat the chaos in the human world.

From the observations made so far about the relationship between God, Wisdom and humanity we can conclude that the two women are not mere poetic embellishments, for while a poetic language and techniques are used, there is no doubt that the sages speak of something they consider very real, with an independent objective existence. Folly is not simply the absence of Wisdom, nor is Wisdom the absence of Folly; they both have an individual existence in their own right. In other words, there is an implicit dualism present in the cosmology of Proverbs. On the one hand we have the sovereign creator and ruler יהוה, on the other hand, within the context of his rule we observe a battle between the two personae of Wisdom and Folly, leaving us with an obvious tension between the tiers, only one of which is dualistic.

It is necessary to consider what led the sages to postulate such a framework. The dualistic aspect of this perspective is simply a reflection of the sage's daily experience. The persistent tension between the righteous and the wicked, between good and evil, is very real to them. The problem with the foolish and wicked, is not, as we will see in chapter 5, that their behaviour is self-destructive, but that it seriously damages, indeed threatens, the community which they are part of. The dualistic framework makes the seriousness of this threat very tangible. Further, it allows the sages to completely disassociate God from the fools; the proverbial God cannot be held responsible for the damage that is the result of Folly's activity.

However, had the sages maintained a purely dualistic view of the world, they would not have been able to affirm a clear pre-eminence of Wisdom over Folly, and, thus, to make any claims that their way was superior to that of the fools; if Wisdom and Folly are equal forces, then the two blueprints offered by them are equally valid approaches to life. To avoid this, the proverbial outlook must not be dualistic in the final analysis. The sages achieved it by eliminating any dualism from the upper tier of their cosmological perspective.

As a result of this ingenious solution, Wisdom and Folly are in principle equals, capable of making a serious impact on the lives of

those who follow them (and thus allowing the sages to make sense of
their daily experience), but Wisdom has a powerful backer while Folly
has none. In this way the wise are given an ultimate edge over the fools
without the seriousness of the impact that folly makes on the life of its
followers being entirely denied.

Several conclusions can be drawn from this framework of the divine
domain. Since it perfectly suits the needs of the basic bipolar paradigm
that we find in Proverbs, yet, from the theological point of view it does
not give an answer to the question of the origins of folly, merely putting
it aside, it is almost certain that this theological framework was derived
from the wisdom paradigm; the theological framework is subservient
to the overall paradigm, not vice versa. Thus, we can see that the
theological questions are, as it was asserted earlier on, of only secondary
importance to the proverbial sages. Further, the fact that theological
conclusions are drawn from the paradigm suggests that the bipolar
nature of the proverbial paradigm goes deeper than merely dividing
people into wise and fools. Rather, the bipolarity is engraved into the
very nature of the entire cosmos; the heavenly realm was seen by the
sages as a place of persistent battle between forces of order and chaos,
and although their theological perspective is not purely dualistic, the
dualism plays a critical part in it, disassociating God from Folly. This
disassociation then makes it possible to lay claim to superiority of the
way of wisdom over that of folly, and insist on the necessity to adhere to
certain basic ethical norms.

Having considered the overall 'layout' of the divine domain, it is time
to turn our attention to the proverbial view of God himself, and the
proverbial religious attitudes. The descriptive rather than defining use
of the divine name, seen in its application to the non-Israelite sections
of Proverbs, implies that the identification of Yahweh in Proverbs must
be based on his character, which can be witnessed in the world, rather
than national, territorial and cultic factors. This perspective explains
the lack of involvement of the book with the cultic issues, since with this
concept of Yahweh's identity, the Yahwistic cult is by its very nature
only a special case, or a particular expression, of the more general
principles which govern interaction between the human and the divine.
The logical conclusion of such a stance is that the harmony with the
divine character must take precedence over the formal conformity with
cultic practice, and this attitude is expressed explicitly in the book on
several occasions. Consider the following passages:

The sacrifice of wicked people is an abomination to Yahweh, but the prayer of the righteous is his pleasure. The wicked person's way is abomination to Yahweh, but he loves one who pursues righteousness. [Prov 15:8–9]

Yahweh is distant from the wicked people, but he listens to the prayer of the righteous ones. [Prov 15:29]

To do what is righteous and just is preferable to Yahweh than a sacrifice. [Prov 21:3]

The sacrifice of the wicked is an abomination, how much more when he brings it in deviousness. [Prov 21:27]

While cultic practice is acknowledged in all of these, only rarely does the book admonish one to engage in cultic activity *per se*. In fact, one could almost gain the impression that the cult is not worth the trouble, that it is dispensable:

In loyalty and truth guilt is atoned for, and in the fear of Yahweh [one] turns away from evil. [Prov 16:6]

The person who says:[34] 'this is holy!', is being trapped, but after vows [have been made, they are] to be bestowed.[35] [Prov 20:25]

However, at least on one occasion [Prov 3:9] the sages encourage involvement with the cult, and this, in combination with the earlier observed systematic use of יהוה, renders the simple conclusion that the sages rejected the cult untenable. Rather, the sages understood the Yahwistic religion in much broader terms than a narrowly defined set of cultic rituals. The proverbial Yahwism finds its centre not in the formal cult but in the concept of *fear of Yahweh*, which we will deal with in chapter 6.

The observations concerning the divine domain made so far can be summarised as follows. The divine sphere is inaccessible to humans, it belongs to one God referred to as יהוה. His influence is not limited by national boundaries, and his character can be witnessed in the world by all those who seek to understand the world. In relationship to this God cultic practice is of only secondary importance, the proverbial emphasis is on ethical obligations rooted in the divine character and demand. In spite of the fact that Yahweh is the only and entirely sovereign deity

---

[34] The root and meaning of יָלַע is unclear, but in the context a *verbum dicendi* is expected.

[35] 𝔐 לְבַקֵּר; 𝔊 renders B colon freely μετὰ γὰρ τὸ εὔξασθαι μετανοεῖν γίνεται, *to change [his] mind having made a vow.*

in the theological framework of the book, a continuous battle between the forces of order and chaos takes place within the divine domain, represented by the figures of Wisdom and Folly. These two are equals in terms of their potential to make an impact on human life, but the former is backed by Yahweh and as a result permanently has the upper hand. Thus, while in theory the proverbial outlook is monotheistic, in practical terms it is dualistic.[36]

Sheol

The next segment of the tripartite world is Sheol, the land of the dead. This sphere is sometimes perceived in terms of two figures in the ANE mythologies and traces of such a concept are also found in Proverbs:

> Sheol and Abaddon are never sated, and human eyes are never sated. [Prov 27:20]

> Sheol and Abaddon are before Yahweh, how much more hearts of sons of men. [Prov 15:11]

While in the first case it needs to be noted that the pair appear here possibly only on poetic grounds, to form a more suitable parallel to the pair of eyes, in the second example there are no obvious poetic reasons; the B colon could easily have been formulated so as to produce rhythmic balance to a shorter A colon with Sheol alone. It is, therefore, likely that the sages' notion of Sheol closely resembled that of other ANE cultures, but otherwise the information contained in the book itself is rather limited. We know that Sheol is entered at the point of death and is inhabited by the רְפָאִים [Prov 2:18; 9:18; 21:16], but it is not possible for us to determine from the book itself who these beings are and what role they play in the underworld.

While we cannot form a very clear picture of what Sheol is like from the book, its significance to the sages is rather unambiguous. Sheol represents to them the complete end of any meaningful existence. Consider the following passage:

> Should they say: 'Come with us, let us lie in wait for blood, let us lie in ambush for an innocent person even though he gave us no cause. Let

---

[36] Thus, the application of the term *monotheism* to the book is problematic, to say the least (*pace* Boström, 1990:88).

us swallow them alive—like Sheol,[37] and in one piece,[38] like those who descend to the pit.' [Prov 1:11–12]

The robbers, waiting to ambush and kill a person, compare themselves to Sheol. By implication, Sheol is a violent and destructive place, one where a person does not want to be of their own choice.

Significantly, Sheol is usually associated with folly [e.g. Prov 5:5; 7:27; 9:18], while wisdom is perceived as capable of preventing one from descending to Sheol [Prov 15:24; 23:14]. Yet, this is not to be understood in absolute terms. Nowhere is it asserted in Proverbs that the wise will not die; having made this claim, some comments are due on three particular sayings. The first of these is Prov 12:28:

בְּאֹרַח־צְדָקָה חַיִּים וְדֶרֶךְ נְתִיבָה אַל־מָוֶת׃

The Hebrew of this verse is clearly corrupt, the B colon being syntactically impossible and making little sense as it stands. The interpreters divide broadly into two groups, one that wishes to preserve the negative אַל found in 𝔏, others who follow the versions and many Hebrew manuscripts reading אֶל instead; in both cases נְתִיבָה has to be emended. The problem with the former approach is that it requires one to assume that the negative is employed contrary to the normal usage, and to ignore its imperative force. Thus, for instance, Dahood (1960) accepts Delitzsch's view that מות is a participle and אַל־מָוֶת means *there is no dying*, but such a construction would normally use אֵין; overall Dahood's proposal to vocalise דְרֹךְ and understand נְתִיבָה as containing 3fs sfx, i.e., *the treading of her path is immortality*, is not convincing. In my view the best solution appears to be Tourney's emendation of נְתִיבָה to פְּתִי בָא (as quoted by McKane, 1970:451). The difference can be plausibly explained by a basic scribal error, since in a number of the ancient Hebrew scripts נ and פ are very similar.[39] Obviously, the meaning of the text is entirely dependent on the particular emendation or exception to the standard Hebrew usage that an interpreter chooses. It is certainly not possible to speak of immortality in Proverbs on the grounds of this verse alone.

---

[37] Or *let us swallow them as Sheol swallows life* (McKane (1970:221). Oesterley (1929:8) points out a personification of Sheol in Isa 5:14, and O'Callaghan (1954:169) brings attention to the image of Mot's hungry mouth in the Baal Epic.

[38] So McKane (1970:269), who sees here reference to Mot, possibly also *completely* (see the note above).

[39] See ANEP 88; I am grateful to David Reimer for bringing this to my attention.

The second saying that needs a few comments in this respect is Prov 14:32:

בְּרָעָתוֹ יִדָּחֶה רָשָׁע וְחֹסֶה בְמוֹתוֹ צַדִּיק׃

The referent of the suffix of בְמוֹתוֹ is ambiguous and may be either the wicked or the righteous. It is most likely that 𝔐 is corrupted and we should follow 𝔊 and read בְּתֻמּוֹ, *in his integrity*, which provides a superior parallel to *his evil* in the first half of the verse. Thus, it is probably best to translate: *by his evil the wicked is brought down, but the righteous seeks*[40] *a refuge in his integrity*.

There is one more saying that could be used to challenge the claim that the notion of immortality is foreign to Proverbs:

> The path of life leads upwards[41] for the intelligent person, so that it turns away from Sheol below. [Prov 15:24]

It is tempting to understand the contrast below/upwards as referring to two kinds of afterlife, but such a reading arises out of a preconceived theological perspective rather than the text itself. As the netherworld is pictured here to be located beneath the surface of the earth, movement upwards is the natural poetic expression for releasing Sheol's hold on a person. It should be noted that in the imagery there is no locality contrasting Sheol. The verse is not concerned with going to some place other than Sheol, but with the ability of the intelligent person to keep a distance from it. Neither of these verses can, therefore, be used to argue for a concept of meaningful afterlife in Proverbs.

Nor is there any indication that the most abstract word for life that BH has, חַיִּים, refers in Proverbs to anything else but the earthly human experience. Consider the following verses:

> My son, do not forget my teaching, may your heart guard my commands. For they will add to you length of days and years of life, and peace. [Prov 3:1–2]

> Blessed is a person who has found wisdom ... length of days is in her right hand, wealth and glory in her left ... She is [the] tree of life,

---

[40] As McKane (1970:475) pointed out, the notion behind חסה is mainly that of seeking refuge, even though there are some occasions in the OT where the less active sense *to find refuge* is clearly intended [e.g. Ps 36:8].

[41] 𝔐 לְמַעְלָה, supported by 𝔖 ܠܥܠ, *upwards*. 𝔊 διανοήματα, *thoughts*, most likely a reinterpretation by the translator. McKane (1970:479) is of the view that 𝔊 did not have לְמַעְלָה and מַטָּה in its Vorlage, but it should be noted that while these are not translated in 𝔊, there are substitutions for both words—𝔊 is clearly not translating Hebrew text that would simply have the two words missing.

whoever grasp her and lay hold of her, each one of them is blessed. [Prov 3:13, 16, 18]

For with me [i.e. Wisdom] your days will multiply and years of life will be added to you. [Prov 9:11].[42]

The overall picture is not of wisdom leading to immortality, but rather of wisdom preventing untimely death. The conclusion that the proverbial sages did not believe in any meaningful existence after death is impossible to escape.

The World of the Living

The sages showed limited curiosity about heaven, and their interest in death and Sheol is limited to avoiding it; the real arena for exercising wisdom is the sphere of the living. It is this tangible world that the sages sought to comprehend, and ultimately use that comprehension to their own benefit. This domain is the result of the creative activity of God. Our primary insight into the proverbial understanding of the origins of the cosmos comes again from Prov 8:22–31 quoted earlier. However, it needs to be pointed out that this text is not intended as a source of detailed information about the process of creation. Rather, its primary purpose is to strengthen the claims that wisdom is the key to successful life by showing that Wisdom knows all that is to be known about the human world. Thus, while the text speaks about the creative activity of God, it quite clearly assumes that the reader has some prior knowledge on the subject.

The human world, designated by the Hebrew words אֶרֶץ and תֵּבֵל, emerges as Yahweh imposes order on the forces of chaos, referred to as תְּהוֹם. This subjugation of the chaos is pictured in three stages:

When he established the heavens, I was there, when he engraved the horizon upon the surface of the primeval ocean, when he made the sky above firm, when he overpowered the springs of the primeval ocean, when he set for the sea its limit (so that water would not cross its edge), when he hollowed out the foundations of the earth. [Prov 8:27–29][43]

First, an upper limit is imposed on תְּהוֹם by which a higher region is created, the heavens. The upper boundary is called here שְׁחָקִים. In the second stage, limits are imposed on the chaos from beneath, when Yahweh overpowers and restrains its sources, עִינוֹת. After this stage the

---

[42] For textual notes see p. 62.
[43] For textual notes see p. 85.

primeval waters cease to be called תְּהוֹם, and are referred to as יָם or מַיִם, which is probably to reflect the diminishing power of chaos. In the final stage, the sea is limited alongside the horizontal plane and the foundations of the land are laid.

The key characteristic of the cosmos in this text is its orderliness. God not only created the world but he also set boundaries to its individual elements by taming the initial chaos. It is this orderliness that lies at the heart of the proverbial understanding and allows the sages to predict how a person's life is to unfold in the future on the basis of their present actions. While the presence of this orderliness in the proverbial perception of the world is broadly accepted by the interpreters, its nature, and more specifically the precise character of the link between actions and their consequences, has been a subject of scholarly debate for some time.

There are two basic models. In the first one, retributive justice is in operation, with God being its administrator. In the second model, there is a simple action-consequence order built-in, where each act produces a particular outcome automatically, without the need for divine involvement. Such an understanding was first formulated in a well known essay by Koch (1983[44]), and later adopted by von Rad (1972:124–37). Koch's fundamental assertion is that

> there is not even a single convincing reference to suggest a retribution teaching [in Proverbs]. … We … find … a conviction that Yahweh pays close attention to the connection between actions and destiny, hurries it along, and 'completes' it when necessary (p. 64).

Rather than being retributive, the mechanism by which actions and their consequences are linked is characterised by an inherent relationship between the nature of the action and its consequence, and further, it operates in terms of either blessing or destruction with no differentiation according to the severity of the triggering action (p. 59–60). Quite clearly the two models are mutually exclusive, and lead to a rather different understanding of the proverbial world and theology. I will, therefore, examine Koch's action-consequence model in some detail, in order to see whether it can be successfully applied to the book.

Much weight is given by Koch to the fact that the relationship between an action and its consequences is simply expressed or assumed

---

[44] The essay was published in German in 1955 as 'Gibt es ein Vergeltungs dogma im AT' in *ZThK 52*: 1–42; all references in the text above are to the English version of 1983.

in the majority of the proverbial sayings, but nothing is said about the mechanism of this relationship. He deduces from this that the consequences are directly and automatically brought about by the action itself. As all conclusions drawn from silence are problematic, it is necessary to consider whether the lack of information about the action-consequence mechanism cannot be accounted for on other grounds, and if so, whether such an explanation may not be more plausible.

First of all, some consideration must be given to the proverbial genre. It was pointed out earlier that the brevity of the proverbial forms has serious implications for the interpretation of the book (p. 42), and this fully applies to the present issue. A proverb typically consists of less than a dozen words. Thus the amount of detail it can deal with is significantly limited. Further, a proverb needs to retain a relative autonomy; it must be possible to understand the sense of the proverb without a fixed literary context. As a result, a proverb cannot but schematisc, and its author will have to make a strict choice about what to include and what to leave out. Therefore, it should be expected that a proverb will express only the minimal information which is essential to conveying the message on the author's mind. If the author's intention is to draw attention to a link between particular actions and particular consequences (and this certainly is the case in much of the material in Proverbs), what he or she cannot omit is the depiction of the action and of the related consequence. The one thing that the author can afford to leave out are the details of the actual process that links them. More so, this is something that the author may even wish to omit, for by leaving out such details, the proverb becomes open to a wider range of applications. Lets take as an example a proverb that we have already looked at earlier (p. 42):

> Who digs a pit may/will fall into it, and who rolls a stone, it may/will roll back over him. [Prov 26:27]

The intention is to warn one from the dangers of digging a pit. This can be understood in a number of ways, literally, metaphorically, even as referring to malicious intent. In any case, it is of little importance whether one may slip into the pit while digging it, or fall into it later having forgotten about it, or any other way. What matters is *what* may happen, not *how* it may happen and the fact that the *how* is not expressed prevents us from limiting the *how* to a single mode.[45]

---

[45] See also Boström (1990:112).

Since the nature of the form is such that it seriously limits the amount of detail discussed, both by necessity and design, no definite conclusions about the nature of the relationship between action and consequence can be made unless this relationship is more explicitly described in the material. This, in turn, requires that we interpret the silence in the light of the limited number of sayings that offer a more detailed insight into the action-consequence chain, and not vice versa; failure to do so is a significant methodological fallacy that casts doubts on the validity of the action-consequence model.[46]

I now want to examine at least some of the material which provides more specific information about the link between actions and consequences in Proverbs, to test the action-consequence model further. The main difference between the two models is in the role God plays in them. In the action-consequence model Yahweh is not a free agent but a passive executor, whose behaviour is determined by the inherent link between action and its consequence; the consequences that one suffers as a result of one's actions are not in any way modifiable by him. The only control he has is over the speed with which the inherent relationship materialises. Further, and possibly more importantly, the mechanism must also be able to function without his involvement, automatically, otherwise it is meaningless to talk about built-in consequences; with this in mind, let us consider several relevant proverbs.

There are a number of occasions in the book, where a particular action is described as pleasing or displeasing to Yahweh, for instance:

> False scales are an abomination to Yahweh, but an honest weight is his pleasure. [Prov 11:1]

---

[46] An objection could be raised at this point that such an approach assumes that the two types of material represent the same school of thought. I wish to make two brief points in addressing such an objection. First, this study limits itself to a synchronic examination of the book. The present aim is to understand the worldview conveyed by the book in its totality and it is from this starting point that this approach stems (in fact Koch does not argue that there are two different schools of thought in Proverbs, so that this approach is fully valid in critiquing his model). Second, all attempts to separate the proverbial material into groups that represent significantly different schools of thought, typically religious vs. secular, have so far failed (the most thorough attempt was made by McKane, 1970, for a critique of which see Wilson, 1987, and Weeks, 1994:57–73). While I do not wish to exclude such a possibility in principle, in the light of the brevity built into the genre it seems that a convincing case could only be made on the grounds of some additional, external information about the origins of wisdom in Israel, not from the proverbial material *per se*.

I cannot but agree with Koch that such verses ultimately imply that God is going to respond in some appropriate way (p. 62). Yet, it should be noticed that by saying that something is an abomination to Yahweh, Yahweh's value judgement on the action is expressed. Thus, it is unavoidably implied that the criteria for the appropriate response is inherent to Yahweh, rather than to the action itself. If the consequences were permanently built-in, Yahweh's value judgement would be irrelevant.

The concept of *fear of Yahweh*, which will be dealt with in detail in chapter 6, points in a similar direction. If the consequences of actions are permanently and unchangeably built-in, humans are not only fully in control of their own lives, but also of God who ceases to be a power to reckon with, to fear, to worship or to trust. It becomes impossible to talk about any real person-to-person relationship between human beings and God, yet, this is precisely what we find in Proverbs:

> As for Yahweh's discipline, my son, do not reject [it] and do not loathe [it] when he rebukes you. For whom Yahweh loves he rebukes, but like a father he delights in his son. [Prov 3:11–12][47]

Here God is not a detached courier of consequences out of his control, but his involvement with a person has a clear emotive element, he is compared to a loving father disciplining a child. Parental discipline is not simply about inflicting punishment, but about moulding the child for his or her own benefit. It is quite clearly implied here that the divine action is not a simple delivery of predefined consequences, but that the relationship between God and human beings is at least as complex as one between a human father and his children.

That the relationship between God and humans is dynamic rather than static is also indicated by the references to prayers of the righteous [e.g. Prov 15:29]. These show that Yahweh's behaviour can be influenced. We cannot conceive of prayer here as yet another simple action with a built-in consequence, because it is implied that only the prayer of the righteous can achieve any positive result [Prov 15:9, 28], i.e., it is not the act of prayer, but the character of the intercessor which determines the outcome. Further, even God's protection of the righteous is not always seen as automatic. Consider the following verse:

> Yahweh's name is a fortified tower, a righteous person runs into it and is inaccessible. [Prov 18:10]

---

[47] For textual notes see p. 67.

The righteous person's protection does not originate in the righteousness *per se*, but in Yahweh's name, i.e., an active invocation of God, here expressed in the poetic terms of running. Again the indications are that the relationship between God and the outcome of a person's behaviour is not entirely straightforward.

We could point out a number of other notions found in the book that speak against the action-consequence model in a similar manner, and I will just briefly list some of them before moving on to one final and major problem of the action-consequence theory. Both humble and glorified states are appropriate for the wise [e.g. Prov 15:16, 33], and the right choices sometimes mean lack of material prosperity. Again, this suggests that a person's present state is not determined by previous actions in any simple manner. Elsewhere, we come across the idea that God considers not only the actions, but also the hidden attitudes [Prov 15:11; 17:3]. This introduces yet another variable that influences what happens to a person, for which a simple action-consequence model cannot account. In Prov 19:14 we find a comparison between receiving an inheritance and finding a prudent wife. The main thrust of the verse seems to be that finding a prudent wife cannot be taken for granted, i.e., the sage does not seem to have any clear advice for the young man on how to find her, or, in other words, there does not seem to be a very clear and predictable action-consequence relationship. An entirely unambiguous statement about God's ultimate control over the results of human undertaking is Prov 21:31. Here it is plainly asserted that human activities that are essential to military success, are no guarantee of it. Prov 21:1 goes even further, declaring that Yahweh has absolute control not only over the consequences, but also over the actions of a king.

While the cumulative weight of the evidence presented so far is in my view sufficient to reject the action-consequence model, there is one further aspect of Yahweh's role in Proverbs that speaks forcefully against it, and which is also an essential part of the Proverbial perception of God and the world. Repeatedly, throughout the book, we find God in the function of a judge and executor of justice. Consider this scene at the gate:

> Do not steal from the impoverished because he is impoverished, and do not crush the poor in the gate. For Yahweh fights their case and will squeeze[48] life from those who rob them. [Prov 22:22–23]

---

[48] 𝔐 קבע is difficult, I follow here the suggestion of Cody (1980:425) based on evidence from Arabic.

The terminology that is employed in v. 23A, יְהוָה יָרִיב רִיבָם, is unmistakably legal. God is portrayed here as an enforcer of justice, who will fight the case of the oppressed with the result of robbing the oppressor.[49] The verse goes far beyond claiming that the oppressor will have to make restitution to the poor, and it is hard not to understand it as implying that Yahweh is going to impose *punishment* on the offender, i.e., the verse is talking about retribution. Consider also the following proverb:

> A good person meets favour from Yahweh, but he convicts a scheming man. [Prov 12:2]

Here we find Hiphil of רשע which Koch suggests means *to treat someone as guilty and thus afflict them* (p. 63). However, the transitive Hiphil of this verb has a technical juridical sense, meaning *to pronounce someone guilty* (KBL-3). There is no indication in this verse that we should not understand the verb in this regular sense. Quite clearly, Yahweh functions here as a judge. Here is yet another picture of a courtroom scene:

> Rescue those taken to death, and those staggering to be killed, surely, you should keep [them] back. Indeed, you may say: 'mercy, we did not know this', does not he who examines hearts understand and he who guards your life, [does not] he know? And he will repay to a person according to his deed. [Prov 24:11–12]

While v. 11 is somewhat obscure, the legal thrust of v. 12 is unmistakable. Koch is aware that the Hiphil of שוב found here has a definite juridical usage, but he suggests interpreting it as Yahweh 'turn[ing] (the effects of) an action back/towards the person' (p. 63). Yet, if we consider the first half of the verse (which Koch does not, referring only to 24:12b!), it is obvious that the whole process involves close scrutiny on behalf of Yahweh, scrutiny that goes beyond the surface action to the motivations of the heart. We can, thus, hardly perceive Yahweh's role here as mechanistic, automatically setting in motion the consequence triggered by the action.

That Yahweh has the function of a judge is also clear in this proverb:

> Many seek the face of the ruler, but man's justice is from Yahweh. [Prov 29:26]

---

[49] For a study of the use of the root ריב see Gemser (1955).

This verse has a chiastic A-B-C-C'-B'-A' structure on the semantic level, which presents us with two courtrooms, earthly and heavenly.[50] In the human court there are many seeking justice, but only the divine judge in the divine court is able to provide it.

There are some places where even Koch is forced to admit that Yahweh plays some active role:

> If one who hates you is hungry, feed him with bread and if he is thirsty give him water to drink, for you are raking burning coals upon his head and Yahweh will recompense you. [Prov 25:21–22]

Koch suggests that the common rendering of the verb שׁלם in v. 22 as *to reward* is unfounded, and that the original sense of the root, *to be complete* is appropriate here. 'Yahweh "completes" the good action of the person ... by means of the appropriate consequences which follow' (p. 60). Koch is right that שׁלם does not mean *to reward*. The notion expressed by the verb is essentially of one person making a contribution to another person to a degree necessary for restoring a disturbed equilibrium. In the present context the person suffers a loss at the hands of someone else but is encouraged not to resort to the natural way to recover this loss. Instead, it is asserted that God will compensate the person, i.e., God will provide whatever is necessary to restore the disturbed equilibrium. שׁלם here does not refer to the completion of the person's inactivity, but of the reversal of the person's initial loss. Thus, God is not completing the 'good' action. Rather, he is supplying the action which would have naturally recovered the loss and which the person was advised to avoid—the source of the compensation is not the human passivity but the divine activity.

It should be clear by now that if one wishes to postulate a system of action-consequence that accommodates the observations made so far, it will have to be more complex than a simple linear relationship between an action and its consequences. Such a model fails to account for what is clearly a rather complex nature of Yahweh's involvement in the chain of events between human actions and their ultimate effect. In the proverbial world, Yahweh is the ultimate decision-maker, one who *determines* the appropriate consequences. These are not decided on the basis of the past actions alone. There is also a relational factor present,

---

[50] מְבַקְשִׁים פְּנֵי ;B' - פְּנֵי מְבַקְשִׁים ;B - אִישׁ ;A' - רַבִּים, A - רַבִּים מְבַקְשִׁים פְּנֵי־מוֹשֵׁל וּמֵיְהוָה מִשְׁפַּט־אִישׁ where מִשְׁפָּט - C ;מוֹשֵׁל - 'C ;יְהוָה - 'C.

and God considers attitudes as well as actions; the divine judge, who is absolutely just, is an inseparable part of the proverbial world.

The observations made here lead to very much the same conclusion as that of Boström (1990:136–39):

> The term 'order' is appropriate as a designation of the world-view of the sages. The book of Proverbs in the main believes in a world which is characterized by regularity, order and harmony. ... [T]he belief in the character-consequence relationship, though forcefully asserted, was to a certain extent 'tentative' and not without vacillation, even though this rarely comes to expression in the book. ... However, ... if one is to make use of the term 'order' to signify the world-view of Israelite wisdom, it must first be qualified theologically as the order which the Lord has established and upholds. ... Our investigation ... has led us to the conclusion that the world-view of the sages was neither built upon a concept of an impersonal order nor of actions with 'automatic,' built-in consequences, but on the active participation of the Lord in the affairs of men in conjunction with man's own responsibility.

The world is orderly, yet, this order is Yahweh's order. It has been put in place by him and it is subjected to his control. The predictability of this order, albeit subject to exceptions, is not due to its fixed nature, but due to the implied stability of Yahweh's character.

The Makeup of Qoheleth's Cosmos

The Divine Sphere

Similarly to Proverbs, Qoheleth's world contains the three spheres that belong to God, to the living, and to the dead. Turning our attention initially to the divine domain, Qoheleth's comments on it are scarce. This he shares with the proverbial sages, with whom he considers it to be entirely separate from the human sphere, completely outside of human reach [Qoh 5:1]. However, Qoheleth has plenty of things to say about God who occupies this domain, referring to God directly some forty times. While in the case of Proverbs a strict definition of the word *monotheistic* did not fully capture the book's outlook, Qoheleth's perspective is thoroughly monotheistic, in the most rigid sense of the word. There is not a single hint in the book that Qoheleth is prepared to consider more than one deity, or a force of any kind, in operation alongside God, nor is there any apologetic against polytheistic views. This latter fact is of some interest, for Hellenistic influence on the society of Qoheleth's day was significant, and the documented tension between traditional Judaism and the penetrating Hellenism would have been impossible to escape.[51] Yet, this tension is not at all reflected in the book. We have to conclude from this that Qoheleth has in mind an audience that needs no convincing with respect to the monotheistic perspective he puts before them.

In the context of Qoheleth's implied monotheistic stance it should be further noted that Qoheleth does not make any explicit references to Israel and its religious institutions, save alluding to Solomon and mentioning Jerusalem. While Proverbs does not show any real interest in these matters either, we saw that an attempt is made in the book to identify the God of the sages with יהוה. In contrast, Qoheleth refers to God exclusively as אֱלֹהִים. Yet, in the light of the aforementioned reference to Jerusalem and the allusion to the splendour of the Solomonic court, it is not only almost certain that this implicit monotheism stems from Qoheleth's Jewish heritage, but also that he does not wish to distance himself from it. Why then does he not at least use the personal name יהוה in a manner the proverbial sages did?

The absence of the tetragrammaton cannot be explained as being due to the later tendency of Judaism not to use the personal name out of reverence, for it can be seen in Ben Sira that the use of it was still acceptable in pious (wisdom) circles of the mid second century. I am, therefore, inclined to think that Qoheleth does not use the personal name יהוה for precisely the same reasons that Proverbs made such a consistent use of it. As I argued previously, the systematic application of the name to all material in Proverbs is an expression of the belief that Yahweh is God of all the earth and of all peoples, and can be universally witnessed by those who seek to understand the world. Once this theological perspective is accepted, it is no more necessary to press the point in the manner attested in Proverbs and the reasoning can move further onto a more abstract level. Since the name is purely descriptive, and since there is but one God, the discussion would naturally move from the question *who is the true God?* solely to the question *what is God like?* It is precisely on this level that Qoheleth operates. In other words, it would appear that the theological environment in which Qoheleth is placed is quite different from the one in which the proverbial sages found themselves. While, as was argued earlier in this chapter (p. 89), the proverbial sages themselves considered יהוה to be a global God, this

---

[51] As I have explained in chapter 3 (see note 41 on p. 70), I agree with the wide scholarly consensus that the book should be dated sometime in the third century BC.

perspective seems to have needed to be defended before those outside of the wisdom tradition; in contrast the book of Qoheleth attests no such need.

The basic image of God in Qoheleth is that of a sovereign despot, who is fully in charge of everything, has no obligations and is accountable to no-one. In no sense can humans deal with him on a par; he is not a God to be trifled with. This is the basic principle of Qoheleth's approach to human-God relationships, as it is expounded in Qoh 5:

> Watch your step when you go to the house of God, and approach[52] more to obey[53] than to offer a sacrifice [as] the fools [do].[54] For they do not know they are about to do[55] evil.[56] Do not be hasty with your mouth and do not let your heart to utter a word before God rashly. For God is in heaven and you upon the earth. Therefore, let your words be few. For the dream comes with much occupation, and the voice of a fool with many words. When you made a vow before God, do not delay fulfilling it, for there is no delight in fools—what you vowed fulfil. One who does not vow is better [off] than one who vows and does not fulfil. Do not let your mouth cause[57] your body to sin, and do not dispute with the

---

[52] The infa. has the function of an impv. (WOC 35.5.1). Fox (1989:210) reads noun/ adjective, but if that was the case, i.e., if 17ab was an explanation of the command in 17aa, כִּי rather than וְ would to be expected, as elsewhere in the book.

[53] Gordis (1955a:237) argues for the sense *to understand*. However, considering the clearly cultic setting, the direct parallel with foolish sacrifices, and especially the emphasis on fulfilling vows, it is far more plausible to understand שׁמע in the sense suggested above, with a close parallel in 1 Sam 15:22.

[54] The syntax of this clause is difficult. The infc. מִתֵּת has two modifiers: (1) it forms a construct chain with הַכְּסִילִים, *giving of the fools*, as indicated by the accents; (2) it has a direct object זֶבַח - *to give a sacrifice*. ⅏, α' and ϑ' read מִמַּתַּן in place of 𝔐 מִתֵּת, but ⅏ ὑπὲρ δόμα τῶν ἀφρόνων θυσία σου, *your sacrifice [will be] better than the gift of fools*, softens the radicalism of the statement, so typical of Qoheleth, namely, that no sacrifice at all is better than a bad sacrifice (similar tendency can be seen elsewhere in ⅏ of Qoheleth). ⅖ in my view understands the text correctly rendering somewhat freely ܐܠܩܒ̈ܐ ܘܡܬܒ̈ܗܐ ܠܟ ܬܝ ܬܫܡܥܬܐ ܠܡܩܪܒ ܩܪܘܒܘ, i.e., *draw near to listen, it is better than offering of sacrifices of fools*.

[55] The infc. is problematic; the idiomatic expression ידע ל with infc. means *to know how to* but that does not seem to make sense in the context. ל + infc. can denote imminent future (WOC 36.2.3d, g), this use is found in elsewhere Qoheleth [e.g. Qoh 3:15] and fits very well with Qoh 5:1–6, especially 5:3 (cf. also Prov 15:8). Crenshaw (1988:114) prefers rendering by a present tense: *they are doing evil*, but it would appear in the context that Qoheleth is speaking from a point of view where foolish sacrifice can still be avoided. The suggestion that the fools are good, because they lack the brains to do evil (Gordis, 1955a:238) is unconvincing in the context (cf. v. 3).

[56] Ogden's (1987b:76) rendering *havoc*, based on the assertion that רַע in Qoheleth refers only to calamities or enigmatic situations while רָעָה is used to refer to moral evil is untenable, for the two words are clearly synonymous in Qoh 8:11.

[57] Reading Hiphil with an apocopated ה.

messenger,[58] saying: 'This is a mistake!'. Why should God be angry on account of your voice and ruin the work of your hands? For amongst multiplying dreams and absurd activities, and excessive words,[59] surely fear God. [Qoh 4:17-5:6]

This is the only place in the book that Qoheleth touches upon cult in any detail.[60] This passage shows that Qoheleth does not reject the cult as meaningless. Indeed, he takes it very seriously, asserting that taking it lightly is seriously short-sighted and self-destructive. Here Qoheleth comes closest to the proverbial belief that God punishes the wicked and blesses the righteous, for while he is unable to affirm the general validity of that principle, it appears that even Qoheleth is not ready to suggest that God will suffer being personally abused and manipulated.

The passage above shows that while Qoheleth never uses the phrase *fear of Yahweh* or *fear of God*, the concept is not foreign to him. It appears for the first time in Qoh 3:

> And I saw the occupation which God gave to human beings to occupy/afflict [themselves] with. He makes everything beautiful in its time, he also put ignorance in their hearts, because of which a person is not able to find out [about] the things which God does—from the beginning to the end. I came to know that there is nothing better for them but to rejoice and to do well in one's life. But also any person who can eat and drink and enjoy the fruit of his labour—it is a gift of God. I came to know that whatever God may do, will be forever—it is impossible to add to it and it is impossible to subtract from it. And God does this so that they would fear him. [Qoh 3:10–14][61]

Qoheleth's God expects humans to fear him, and in fact took active steps to ensure that it would be so, by limiting human intellectual capacity and the resulting practical capabilities to interfere with his designs. Thus, the fear of God derives from the awareness of the divine superiority; it is the awareness and acceptance of the qualitative divide between God and the human race. In practical terms, it means avoiding any attempts to trifle with God, to make promises with no

---

[58] 𝕲 (𝕾) + τοῦ θεοῦ which is almost certainly interpretative.

[59] Barton (1908:125) suggests that הַבְלִים and דְּבָרִים should be transposed, but 𝔐 is supported by both 𝕲 and 𝕾, and there is no internal need for such an emendation.

[60] Additional passing reference to cultic practice can be found in Qoh 9:2.

[61] For textual notes see p. 74.

intention to fulfil them, and in general to take the cult light-heartedly. Therefore, although Qoheleth never uses the popular wisdom saying found in Proverbs and elsewhere that fear of God is the beginning of wisdom, he makes it quite clear that not fearing God is an act of sheer madness, and so at least implies that wisdom and fear of God go hand in hand.

The problem Qoheleth is facing is not that he does not consider fear of God to be a wise and sensible attitude, but that he is unable to affirm that those who fear God fare any better than those who do not:

> Since the sentence of the evil deed is not carried out quickly, therefore, the heart of human beings which is within them is full to do evil — because a sinner does evil a hundred [times], yet his [life] is prolonged— although I know that it should be well with the fearers of God, those who continue to fear him. And it should not be well with the wicked, and [his] days should not be prolonged like a shadow, because he did not fear God. There is absurdity which happens upon the earth, that there are righteous men to whom it happens as if they were wicked and there are wicked men, to whom it happens as if they were righteous. I said that also this is absurd. [Qoh 8:11–14][62]

Qoheleth's experience teaches him that in the real world there are righteous people who suffer and wicked who prosper. Therefore, there is a tension between the last two quoted passages, one encouraging to fear God, the other admitting that it may make no observable difference. It is tempting to relegate the former text to a pious editor, but I am inclined to think that both of these texts originated from the same hand. The tension observed here is at the heart of Qoheleth's world which does not subject itself to human rationality—this is the way, Qoheleth believes, God intended it. The rationale for fearing God is not simply that it pays off, but that God is beyond human reach.

Sheol

In contrast to Proverbs where Sheol appears only as an acknowledged reality, but never the subject of deliberation, Qoheleth gives it some thought, but even for him it remains a great unknown:

---

[62] For textual notes see p. 72.

I thought to myself concerning[63] human beings: God makes clear[64] to them and shows[65] them that they are animals.[66] Indeed, as for the fate of[67] human beings, and the fate of an animal—[68]they have the same fate: as [is] death of this, so [is] death of the other and there is one breath to both. And there is no advantage to a person over an animal, for both are passing.[69] They both are on [their] way to the same place—both came from the dust and both are returning to the dust. Who knows? Is the breath of the human beings ascending above and the breath of the animals descending beneath to the earth?[70] And I saw that there is nothing better than [if] a person rejoices in his deeds for this is his portion. For who shall take him to look at that which will be afterwards?[71] [Qoh 3:18–22]

The deliberation about what happens to the human and animal רוּחַ at the point of death reflects familiarity with a belief in a meaningful

---

[63] Delitzsch (1982b:267) links עַל־דִּבְרַת not with Qoheleth's thinking but with the divine activity, i.e., God does this *for the sake of sons of man*. However, if that was the case, one would expect some statement explaining what it is about this particular divine activity that is done for the sake of man. It is far more natural to link the clause with the preceding *verbum dicendi*.

[64] MH sense of ברר (see Jas). The BH sense is generally more concrete: *to purge out, to select, to polish*, but the process of abstractisation is already on the way, as is seen from the application of the adj. בָּרוּר to speech (e.g. Zeph 3:9). The sense *to select* is not appropriate in the context which does not assert exclusiveness of humanity (or some human beings) but rather the exact opposite. Gordis (1955a:226) thinks that לברם is a case of asseverative ל before Sx. I am more inclined to understand it as an infc. used as a finite form, a phenomenon that occurs in LBH (WOC 36.3.2a).

[65] Reading with 𝕲, 𝖁, and 𝕾 as a Hiphil with an apocopated ה.

[66] 𝔐 שֶׁהֶם־בְּהֵמָה הֵמָּה לָהֶם; reading שְׁהֶם־בְּהֵמָה לָהֶם. The pronoun הֵמָּה is not attested in 𝕲, and is probably a result of a dittography. The final לָהֶם functions as an indirect object of the preceding verb.

[67] Reading with the versions as a construct form.

[68] With many Hebrew manuscripts and the versions omitting the conjunction ו found in 𝔏, which is likely to be a scribal error caused by parablepsis.

[69] Hebrew הֶבֶל, which I elsewhere translate *absurd*, but here the emphasis is clearly on ephemerality.

[70] I follow the versions in understanding the initial ה of הַעֹלָה and הַיֹּרֶדֶת as interrogative particles, for, as Gordis (1955a:228) notes, there is a tendency to vocalise in the same manner as the article when standing before י or א (cf. Lev 10:19). Furthermore, even if one understands these as articles, the whole clause still clearly remains a question because of the initial מִי יֹדֵעַ.

[71] The question can be understood in two ways, depending on the referent of the sfx on אַחֲרָיו: (1) no-one can come back from the dead to look at what will be after *him*; (2) no-one can be taken while still alive to have a preview of what will be *afterwards*, i.e., after death. The latter interpretation fits the context much better. The 3ms sfx is purely adverbial, cf. יַחְדָּו (Gordis, 1955a:228); for such an adverbial use of אַחֲרָיו elsewhere in the book see Qoh 9:3 (note 76 on p. 154).

afterlife, but it is not something to which Qoheleth himself appears
to adhere. Irrespective of which interpretation of אַחֲרָיו is adopted (see
note 71), the basic implications remain the same. There is no way
that Qoheleth, or anyone else, can describe what happens after death.
The world of the dead is not accessible to the living and vice versa.
Consequently, Qoheleth's empirical methodology does not provide him
with a definite answer to the possibility of a meaningful afterlife, yet, it
is obvious, that he himself is sceptical in that matter. Sheol is a place of
oblivion, where all that is characteristic of human earthly striving ends,
and it is quite possible that Sheol is nothing more for Qoheleth than a
poetic image for non-existence:

> Whatever you may be able to do, do it with your vigour, for there is
> no doing or devising or knowledge or wisdom in Sheol, where you are
> [already] going. [Qoh 9:10][72]

Before moving on to consider the human domain, I wish to draw
attention to two further passages in the book immediately relevant to
the present discussion:

> And I turned[73] and I saw all the oppression which happens under the
> sun. And behold, the tear[s] of the oppressed, and they do not have
> a comforter, and from the hand of their oppressors [comes][74] power,
> and they do not have a comforter. And I congratulated the dead, who
> already died, over those still living. And more than both of them [I
> congratulated][75] the one who has not been yet, who has not seen the
> evil that happens under the sun. [Qoh 4:1–3]

> If a person begets a hundred [children] and lives many years, as many as
> the days of his years may be, but his soul would not be satiate from the

---

[72] For textual notes see p. 191.

[73] I am inclined to agree with Fox (1989:201) that the verb is not used here idiomat-
ically, since this is Qoheleth's first observation of oppression. If it was to modify ראה
alone in the sense *I had yet another look at the world and saw* יסף and not שׁוּב would be
expected (for the distinction between the two verbs see Jöu § 177b). Further, such an
understanding is in harmony with 𝔐 accents.

[74] Gordis (1955a:228) suggests that וּמִיַּד עֹשְׁקֵיהֶם כֹּחַ is a nominal expression parallel
to דִּמְעַת הָעֲשֻׁקִים and following the וְהִנֵּה. However, the conjunctions indicate in my view
that וְהִנֵּה is part of the first clause, with וּמִיַּד עֹשְׁקֵיהֶם כֹּחַ being parallel to וְהִנֵּה דִּמְעַת
הָעֲשֻׁקִים.

[75] The אֵת indicates that *those who have not been yet* is the object of the verb from the
previous verse, *pace* Gordis (1955a:229) who sees here a nominative absolute, on the
grounds that the verb would be too distant from the object. However, a dozen words
hardly creates a distance that would interrupt the flow of thought.

good things, and he[76] even did not have[77] a burial, I say: 'the miscarried one is better off than him'. For in absurdity he came and in darkness he will go[78] and in darkness his name is covered. He did not see the sun either and did not get to know [anything], there is more peace[79] to this one than the other. Even if[80] he lives a thousand years twice, but does not enjoy himself, do not they both go to the same place? [Qoh 6:3–6]

Here Qoheleth touches on the question of the nature of the existence of the unborn. It is probably necessary to make a distinction between the two passages. In the latter Qoheleth is concerned with a miscarried baby, i.e., someone who bypasses the world *under the sun*. The former text would, on the other hand, seem to be talking not about a person in a prenatal stage, but simply one that has not come into being at all. This raises a question of where the one *who has not been yet* is located. Qoheleth made it quite clear that those who are in Sheol cannot enter the world under the sun; the traffic between these two domains flows in one direction only. Thus, the one *who has not been yet* is found neither in Sheol, nor in the world under the sun. It is possible that such persons are somewhere in the divine domain, but in the light of the strict separation of the human from the divine which Qoheleth maintains, it is more likely that he in fact tacitly assumes yet a fourth domain that serves as a storage place for human beings before they are born

---

[76] Crenshaw (1988:120) takes this as a reference to the miscarried child. However, the miscarried child is not introduced until the very end of the verse, and the 3ms sfx is used throughout the verse to refer only to the unfortunate man (consider מִמֶּנּוּ which comes *after* the sfx in question). This makes Crenshaw's interpretation unlikely. The above rendering finds further support in the accents.

[77] Gordis (1955a:249) asserts that the text as it stands does not make sense, and reads לוֹא הָיְתָה, in the sense *even if he has a proper burial*. However, there are a number of objections against this reading. (1) it has to be assumed that the particle לוֹא is used incorrectly, because for this interpretation the condition must be real; (2) the particle would be superfluous for a real condition, fulfilling identical functions as the already present וְגַם; (3) the particle לוֹא would stand at the beginning and not between the subject and predicate. Gordis fails to appreciate that the conjunction *and* does not have to be taken in a strictly Boolean sense, i.e., the clause as it stands does not necessarily imply that a failure to be satiate in life could somehow be compensated for by a proper burial. Rather, Qoheleth, in his typical style, pictures a person at the extreme, who is both not satiate and does not get a proper burial.

[78] Following 𝔊 יֵלֵךְ; 4QQoh^a הלך.

[79] Reading with 𝔊 נַחַת; 4QQoh^a נוחת. Gordis (1955a:249) renders *satisfaction* because he considers the statement *there is more rest* to be self-evident. However, satisfaction requires self-consciousness, and it is precisely the point Qoheleth is making that the miscarried child has no consciousness at all.

[80] Reading with 𝔐 אִלּוּ; 4QQoh^a ואם לוא.

into this world. Thus, it is possible that we meet here the later rabbinic notion of גוּף in an incipient form.

The World of the Living

While Qoheleth offers us some insights into the different segments of the larger cosmos, he is mainly concerned with what he typically designates as the *under the sun*, the sphere which is exclusive to the living and out of bounds to both those not yet born [Qoh 4:3], and those already dead [Qoh 9:6]. Qoheleth never speaks explicitly of the origins of the world in a manner similar to Prov 8:22ff., yet, it is implied clearly enough that the world was created by God [e.g. Qoh 7:13; 12:1, 7]. There are two passages in the book that have special bearing on our understanding of Qoheleth's cosmological perspective, and it is these that I will concentrate on next.

The first of these is the opening poem [Qoh 1:4–11]. This text, wedged between the opening inclusio and the Solomonic experiment, can easily be dismissed as being of little real significance. Yet, it is not some unnecessary embellishment, but rather the whole of Qoheleth's reasoning stems from the outline of the cosmos that this passage spells out. The poem follows immediately after the programmatic question of Qoh 1:3 *what profit is there for a human being in all his labour which he carries out under the sun*, dealt with in chapter 2, and it is the beginning of Qoheleth's reply to this question:

> A generation is going, and a generation is coming, but the earth stands for ever.
>
> The sun is rising[81] and the sun is setting, panting to its place, there it is rising [again]. Going to the South, going to the North, circling, circling,[82] the wind[83] is going, and the wind [keeps] returning on its circular path.[84]

---

[81] Reading זוֹרֵחַ instead of זָרַח אֶל in the light of the string of ptcs in vv. 4–6.

[82] The repeated סוֹבֵב should be retained, note the 2+2+2+2 beat up to the *zāqēp̄ qāṭōn*.

[83] The gender disagreement of the preceding participles with רוּחַ is most likely due to the fact that the noun follows the opening verbs at a significant distance, and thus the text uses the generic unmarked form which is retained once the subject has been stated. Such syntax is found several times in the book [e.g. Qoh 7:7, 24] and elsewhere in the OT [e.g. 1 Kgs 19:11].

[84] The final part after the *zāqēp̄ qāṭōn* should be retained—the basic notion in the poem is that of circularity, and this part closes the circle.

All the rivers are going to the sea, and the sea is [never] filled up. To the place where the rivers are going, there they are returning to go.[85] All the things[86] are wearisome[87]—one is not able to describe [them]. The eye will not [ever] be satisfied by watching, nor will the ear be [ever] filled from[88] hearing.

Whatever has been, is that which will be, and that which has already happened, is that which will happen. And there is nothing new under the sun. Is there[89] such a thing about which one could say: 'Look at this! This is new!'? It already has been during the ages which were[90] before us.

There is no remembrance of the previous [generations],[91] and also concerning the later [generations] who will be, there will be no remembrance of them with those who will be afterwards. [Qoh 1:4–11]

---

[85] Here I am inclined to side with those commentators who argue that שָׁם הֵם שָׁבִים לָלֶכֶת in 7b should be translated *there they are returning to go*, since, as Whybray (1988) pointed out, the idiomatic use of שׁוּב in the sense *to do something again* is employed in reference to repeated activities separated by a lapse of time, not to a single continuous activity and thus the phrase cannot be very well rendered *there they continue to go*. Continuity, I think, would more likely be expressed by the idiomatic use of יסף.

[86] Fox (1989:171) argues for the sense *words*, because דָּבָר is never used in reference to material things. However, here the reference is not to the four material objects, but to the phenomena associated with these, and דָּבָר is regularly used of action or activity (e.g. Exod 9:6; 2 Sam 11:11). Loader (1986:21) also prefers to render דְּבָרִים as *words*, because of the later reference to hearing and speaking, and interprets this verse as an attack on traditional wisdom. However, since the reference is not only to hearing but also to seeing, it does appear that הַדְּבָרִים does not refer to words, but to the observable phenomena.

[87] The context, with its reference to human failure, strongly favours the rendering proposed here against a more passive sense, i.e., *all things are weary* (pace Barton, 1908:74–75; Delitzsch, 1982b:223); the phenomena described are characterised by constancy, not weariness, thus the passive sense is wholly inappropriate here. Ogden's (1987b:32) understanding that *toiling toward a goal* is denoted here is precluded by the circular, i.e., goal-less nature of the phenomena in question; similarly Whybray's (1988) understanding that the word denotes not weariness but purposeful activity fits ill with the context in which nothing at all is achieved in spite of the continuous effort.

[88] Gordis (1955a:197) observes that מלא normally takes a direct object without preposition. However, it should be noted that in this case *hearing* is not the substance of the filling, but rather the process, the instrument. Consequently, a simple accusative would not be appropriate here.

[89] The B colon requires this to be interpreted as a question. Gordis (1955a:197) suggested that this is a protasis of a conditional sentence, but against that view speaks the lack of any formal co-ordination between the two colons.

[90] Reading pl. with some Hebrew manuscripts.

[91] In the context the other possible referent are the ages from v. 10; however, this verse refers to three successive cycles, and since remembering associated with the final cycle is a function of a human mind it is clear that the ultimate referent is personal (Gordis, 1955a:198 pointed out that an impersonal referent would most likely have used a feminine form).

I have adopted a formal division of the text suggested by Rousseau (1981), who argued that the poem consists of three two-verse stanzas framed within an opening bi-colon and a closing tri-colon. It can be observed that the first two stanzas are made of two successive statements resembling each other. In the first stanza we find a description of two natural phenomena, sun and wind. A basic macroscopic pattern of behaviour is suggested for each, followed by a further detailed description of the nature of that movement and concluded by a statement implying that the whole behaviour is repetitive. The two statements can be schematised as follows:

> sun: rising + setting; panting; cyclic repetition
>
> wind: southward movement + northward movement; spinning; cyclic repetition

In the second stanza we find an observation concerning the character of the movement of water and of the nature of all things from the perspective of a human observer. Again, both of these statements have a similar structure: a claim is made about the basic nature of the phenomenon, followed by a description of a result that is produced, in both cases in terms of a failure, followed by a reason for the failure:

> rivers: going to the sea; *fail* to overfill the sea; *because* they return to the starting point
>
> all things: wearisome; *impossible* to describe; *because* of endless flow of information

In the third stanza the pattern changes. The arrangement here is chiastic. The stanza opens and closes with declarations that everything repeats itself, linking together past, present and future, between which we find two statements that there is nothing new:

> past = future, past = future
>
> nothing new; nothing new
>
> present = past

The initial bicolon and the closing tricolon form a frame for the three stanzas, that indicates Qoheleth's real interest. Verse 4 represents the main topic, the movement of the generations with the seeming stability of the earth as its reference point.[92] Having introduced the key issue,

---

[92] Ogden (1986) proposed that דּוֹר here refers not to human generations, but to the cycles of nature; this has been convincingly refuted by Fox (1988b). However, Fox's

the replacement of one generation by another,[93] Qoheleth seeks better understanding of the character of this passing movement by drawing a parallel with other observable phenomena, namely the sun, wind and water; the conclusions from his observation of the natural phenomena are applied to the relationship between the individual generations, and it is asserted that human existence is subject to the same pattern of behaviour. That which is true of any particular generation is also true of any other generation, i.e., in a certain sense the temporal movement of generations is cyclic. However, this cyclic temporal movement is accompanied by an additional linear element that accounts for the displacement of one generation by another, and yet a wider, supra-generational cyclicity, one which accounts for things that have the appearance of being new, but in reality are merely a repetition of something that took place outwith the reach of the present human memory.

From Qoheleth's point of view, the cyclic elements of the flow of time are the most important, and are referred to by him later:

> Whatever has been, still is, and what [is] to be, already has been; and God chases the pursued.[94] [Qoh 3:15]

As a result of the cyclic nature of human existence, on the macroscopic level, Qoheleth's world is uniform, unchanging and, therefore, predictable. Human experience has universal validity, and so Qoheleth's own observations can be used to draw more general and widely applicable conclusions, i.e., Qoheleth is able to turn his experience into a

---

suggestion that אֶרֶץ here denotes humanity as a whole is to be rejected; it refers to the stage for the movement of the generations and the reference point for the activity of the other natural phenomena, the earth.

[93] A note is due on the sequence in v. 4. It would seem more natural to have *generation comes and generation goes* instead of Qoheleth's *generation goes and generation comes*. However, the order which Qoheleth uses is significant as it shows that his concern is with the succession of generations. The suggested *generation comes and generation goes* would picture only one generation, which would do both the coming and leaving while the statement *generation goes and generation comes* pictures two generations, coming in succession. (That this order is not accidental is shown by the same organisation of v. 11.)

[94] When בקשׁ is found in the OT together with רדף it is always in the sense *to pursue* [Josh 2:22; Judg 4:22; 1 Sam 23:25; 25:29; 26:20]. I follow here Ibn Ezra's understanding that *the pursued* here is the never ending time (see Rottzoll, 1999:87–88). Ogden's (1987b:58) suggestion that vv. 14 and 15 are closely parallel and that in the light of the parallelism the sense of v. 15 is 'God requests that it be pursued,' *it* being either *enjoyment* or *the eternity*, finds no tangible support in the text (it is unlikely that אֶת־ is an abbreviated form of אֶת־אֲשֶׁר).

paradigm that describes the way in which the world is. However, this uniformity is of an entirely different type than that of the proverbial world; *macroscopic* is the key word here. The predictability of Qoheleth's world happens on an abstract phenomenal level, pertaining to issues such as birth and death, joy and sorrow, but does not extend to the lower detailed level of specific human actions and their consequences. The macroscopic regularity stems from the fact that there is no real progress in time. The only forward movement is limited to the exchange of the generations on the surface of the earth, while the principal nature of human existence and experience does not change.

The individual generational cycles of human existence lack any tangible and persistent link; they are connected by human memory alone. This has got only a limited reach, and does not encompass the entirety of the supra-generational cycle. It is, therefore, possible to gain the impression that the world is progressing and new things are taking place. This, Qoheleth says, is merely an illusion, and the lack of a persistent inter-generational link means that any human achievement is bound to disappear from human memory at some point. From the point of view of Qoheleth's enquiry this means that to answer the question of persistent and absolute יִתְרוֹן, he only needs to scrutinise what can be achieved within a single-generation cycle of time; if a particular human activity cannot produce lasting benefit within the individual's life span, even less can it do so as new generations come and go.

So far, I have argued that Qoheleth's world is principally cyclic and, thus, essentially predictable. The precise nature of this predictability is explained by Qoheleth in the famous poem on time. This passage has some intriguing characteristics. It contains three quarters of the occurrences of the word עֵת found in the book, but its even more striking feature is a carefully worked out formal structure. We find in the poem three stanzas placed within a frame. Within each of the stanzas as well as within the opening bicolon of the closing section, we find a careful antithetical parallelism—the time of birth is juxtaposed with the time of death, the time of planting with time of uprooting, etc. At the same time the sequence positive/negative in the two halves of each stanza is reversed, creating a semantic chiasm. The intricacy of the arrangement goes even further, as there is a mutual chiastic arrangement between the neighbouring stanzas.[95]

---

[95] For a detailed examination of the formal characteristics of the poem see in particular Loader (1969;1979:11–14, 29–33).

It is not my intention to go into a detailed discussion of the significance of the individual lines of this poem. Some seem self-explanatory, some have puzzled commentators for two millennia. For the present purposes, the most crucial is the significance of the word עֵת as it is used here. I will start with some general comments on its semantics in the OT. עֵת is the basic OT word denoting a *specific* time, referring either to a point [e.g. Deut 1:9] or an interval [e.g. Deut 3:8] on the time continuum. Significantly, עֵת *per se* is temporarily non-specific. Its meaning is similar to the English *time* in constructions such as *point in time* or *during this time*; in contrast to the English *time*, however, עֵת lacks any abstract sense such as when *time* is used in modern sciences. In order to denote more specific temporal information עֵת must be further qualified, and this can be done in two distinct ways. First, עֵת can be qualified by some temporally specific expression, and the whole phrase then refers to an absolute time. An example of this use can be found in phrases such as the very common לְעֵת עֶרֶב [e.g. Gen 8:11]. Second, עֵת can be qualified by a non-temporal circumstantial expression. The whole phrase then can be translated to a fixed point on the temporal axis when the specific circumstances occur, but this can only be done with hindsight. The expression itself does not carry temporal information; the time it denotes is relative. This is the case, for instance, in the phrase בְּעֵת צָרָה [e.g. Isa 33:2].

Returning to the time poem, it is tempting to read it as a statement of temporal determinism of existence. Everything has been pre-set in time and it will occur at the point on the temporal continuum that has been allocated to it.[96] The opening line of the first stanza: *there is a time to give birth and there is a time to die*, quite clearly lends itself to such a reading. However, such an understanding encounters a number of difficulties. To start with, it is in ill harmony with the role the text plays within the larger structure of the book. The poem serves as an eloquent answer to the programmatic question of Qoh 1:3, as is indicated by its restatement in Qoh 3:9. It follows directly after the basic investigation into life which Qoheleth, alias Solomon, undertook in chapters 2–3, and contains the essence of Qoheleth's explanation why the Solomonic experiment failed. Since the mode of operation of this experiment implies free decision-making [Qoh 2:10], and since the Solomonic experiment did not fail because Qoheleth, alias Solomon,

---

[96] Thus von Rad (1972:263) speaks of 'the time and the hour which are set for all human projects'.

was not able to do what he pleased, it is unlikely that the explanation
is to be found in the conviction that the world is predestined in a rigid
temporal fashion. Further, if the explanation for the failure was such
a strict temporal determinism of existence, then this would have been
a natural place to end the book. It is hard to accept that Qoheleth
believed in a strict temporal predestination and at the same time to
account for the almost 50 command forms that are located after the
time poem,[97] at least some of which are clearly intended as genuine
guidelines for making the most of life.

However, by far the most significant objection to reading the poem
as a declaration of temporal predestination is the fact that Qoheleth
makes a statement that shows explicitly that he does not consider one's
death to be fixed in time. He advises the reader *do not be too wicked and
do not be a fool, why should you die when it is not your time?* [Qoh 7:17]. Quite
clearly the time of death is the function of circumstances here. While it
cannot be avoided (there is some limiting natural time of death, one's
time), it can be speeded up by one's course of action. Time to die is
then not an absolute point on the temporal continuum, but rather a
set of circumstances, natural or unnatural, resulting in death. This precludes Qoh 3:2 being a statement about a fixed temporal predetermi-
nation of a person's death; in the expression עֵת לָמוּת it is not עֵת that
qualifies לָמוּת but rather לָמוּת that is the circumstantial qualifier of עֵת.

Circumstantial understanding of עֵת required in Qoh 3:2 not only
makes good sense throughout the poem, but in some of the other verses
it is clearly preferable. Thus, there are certain circumstances which are
required for successful planting, and certain circumstances that lead
to uprooting of plants.[98] When considered on its own it is very unlikely
that one would wish to interpret this line as a statement of fatalism. The
same is true in respect of time of weeping and time of laughing in Qoh
3:4A, or even more so, speaking and being silent in Qoh 3:7B, which is
most naturally understood as a time when it is, or is not, *appropriate* to
speak, not a time when it is or is not *possible* to speak.

The circumstantial understanding of עֵת in the poem also makes very
good sense of the so carefully worked out polarity and the comments

---

[97] As a matter of fact, the overwhelming majority of command forms and direct
address to the reader in the book are located after the poem, in chapters 7–12.

[98] I disagree with Loader (1979:30) that the reference in 2B is to planting and
weeding. The parallelism between 2A and 2B and the pass. ptc. נָטוּעַ suggest the object
affected is identical in 2Ba and 2Bb.

that follow it. God designed the world in such a way that for every set of circumstances leading to some positive outcome, there is a corresponding set of circumstances producing a negative outcome and the negative and positive are in balance, maintaining an equilibrium which is neither positive nor negative, but simply neutral, or, in Qoheleth's own vocabulary, הֶבֶל. Qoheleth's concern in this poem is not *when* things happen but *that* they happen, and that they come in mutually annulling pairs.

The system Qoheleth pictures is not self-maintaining in a deist sense. Rather, God is involved and is in full control. He leads everything to perfection in its time, i.e., it is God who makes certain that eventually everything is brought into perfect balance, that within the *under the sun* sphere no event will be left without its counterpart. His ultimate control over the whole system and the inability of human beings to cheat it, clearly implied by Qoheleth, is based on two things. First is the fact that God imposed limitations on human abilities, and neither speed, nor strength, nor wisdom can guarantee success, but time and chance happen to all; indeed, no-one is able to know one's time [Qoh 9:11–12]. The second factor responsible for human inability to overcome the equilibrious nature of the world is the reality of death. Death functions as a wild card that can be played by God at any time and always results in neutrality. In order for death to function this way, its value must be ambiguous, sometimes positive, sometimes negative. This is precisely what we find in Qoheleth. Sometimes death cancels one's earthly achievements [Qoh 5:13], and thus thwarts any seeming positive bias of the world; on other occasions death brings redemption from a thoroughly negative experience of life [Qoh 4:2]. Similarly, birth can be perceived not only positively but also as a negative event [Qoh 6:3].[99]

While the inevitability of death is the ultimate reason why no profit can be made during human life, it needs to be pointed out that it is not the sole reason. Rather, the paring birth/death is only an extreme case of many such pairs that human experience is made of. As a result, not only can no gain be carried past death, but essentially no real profit can be made even in the time framed by birth and death; every success is, given enough time, replaced by a failure. Qoheleth considers this to be an intentional feature of the design of the *under the sun*. He touches on this issue early on,

---

[99] For an extensive examination of Qoheleth's view of death against the background of attitudes found in the ANE see Burkes (1999).

> I saw all the things that happen under the heaven, and behold, all this is absurd and striving after wind. What is crooked, cannot be straightened, and a deficit cannot be counted. [Qoh 1:14–15][100]

but it is only later on that the full significance of the statement becomes apparent:

> See the activity of God, for who is able to straighten that which he made crooked? On a good day, enjoy [it]![101] And on a bad day, consider: also this alongside that God did, so that a person may find nothing to complain against him.[102] [Qoh 7:13–14]

The world of Qoheleth's experience is one where the positive and enjoyable is always accompanied by the negative and unpleasant, and it is precisely because God wished it to be so. In Qoheleth's understanding, God is ultimately responsible for everything. For him everything that happens is linked to God, and both the positive and negative experience of human life is a part of the intentional design. Qoheleth is even prepared to go as far as to suggest that God is responsible for evil perpetrated by humans, at least to a degree [Qoh 8:11–14]. Yet, Qoheleth does not condemn God, but equally there is not a hint of dualism in the book that would allow the responsibility to be passed onto someone else. One can sense in Qoheleth an echo of the Isaianic 'does the clay say to the potter, "What are you making?"' [Isa 45:9 NIV].

However, the pairing of events outlined by the time poem is not strictly synchronised, death does not necessarily coincide with birth, nor does joy turn immediately into sorrow on every occasion. This temporal discrepancy is a critical part of Qoheleth's perception of the world, for it leaves some paradoxical hope; life may not produce anything of real value, but it can still be worth living. It is from here that Qoheleth's positive attitude toward life and his calls for enjoyment originate, and the whole of Qoheleth's wisdom is built around this feature of the design of the world, as we will see in chapter 6.

---

[100] For textual notes see p. 151.
[101] 𝔐 הֱיֵה, be (in good)!; 𝔊, α', ϑ' חֲיֵה, live (in good)!
[102] This is an idiomatic use of אַחֲרָיו; see 𝔙, σ', 𝔖 and the rabbinic interpretation; Driver (1954:230) points out loosely related Aramaic and Syriac idioms.

Cosmology and Theology of the Epilogue

Finally, before we leave Qoheleth, a few words are necessary with reference to the epilogue. It is not possible to reconstruct fully the epilogist's
cosmological and theological perspective from the few verses, but a few
observations with respect to his view of God are possible. In contrast to
Qoheleth's understanding, and similarly to Proverbs, the epilogist's God
is prepared to reveal to humans what he demands of them. Further, the
exhortation to obey divine commandments, in spite of the obscurity of
the final phrase of the epilogue, does betray God pictured as a judge,
and certainly involved in the human world much more directly than we
find in Qoheleth proper. In the light of this emphatic exhortation it is
unlikely that the epilogist would affirm Qoheleth's conviction that the
righteous and wicked have the same chances of success; it is only those
who obey God that prosper. In this respect the epilogist would seem
much closer to the proverbial point of view, but it is necessary to keep
in mind that these two perspectives have been arrived at differently. As
pointed out earlier, the epilogist's understanding is based on knowledge
of specific divine commandments, i.e., verbal revelation, and thus is by
necessity originating within the cult.

Summary

Again, there are some significant similarities in the cosmological and
theological perspectives of the two books. In both, the world of the
living is entirely separate from the divine sphere and the realm of the
dead, and humanity does not have free access to either of these two.
Neither of the books reflects adherence to a belief in a meaningful
afterlife; the concern of both Proverbs and Qoheleth is with earthly
existence. As far as the world of the living is concerned, it is considered
orderly and predictable so as to allow a formulation of a paradigm
that describes its behaviour. Yet, the orderliness is of a different kind.
In Proverbs a fairly stable link between a person's behaviour and its
consequences is maintained by a just God, and it is possible to exploit
this link in order to achieve a significant degree of progress in life.
In contrast, for Qoheleth the uniformity of the world lies on a more
abstract, phenomenal level and guarantees that no real progress can be
achieved during a human lifespan, nor beyond it.
    The cosmological perspective is closely linked to the overall image of
God in the two books. While both of the main voices think in terms of

one God with a universal sphere of influence, not limited to any single territory, in Proverbs God is much more open toward humanity. He is likened to a father figure, he wishes to be known, and he reveals himself abundantly to those who seek to understand the world with the right motives. Qoheleth's God is much more remote, closely guarding his unique position by limiting what human beings can know. Further, in the semi-dualistic outlook of Proverbs, God is essentially disassociated from evil which stems from the forces of chaos, the origin of which is silently passed over. In stark contrast, no such dualism is found in Qoheleth. For him God is ultimately responsible for everything, and humanity has no other choice but to live within the framework that God set up for it. The theo-cosmological perspective of the epilogue of Qoheleth is different from both Proverbs and the core of Qoheleth. The semblance of similarity with the view of the Proverbial sages is only superficial, for even though the epilogist's God appears to be involved in the human world in a very direct manner, the overall theological perspective centres virtually exclusively around direct revelation.

CHAPTER 5

THE HUMAN WORLD

In the previous chapter I pointed out that the wisdom undertaking, as we find it in both Proverbs and Qoheleth, is an earthly exercise with earthly concerns. This statement can be further qualified: the wisdom enterprise is not only earthly, but it is anthropocentric in its aims. Its goal is not simply to understand the world *per se*, but rather to understand the place of a human being in the cosmos. Ultimately, the sages wished to understand the world in order to improve the quality of their existence, to use a modern phrase. Therefore, an attempt to formulate the sages' worldview cannot be made without close examination of their anthropological perspective, their social views and the socio-economic structures reflected in the two books.[1]

The Human World of Proverbs

Proverbial Anthropology

I will start with the elementary question 'what is a human being' from the proverbial perspective. While I have suggested in chapter 3 that the sages had a fairly homogenous view of the world in which human beings could learn from other creatures, there is evidence in the book that humans occupy a special place in the created world. Humanity is, for instance, singled out from the whole earth as Dame Wisdom's source of pleasure [Prov 8:31], and on a couple of places it becomes

---

[1] I must clarify that I do not wish to imply here that wisdom is, as it is sometimes claimed, solely or predominantly anthropocentric in its entirety, i.e., that it is concerned only with questions of human nature and activity. I fully agree with Perdue (1994:46–48) that in order to do justice to wisdom, it is not possible to consider it merely as an attempt to understand humanity, nor is it possible to relegate wisdom entirely to the sphere of cosmological deliberation. Rather, both of these elements are key aspects of the wisdom quest. Wisdom is about understanding the whole world for the sake of, and with special emphasis on, humanity; it is about human players on the cosmic stage. Thus, its concerns are anthropocentric, but these concerns are addressed in a wider cosmological context.

apparent that the sages had a high anthropology, somewhat resembling the *imago dei* perspective of Genesis:

> He who oppresses the poor reproaches his maker, he who shows grace to the underprivileged respects him. [Prov 14:31]

> He who derides a poor person scorns his maker, he who rejoices over disaster will not go unpunished. [Prov 17:5]

> A rich person and a poor person share this:[2] Yahweh made both of them. [Prov 22:2]

> A poor person and an oppressor share this:[2] Yahweh gives light to the eyes of both of them. [Prov 29:13]

There is an apologetic concern in the background of these verses; they are aiming to refute an implied claim that the poor can be freely oppressed, because the socio-economic divide is evidence that such oppression is permissible, and most likely, that it is a right that the rich are divinely granted. It is in this context that the theologically-based argument of the previous verses makes best sense; the sages argue that all human beings, irrespective of their social standing, are due a certain dignity because they all have the same maker. This is not to say that Proverbs principally rejects any social arrangement that is hierarchical, nor that the sages considered poverty and wealth as arbitrary states outside of a person's control. On the contrary, poverty is most frequently portrayed as self-inflicted and riches the product of wisdom. The quoted verses are not intended as a critique of the existing social arrangement, only of using it as a justification for behaviour otherwise considered unacceptable; that which is unacceptable with respect to the rich is also unacceptable with respect to the poor.

A human being, as envisaged in Proverbs, could be called *homo docilis*; when humanity was created by God, it was endowed by him with certain abilities such as those exemplified in the following proverb:

> Hearing ear and seeing eye, Yahweh made both of them. [Prov 20:12]

This has two main implications. First, human senses are God-given and should, therefore, be cultivated and used in coming to grips with the larger created world. God equipped people to observe, to learn and so gain knowledge and skills; it is, therefore, wrong not to employ these faculties. Yet, an additional and more cautious tone can be detected in the proverb. Since these senses were created by God, their perception

---

[2] Lit. *meet.*

lies within the sphere of divine control and nothing can be acquired by them that would be hidden from God himself; the sage who acquires wisdom using his God-given senses should not think that such wisdom can make God dispensable. This perspective is explicitly expressed elsewhere in the book:

> A person's mind plans his ways, but Yahweh establishes his step. [Prov 16:9]
>
> A man's steps are from Yahweh, but a human, how can he understand his way? [Prov 20:24]
>
> There is a path that [seems] straight to a man, but at its end are paths of death. [Prov 14:12]
>
> All the ways of a man are pure in his eyes, but Yahweh tests spirits. [Prov 16:2]

Apart from the aforementioned implication that proverbial wisdom can never threaten the sovereignty of Yahweh, an additional notion can be seen in these verses: there are general limits to what human senses can ascertain, not necessarily linked to direct divine intervention. Consequently, the wise person is never entirely self-reliant. The sage knows that people are under the thorough scrutiny of God, their destiny is firmly in divine hands, and their abilities have inherent limits. It is from this basic anthropological perspective that the *fear of Yahweh* emerges as the cornerstone of proverbial wisdom:

> Trust in Yahweh with all your heart, and do not lean on your understanding, know him in all your ways, and he will straighten your paths. Do not be wise in your own eyes—fear Yahweh and turn away from evil. [Prov 3:5–7]

Yet, in spite of the acknowledgement that there are limits to human ability to be in control, Proverbs in general is rather optimistic about human potential and within the world subjected to divine order the life of the *homo docilis* is understood in linear terms, as progressing forward. Wisdom and righteousness promote advancement and facilitate one's success; folly hinders progress in life and leads to failure and loss. This sense of progress is best seen in the sayings which employ the imagery of a path, such as the following two:

> The righteousness of a blameless person straightens their way, but the wicked will fall on the account of his wickedness. [Prov 11:5]

> The way of the sluggard is like a hedge of nightshade,[3] but the path of the upright ones is a highway. [Prov 15:19]

The positive view of human abilities is not to be confused with a conviction that humans are principally good. The inborn human tendency in Proverbs is toward folly and evil:

> There is wickedness tied to the heart of a boy, the disciplining rod will drive it away from him. [Prov 22:15]

> Who can say: 'I have cleansed my heart, I have purified [myself] from my sin!'? [Prov 20:9]

> Many a person summons his confidant, but a trustworthy man who shall find? [Prov 20:6]

This, though, is not to be understood as a doctrine of total depravity of human nature; the sages believed passionately, as the initial quoted verse indicates, that the natural tendency can be overcome if sufficient effort is made. The means by which this is accomplished is wisdom. Wisdom is not something that comes naturally, rather, wisdom is gained through discipline and hard work; only folly comes easily and without effort. It is, therefore, not at all surprising that the sages despised laziness and that they derided the sluggard, as in the following joke:

> The sluggard buries his hand in the pot, yet, he does not carry it back to his mouth. [Prov 19:24]

The natural human tendency toward folly is also reflected in the fact that the majority of the human qualities mentioned in Proverbs are negative, ones to be overcome. The most important of these is probably short-temper:

> Do not associate with an angry person, and do not walk with a short tempered man, lest you learn his ways and get yourself a trap for your own life. [Prov 22:24–25]

> An angry man gets engaged in a strife, but a patient person appeases a dispute. [Prov 15:18]

> An angry man stirs up strife, and an irritable person multiplies transgression. [Prov 29:22]

The basic shortcoming of irritability that makes it so unpalatable to the proverbial sages is the spiralling out of control of events in the life of

---

[3] Probably *Solanum coagulans, Solanum incanum,* Jericho potato. Grows to up to 1m and is thorny (Hepper, 1992:55).

an anger-driven person; such a life descends into chaos. In contrast,
a proper life is one that shows orderliness, for it is order from which
success stems.

Self-control is a prime characteristic of a wise person and the ad-
monishment to exercise it is not limited to anger-management, but
applies to other human dispositions. The sages observed that human
appetite is limitless and held the opinion that excess devalues experience and, thus, deprives a person of possible satisfaction:

> Sheol and Abaddon are never sated, and human eyes are never sated.
> [Prov 27:20]

> [When] you find honey, eat what is sufficient for you, lest you overeat
> and vomit it. [Prov 25:16]

> A sated appetite treads down the honey comb, as for a hungry soul, any
> bitterness is sweet. [Prov 27:7]

Another emotion that the sages observed and commented on, and
which they considered particularly powerful, is jealousy:

> Anger is cruel and rage is a flood, but who can withstand jealousy? [Prov
> 27:4]

> He who commits adultery with a woman lacks sense, he who does so,
> is destroying his life. Beating and disgrace he will find, his dishonour
> will not be wiped out. Since jealousy [drives] the husband's anger, he
> will have no compassion in the day of revenge. He will not accept any
> satisfaction and will not consent no matter how big the gift. [Prov 6:32–
> 35][4]

These comments on particular emotions, such as anger or jealousy,
are only an element of a much deeper psychological insight. The
sages believed that the emotional and mental part of human existence,
largely hidden from the outsiders, is of the utmost importance; to quote
only few relevant sayings:[5]

> Anxiety in the mind of a man bows him down, but good news makes
> him happy. [Prov 12:25]

> A deferred expectation makes the mind sick, but a fulfilled desire is a tree
> of life. [Prov 13:12]

> A joyful mind makes the body to be well,[6] but a crushed spirit dries up
> the bones. [Prov 17:22]

---

[4] For textual notes see p. 184.

[5] See also Prov 14:10, 30; 15:13,15.

[6] Reading with ܓ ܪܲܓܘܼܫܵܐ, *the body*, i.e., גְּוִיָּה. 𝔐 גֵּהָה, *medicine*, but both the par-

> A man's spirit endures his infirmity,[7] but who can lift up a crushed spirit?
> [Prov 18:14]

It is quite clear that the sages considered mental well-being as even more essential than physical health; mental strength was seen by them as essential to the ability to endure physical illness or hardship. These verses also indicate that the sages did not assume that the wise are spared all difficulties in life. Instead, they saw them as the testing stone of real mental strength:

> [If][8] you become disheartened in the day of trouble, your strength is small.[9] [Prov 24:10]

A small detour is necessary at this point. In the verses quoted previously inner well-being is often conveyed in terms of joy or happiness. Yet, it should be observed that joy *per se* is not the sages' aim; they differentiate clearly between what they consider proper and improper sources of joy. Thus, it is wrong and unwise to rejoice in someone else's misfortune [Prov 17:5; 24:17–18], enjoy doing what is evil [Prov 2:14], find joy in gluttony and drunkenness [Prov 20:1; 23:29–35], in adultery [Prov 5], or folly in general [Prov 15:21]. Rather, one finds proper joy in doing what is right and just [Prov 21:15], in the knowledge and ability to advise others [Prov 15:23], in the relationship with one's wife [Prov 5:18], in one's offspring being properly brought up [Prov 10:1], in friendship, in being a peacemaker [Prov 12:20], but also in the luxury that comes with wisdom [Prov 27:9]. The sages further appreciated that joy can be easily thwarted, cannot obliterate all pain and that sometimes the two co-exist:

> Even in laughter the heart does not stop aching,[10] and as for its end—joy is depressed.[11] [Prov 14:13]

---

allelism and the syntax (the Hiphil requires an object) support 𝔊 (*pace* McKane, 1970:506).

[7] 𝔊 θυμὸν ἀνδρὸς πραΰνει θεράπων φρόνιμος, *an attendant of a sound mind soothes man's spirit*. This is unlikely due to a difference in the Vorlage, and more probably an interpolation by the translator. 𝔊 ܪܘܚܗ ܕܓܒܪܐ ܡܣܝܒܪ ܟܘܪܗܢܗ, *man's spirit endures his suffering*, reflects the same Hebrew as 𝔐.

[8] The conditional nature of this saying, albeit only implied, is unmistakable.

[9] 𝔐 צַר, *narrow*, which is a play on צָרָה, *trouble*, in the A colon.

[10] Toy (1899:239) prefers to render the Px as modal, i.e., *may be sad*; this is a possible rendering, but the parallel verbless clause in the B colon suggests a non-modal sense, such as the usual habitual one.

[11] Reading תּוּגֶה, i.e., 3fs Niphal of יגה in place of 𝔐 תּוּגָה, *grief*. This reading is favoured by the parallelism which suggests construction of the type *adverbial modifier*

The feeling of joy is, thus, better seen in Proverbs as an important by-product of wise living than its centre of gravity. Joy comes naturally to the wise, it is the trait of wise living. In contrast, excessive pursuit of pleasure leads to poverty:

> Who loves enjoyment [ends up] an impoverished man, who loves wine and oil will not become rich. [Prov 21:17]

Returning to the sages' psychological insights, it can be observed that their evaluation of people does not hinge on external appearances but on character; it is the inner person that is the real person in the proverbial perspective:

> As water reflects the face[12] so person's heart the person. [Prov 27:19]

That which is visible on the surface is often misleading, covering an inner reality that can be significantly different:

> A gold ring in the nose of a pig is a beautiful woman turning aside from discernment. [Prov 11:22]

> Charm is deceitful, and beauty is a vanity, but a woman who fears Yahweh,[13] she should be praised! [Prov 31:30]

> A person is desirable[14] for his loyalty, and a poor person is better than a liar. [Prov 19:22]

> Do not eat the bread of a greedy person, and do not desire his delicacies … 'eat and drink', he says to you, but his mind/heart is not with you. As for your morsel, which you ate, you will vomit it, and you will destroy your pleasant words. [Prov 23:6–8]

+ *verbal clause*. Even if the 𝔐 pointing is followed, שִׂמְחָה תּוּגֶה has to be rendered as a nominal clause, for the accents, placing the secondary division after וְאַחֲרִיתָה, show that וְאַחֲרִיתָה is a *casus pendens*.

[12] Lit. *as water face to face*; 𝔊(𝔖) ὥσπερ οὐχ ὅμοια πρόσωπα προσώποις, most likely an attempt to make sense of the text.

[13] 𝔐 יִרְאַת־יְהוָה where יִרְאַת should probably be understood as a fem. ptc. However, as the pointing stands, the text would need to be rendered *woman, fear of Yahweh*, i.e., the woman is equated with *fear of Yahweh*. This is exploited by McCreesh (1985) who argues that the woman is Wisdom. 𝔊 γυνὴ γὰρ συνετὴ εὐλογεῖται, φόβον δὲ κυρίου αὕτη αἰνείτω is not an exact rendering of 𝔐, but contrary to the claim that it read נְבוֹנָה in place of יִרְאַת־יְהוָה (e.g. Toy 1899:549; Oesterley, 1929:287), the Greek text quite clearly attests *fear of Yahweh* as an attribute of the woman.

[14] 𝔐 תַּאֲוַת, i.e., *desire of*, supported by 𝔖 ܪܓܬܐ, *desire of*. 𝔊 καρπὸς, i.e., תְּבוּאַת, is followed by McKane (1970:532) who renders *man's productivity is his loyalty*. However, there is a superior semantic parallelism between the two colons in the Hebrew, since both *desire* and *better than* imply a value judgement; the 𝔊 reading is probably a result of an audible error. In the light of the parallelism the genitive *desire of* is best interpreted as objective.

The picture of the human being that emerges from these observations is that of a special creature which reflects its divine maker. It is a creature endowed with great potential, which, however, can only be unleashed when the raw material has been systematically and persistently moulded according to the way of wisdom. The natural human inclination is toward folly and evil. Wisdom is a potent means to overcome this tendency, to bring forward that true human being that Yahweh rejoices in, offering external success and internal satisfaction, both of which together form a healthy human existence.

The Social Perspective of Proverbs

The impression could be gained that the proverbial perspective is strongly individualistic, concerned with the success and prosperity of a single person at a time.[15] This would be to misunderstand the sages. While the book addresses itself to an individual and the depiction of success is largely in individual terms, in general, prosperity is understood in the book as happening in the context of the progress and affluence of a community to which the individual belongs. Wisdom is not simply a tool of bringing order and success to an individual's life, but also a means for creating order on the social level. The righteous and wise uphold such an order, principally to do with justice, while the fools reject and pervert it. The most elaborate expression of this sentiment is in my view found in the following passage:

> To be partial in judgement is not good. Who pronounces the guilty innocent—people will curse him, nations will scold him. But those who reproach [him] will be pleasing, and good blessing will come upon them. He kisses lips,[16] who gives straight answers.

> Get done your business outside, make it ready in the field that belongs to you, after that, also build your house.

> Do not be a witness against your neighbour when there is no cause,[17] and [do not] mislead[18] with your lips. Do not say: 'As he did to me, so I will do to him! I will repay the man according to his deed'.

---

[15] So, for instance, Rylaarsdam (1946:52).

[16] 𝕲 χείλη δὲ φιλήσουσιν ἀποκρινόμενα λόγους ἀγαθούς, *lips that love answer good words*, is a free rendering of 𝔐.

[17] 𝔏 עֵד־חִנָּם; one manuscript עֵד־חָמָס; 𝕲(𝕾) ψευδὴς μάρτυς. The versions are most likely reading the same text as that of 𝔏 and interpreting it; they do not offer clear support for the alternative Hebrew (*pace* BHS).

[18] 𝔐 וַהֲפִתִּיתָ is difficult. The initial ה could be understood as a question marker, e.g. Toy (1899:456) who deletes it. Another possibility is that it was originally a ת, thus,

I crossed[19] over a field of a lazy man, and over a vineyard of a person with no sense. And look: all over it weeds were coming up, chickweed covered its surface, and its stone wall was breached. And I observed [it] and I took [it] to my heart, I saw [it] and I learned a lesson: A little sleep, a little slumber, a little folding of hands to lie down, and your poverty comes like a tinker,[20] and your need like a shielded warrior.[21] [Prov 24:23b-34]

The key to understanding this final sub-collection from Prov 10–24 is in my view in its interlocking structure. The text consists of two thematic groups of material, 23b-26, 28–29 on the one hand and 27, 30–34 on the other hand. The first group deals with the need to uphold justice in all circumstances, irrespective of personal feelings, and hints at the importance of justice for the community. The second group has an agricultural theme, explaining the need to take care of the primary asset, the land, and emphasising the priority of the stewardship of the land over everything else. These two thematic groups, however, were not simply juxtaposed, but rather locked together by placing v. 27 within the former group. This arrangement is in my view intentional, turning the literal meaning of the second group into a metaphor explaining the consequences of the failure to follow the advice of the former sayings.[22] Just as the sensible farmer knows that caring for the external assets has to take priority over that which may seem to produce more immediate benefit, such as building a comfortable house, so the upholding of justice within one's community must take priority over

---

Driver (1951b:189) proposes to read תפתהו, rendering *and do (not) break, i.e., slander, him with thy lips*. I prefer to read the verb as a Hiphil, with the negative in the A colon carrying its force over. The verb has an imperative force, the tense following the usual rules after wav relative.

[19] Omitted by 𝕲, instead inserting ὥσπερ, see also n. 22 below.

[20] מִתְהַלֵּךְ, possibly iterative sense of Hithpael which some argued appears with the root הלך (see WOC 26.1.2b). Some manuscripts and 𝕰 read here כִּמְהַלֵּךְ as in Prov 6:11. This is a preferable reading, producing better parallelism between the two colons and is adopted here; the Pi implies state. For the adopted rendering see McKane (1970:324).

[21] Albright (1955:9–10) derives מָגֵן from Ugaritic root *mgn, to beg, i.e., like a beggar*; such a rendering is a distinct possibility.

[22] Note that while the instruction of vv. 23b-26 has a formal motive clause and vv. 30–34 form a motive for the instruction of v. 27, the instruction of vv. 28–29 is left without motivation, which in the proposed reading is supplied by the combined text of vv. 27, 30–34. Further, it is likely that this is how 𝕲 understood the text, because by omitting the verbs in v. 30, and replacing them with ὥσπερ, vv. 30–34 are explicitly linked to what precedes (there is no referent for ὥσπερ in vv. 31–34). The added clause ἐὰν δὲ τοῦτο ποιῇς then refers not only to v. 33, but also to v. 29.

settling of personal grievances; individual welfare stems from that of the surrounding community.

This perspective is implied in a number of other places, and in particular, the concept of righteousness is set in a communal context; a righteous person is someone whose actions benefit the community:

> The lips of a righteous person feed[23] many, but fools die in lack of sense. [Prov 10:21]

> In the success of righteous people the city rejoices, and in the destruction of the wicked ones there is shouting of happiness. In the blessing of upright people a city is exalted, but by the mouth of the wicked it is torn down. [Prov 11:10–11]

> When the righteous multiply, people rejoice, but when the ruler is wicked people sigh. [Prov 29:2]

> The memory of the righteous [leads] to blessing, but the name of wicked people rots. [Prov 10:7]

It is, therefore, necessary to conclude that in the proverbial perspective, where wisdom and righteousness are virtually synonymous, the individual is always intrinsically linked to a community and the book's focus on the individual cannot be equated with individualism in the modern sense of the word. Proverbs does not see a person as an isolated self, but always implicitly interacting with others, as belonging to a collective.

The collective and the individual form an inseparable unity and by distancing from the community, an individual suffers loss. The following saying expresses this sentiment quite explicitly:

> Like a bird fleeing from his nest, so is a man fleeing from his place. [Prov 27:8]

Such a perspective is also reflected in the fact that the vast majority of the proverbial advice pertains to inter-human relationships. Alienation from one's neighbours is seen as having most severe consequences to a person's well-being:

> He who brings trouble on his household will inherit wind, and a fool will be a slave to a wise heart. [Prov 11:29]

> He who gathers dishonest profit brings trouble on his household, but who hates bribes will live. [Prov 15:27]

---

[23] 𝔐 יִרְעוּ; 𝔊 reading יֵדְעוּ which corresponds well with *in lack of sense* in the B colon, but does not fit the immediately following רַבִּים which is unlikely to be impersonal (note also that the B colon is modified in 𝔊, לֵב being omitted).

The verb עכר rendered here *to bring trouble* generally implies unintended collateral damage rather than direct destruction, most often referring to causing alienation between two parties. The meaning of these verses is illuminated by the following text:

> Simeon and Levi, Dinah's brothers, took their swords and attacked the unsuspecting city, killing every male. ... Then Jacob said to Simeon and Levi, 'You have brought trouble on me [עֲכַרְתֶּם] by making me a stench to the Canaanites and Perizzites, the people living in this land. We are few in number, and if they join forces against me and attack me, I and my household will be destroyed.' [Gen 34:25, 30, NIV]

For a family to be alienated from the community is not simply a question of loss of honour and dignity, but of economic downfall, a matter of life and death. Thus, while the conviction that an individual is co-dependent on the community may not be considered particularly revolutionary or significant, we need to appreciate the degree of such dependency that is implied in Proverbs.

If an individual's success is directly dependent on the well-being of the community, then it follows that a person's responsibility is to behave in a manner that promotes such collective well-being. In Proverbs this is reflected mainly in two ways. First, one of the primary duties of the wise is to uphold justice for all, both rich and poor. This takes a number of different forms, from honest business practices to juridical justice. The need to uphold justice is then accompanied by the second contribution to the well-being of the community, showing mercy to the poor. The practical application of both of these aspects of wise living will be dealt with in detail in the following chapter, at the moment only a brief comment concerning the sociological implication of the latter principle is needed. We have observed earlier, when looking at the anthropological perspective of the book, that the sages argued that even the poor in society deserve fair treatment because all people have the same creator. The requirement to show mercy to the poor goes further than this, consider the following passage:

> A poor person is hated even by his neighbour, but a rich person has many friends. Who despises his neighbour[24] sins, but who is gracious to the poor—it is to his blessing. [Prov 14:20–21]

These verses show concern that the poor should not be excluded from the life of the community on account of their poverty. It is important

---

[24] 𝔐 לְרֵעֵהוּ, 𝔊 πένητας, *a labourer*, most likely an attempt to create a closer parallel

to appreciate that this attitude to the poor does not originate merely in feelings of pity for those who suffer. Rather, it appears to stem from a deeper insight into the nature of life in a community:

> The righteous person knows the justice of the poor, the wicked person does not understand knowledge. [Prov 29:7]

The person who perverts justice for the poor is not seen solely as wicked, but essentially as ignorant, not appreciating the wider implications of such a behaviour. The sages on the other hand do:

> Who closes his ears to the cry of the poor—he also will cry and he will not be answered. [Prov 21:13]

The exclusion of the poor from the society, whether by denying them justice or not caring about their needs starts a process in which the cohesion of the community breaks apart. This is the worst possible scenario in a world an individual's prosperity depends closely on the prosperity of that community.

The proverbial society is not only tightly-knit, but it also appears to be fairly closed-off. This is best seen in the warnings of Prov 1–9 against strange women. While the precise identity of the woman in Prov 7 is debated,[25] on one occasion she is designated as a נָכְרִיָּה which most often denotes a woman of different ethnic origins. Yet, even if she is not a foreigner in an ethnic sense, she lives in a manner that is foreign to the proverbial community. She dresses differently (in the father's judgement as a whore), the manner with which she approaches the youth in the street is different from the customs of the proverbial society, she surrounds herself with imported things such as costly Egyptian linen and expensive spices. Further, her husband appears to be a travelling merchant, leaving his home for long periods of time. In this respect he fits the description of Prov 27:8 cited earlier, of a man leaving his nest; he does not belong to the proverbial world which for all practical purposes cares little about what is beyond its boundaries. Thus, the whole household of the woman of Prov 7 stands outside of the customs of the proverbial world, and there is no doubt that it is not welcome; they are tolerated, but not accommodated.[26] In

---

with the B colon. It would seem to reflect a different social setting.

[25] See in particular Snijders (1954), Perdue (1977:150–51), Yee (1989), Washington (1994).

[26] This attitude toward outsiders raises certain questions in relationship to the proverbial theology. It was pointed out in the preceding chapter that Yahweh is a non-

addition to this attitude to outsiders, it appears that in the proverbial perspective the local community ties can be seen as stronger than ties with distant relations:

> Do not abandon your friend and the friend of your father, and into the house of your brother do not go in the day of your calamity. A nearby neighbour is better than a distant brother. [Prov 27:10]

These observations suggest that the proverbial material originated within a social system based on a small, close-knit community that would have been economically self-contained, with little systematic contact with other communities, and that it was closed to outsiders who were not prepared to accept its own standards. It is only in such a small and economically isolated community, where nothing one does remains anonymous and on which one totally depends for livelihood, that becoming an outcast results in such severe repercussions as the material portrays.

What then was the socio-economic make up of the proverbial society? I have suggested above that the sages believed that all human beings represent their maker and deserve a certain dignity. This suggests that the proverbial society is, at least on the basic anthropological level, composed of equals. Some qualification for that statement is necessary. It has to be acknowledged that Proverbs is written from a male perspective, with the primary voice introducing the material being that of the father, and that it has a male as its intended addressee. Further, most of the proverbial characters, whether it is the righteous, the wise, or the villains are implicitly male, and the proverbial society as a whole is unmistakably patriarchal. References to women are limited to wives, maids and the stray women of Prov 1–9; women are never addressed, and no reference to daughters is made along the repeated addresses of the son.[27] In other words, women are only spoken of with the male

---

local deity in Proverbs and that the sages are prepared to learn from people of other ethnic origins. It might seem, therefore, that the present observations about the nature of the proverbial community contradict such a perspective. However, this is not so. The pivotal conviction from which the proverbial willingness to learn from outsiders stems is one of uniformity of the cosmos, and thus, of uniformity of human experience irrespective of local or national boundaries. Within this framework the sages do not expect that wise people anywhere could derive from their experience standards for living that are significantly different from their own. The cross-cultural unity is based on a shared framework of wisdom, the cross-cultural division on rejection of the proverbial wisdom. The foreign woman in our material is not rejected on grounds of ethnicity, but on grounds of different, incompatible ethos.

[27] Unless one counts the metaphorical use of בַּת in Prov 30:15, or the occurrence of

world and social structures as the reference point, and are clearly perceived as dependent on the males. Therefore, it is more appropriate to
speak of a society of equal males. Yet, to do justice to the proverbial
outlook, it should be noted that there is no indication that the verses
asserting the basic human dignity irrespective of wealth or poverty
apply exclusively to males. Rather, the mother figure has a role in the
education of the son that appears to be on a par with the father and
the son is urged to honour her [Prov 1:8; 6:20; 23:22]; in fact, Brenner
(1993:194–98) argued that some of the proverbial sayings about women
are likely to have a woman as a speaker. Further, the woman of valour
in Prov 31 shows a great degree of freedom and independence in her
activities; notably she manages significant financial funds of her own
and she has a position of a great authority in running the household.
Thus, while the proverbial world is undeniably patriarchal, it must also
be acknowledged that a woman is accorded in it a position that has
dignity.

Within the proverbial world the most important socio-economic unit
is the family. Altogether, words that have family as the point of reference, such as father, mother, son, brother, wife, husband or household, appear nearly 140 times in Proverbs. It has become almost critical
orthodoxy to understand the father-son relationship in the book as a
metaphor for what is in fact a relationship between a teacher and a
pupil. Yet, there is not a sufficient support for such an understanding
in the material itself. It is beyond doubt that the real father is intended
where he is accompanied by the mother in the parallel colon. The very
first instruction of the book is of this type, commanding obedience to
both parents:

> Obey, my son, the instruction of your father, and do not abandon the
> teaching of your mother. For they will be a wreath of grace to your head,
> and a necklace to your neck. [Prov 1:8–9]

The strategic position of this admonition should not be ignored; by
opening the book with a command to obey both parents, the editor
makes it very clear that the context within which the proverbial instructions and admonitions are set is the family. We should further observe,
that the roles played by the two parents in this saying are virtually identical, for the Hebrew terms מוּסַר and תּוֹרָה are to a large extent synonymous and can both be translated as *instruction*.

בָּנוֹת in Prov 31:29 where it is used as a poetic equivalent of נָשִׁים.

There are several more sayings in which both parents appear. In Prov 4:3ff. the father supports his earlier demand for obedience by the claim that he also once was a child subject to the authority of his parents, and goes on the speak about the relationship between himself and his father. It should be noted that not only the earlier reference to the grandmother [Prov 4:3] makes it impossible to see the father/son relationship here as a metaphor, but also a reference is made to the father's teachers, who are clearly distinct from the grandfather [Prov 5:13]. In Prov 6:20, the original command from Prov 1:8 is restated, again the reference is made to the mother's teaching. Several sayings then depict a close link between being wise and having a proper relationship with one's parents [e.g. Prov 10:1; 15:20; 23:22–25; 28:24; 30:11, 17]. In the case of Prov 10:1 we should again observe the strategic position of this saying, which opens the first collection of Solomonic proverbs, indicating the principal setting on the editor's mind.

Overall the proverbial material itself does not give even the slightest impression that the references to the father on his own are in any way different than those to the father and mother together. Rather, the metaphorical reading of the father/son relationship originated in similar interpretations given to certain Egyptian texts. However, both the methodological validity of comparing Proverbs to these texts, and the correctness of such a reading of the Egyptian material *per se* is questionable, for as Fox (1996b) pointed out, the Egyptian instructions are not intended for young pupils but for adults with serious responsibilities of their own, and, irrespective of whether the characters are real or fictional, a genuine father-son relationship is intended in all instances. Thus, we are obliged to conclude that the primary identity of the addressee is that of a son, i.e., as belonging to the family structure.

A person who rejects this structure and its arrangement is an abomination to the sages:

> A fool reviles his father's discipline, but he who accepts rebuke is prudent. [Prov 15:5]

> He who maltreats [his] father and drives away [his] mother is a disgraceful son and behaves shamefully. [Prov 19:26]

> He who curses his father and mother, his light will be quenched in time[28] of darkness. [Prov 20:20]

---

[28] So KBL-2 for Q בְּאֶשׁוּן, K(𝔖) בְּאִישׁוֹן, *in the eye of darkness*, i.e., midnight; omitted by 𝔊.

> As for an eye that mocks [its] father, and despises obedience[29] [to its] mother, wadi ravens will pick it out, and vultures will eat it. [Prov 30:17]

As the preceding verses indicate, the family has a clear hierarchical structure. In general, old age commends respect in the proverbial society:

> The splendour of young men is their strength, but the adornment of the old men is grey hair. [Prov 20:29]

The young have to prove themselves to gain respect, for youth is synonymous with lack of experience and wisdom. In contrast, old age is enough to grant someone high esteem, because only wise people live long, while fools die prematurely. That this age-based hierarchy applies fully to the family unit transpires through the father's invocation of the grandfather's authority in Prov 4:1ff., and is seen very explicitly in the following proverb:

> Listen to your father who begot you, do not despise your mother because she grew old. [Prov 23:22]

It can be observed that the proverbial family is a cohesive unit accountable for its individual members. A person's folly brings disrepute on the whole family, the entire house is shunned on account of an individual while a son's/wife's wisdom has direct bearing on the reputation of the father/husband:

> The crown of the old people are [their] grandchildren, and the splendour of sons are their fathers. [Prov 17:6]

> A foolish son is a destruction to his father, and a contentious wife is a continuous dripping.[30] [Prov 19:13]

> He who returns evil for good—evil will not depart from his house. [Prov 17:13]

> … her husband is known in the gate, when he sits with the elders of the land. [Prov 31:23]

Further, the family is not just a basic social unit, but also the key economic cell of the proverbial society. The proverbial economy is land-based and the family unit is tied to a specific portion of the land:

---

[29] The meaning of 𝔐 לְיִקֲּהַת is uncertain. 𝔊 γῆρας, *old age* for which BHS proposes לְזִקְנַת, but possibly the translator did not know how to deal with the Hebrew, or, assuming metathesis of ק and ה in the Vorlage knew a root להק, *to be old* (so Greenfield, 1958:212–14).

[30] For discussion of the verb טרד see Greenfield (1958:210–12).

> Do not move the ancient boundary, which your fathers established. [Prov 22:28]

> Do not move an ancient boundary, and do not enter the field of orphans, for their defender is strong, he will fight their case against you. [Prov 23:10–11]

These verses (and the related Prov 15:25 quoted earlier) show that the allocation of land to individual families was based on a long-existing tradition and was considered as fixed—the land was to remain in the particular family even when the male head of the family died leaving a widow and orphans behind. Considering that nowhere in Proverbs we find an indication that land was considered a commodity, it appears likely that the underlying economic system is similar to that depicted in the book of Ruth (it is certainly significant that Prov 23:11 uses the term גֹאֵל in the context of land belonging to an orphan), or presumed by the Law of the Jubilee [Lev 25].

While the family appears to be the key element of the socio-economic makeup of the proverbial world, there are additional superstructures identifiable in Proverbs. Certain issues are settled at the gate:

> Do not steal from the impoverished because he is impoverished, and do not crush the poor in the gate. For Yahweh fights their case and will squeeze life from those who rob them. [Prov 22:22–23][31]

The language of this verse shows that the gate was a place where legal disputes between individuals would have been heard. It, however, should not be envisaged as a formal courtroom with appointed judges. Rather, it appears to be a less formal assembly where resolutions were reached through collective deliberation by those respected in the community for their wisdom and status. The openness of the gate proceedings to contributions of the broad public is indirectly indicated by the following proverb:

> Wisdom is high for a fool,[32] he does not open his mouth at the gate. [Prov 24:7]

This text implies that if the fool had been in possession of wisdom, he could have made a contribution that would have been taken seriously, i.e., the authority of one's voice at the gate is based on merit rather than formal appointment.

---

[31] For textual notes see p. 104.

[32] רָאמוֹת אM; the translation follows a suggestion by Driver (1951b:188) to read רָמָה, *high*.

The gate was not only a place where legal matters were heard, but also a place where individual members of the community were scrutinised and either praised or criticised; what would have been said of someone at the gate had a major impact on the individual's life:

> Charm is deceitful, and beauty is a vanity, [but] a woman who fears Yahweh, she should be praised! Give her from the fruit of her hands, and let them praise her in the gates [on account of] her deeds. [Prov 31:30–31][33]

> How I used to hate instruction, and my heart despised rebuke and I did not listen to the voice of my instructors, and I did not stretched my ear to my teachers. I came so near to a total disaster in the midst of the assembly and congregation. [Prov 5:12–14]

The latter text does not in fact refer to the gate *per se* but instead uses the terms עֵדָה and קָהָל. These words refer to a formal gathering of the community. References to such an assembly are found elsewhere in the OT and Gottwald (1979:243) evaluates these in the following manner:

> Although the total number of references to 'the assembly' in demonstrably or probably early sources is not great, the impression is strong that the body of free-and-equal males gathered for stated cultic celebrations, for periodic redistribution of land, and for exceptional deliberations on matters of war and of internal dispute … The *qāhāl* is, as it were, an instrument by which Israelites come together to reach collective decisions and to carry out ceremonial activities.

While קָהָל in Prov 5:14 may not refer to a large scale gathering, but only an assembled community of a village or town, Gottwald's depiction of the assembly as a 'body of free-and-equal males' fits the proverbial context. The exceptions to this picture of equality are few; Prov 19:10 objects to עֶבֶד gaining an influential position in society, and a rather inflexible social hierarchy is painted in the following passage:

> Under three things the earth shakes and four it is not able to bear: under a slave, when he becomes a king, and a fool when he is sated with food, under a hated woman that is married,[34] and a maid when she dispossesses her mistress. [Prov 30:21–23]

However, it has to be appreciated that in Proverbs עֶבֶד is not usually a servant working for hire, but a slave, who is land-less and thus stands outside of the proverbial land-based socio-economic structures

---

[33] For textual notes see p. 133.

[34] 𝔐 תִּבָּעֵל; Van Leeuwen (1986:608), following van der Ploeg, argues that we should read Qal, *under a despised wife when she rules*, but such a rendering has no obvious merit.

by default. This he shares with the עָנִי, but in contrast to the poor he is
a possession of his master, whom he is expected to obey, yet, has no real
motivation to such obedience:

> A slave cannot be disciplined by words, for he understands, but does not
> respond. [Prov 29:19]

It appears that one could become a slave either by birth or due to
imprudence:

> … and a fool will be a slave to a wise mind. [Prov 11:29]

> He who pampers his slave from childhood, in the future he will be ???.[35]
> [Prov 29:21]

It is also clear that only the wealthy members of the society were
able to afford slaves, who were in a certain sense the true sign of
sound economic standing; the relative paucity of sayings concerning
עֶבֶד indicates that the slave was not an essential element of the world to
which the sages addressed themselves. Further, while the verses above
say that such a state of affairs is undesirable, they indirectly witness
to the fact that slaves sometimes gained a position of influence and
maids became wives. In addition, these isolated statements have to be
held together, for instance, with Prov 17:10 that judges a slave on merit
rather than social origins and accords him a place within the regular
family structure. Thus, while we encounter a certain tension in the
book concerning the status of slaves, all indications are that the slave
played only a marginal socio-economical role in the proverbial world.

However, there is one character in Proverbs that stands out from
the society the members of which are in principal equal, the king.
Altogether there are some 40 references to the king, and he is perceived
as a part of the established divine order represented by Dame Wisdom
[Prov 8:15]. At the same time the association between the king and
God is much weaker than is found elsewhere in the OT. Some sense
of link between the divine and royal realms is conveyed through the
juxtaposition of the Yahweh and king sayings in Prov 16 and is found
more explicitly in the janus verse of this section:

> [When?] there is divination on the lips of a king when he administers
> justice, his mouth does not act unjustly. [Prov 16:10]

---

[35] מָנוֹן אֵ is unexplained. 𝕲(𝕾) has ὃς κατασπαταλᾷ ἐκ παιδός, οἰκέτης ἔσται, ἔσχατον
δὲ ὀδυνηθήσεται ἐφ' ἑαυτῷ, *who lives wantonly from childhood, will be a servant; at the end will
suffer pain upon himself*, which is most likely a free rendering.

However, it is difficult to say, whether this verse is to be taken as a declaration or as a conditional statement. Overall, there are only two places in Proverbs where both God and the king appear:

> It is glory of God to conceal a thing, and glory of kings to explore a thing. [Prov 25:2]

> My son, fear Yahweh and the king, do not associate with revolutionaries.[36] [Prov 24:21]

Neither of these verses points to an intimate relationship between the king and the deity, and in the former proverb it even appears as if the king is in a sense working against the divine activity, uncovering what God has concealed. Overall, it is necessary to conclude that while the king is perceived as a part of the divine order, he is not portrayed in Proverbs as a direct divine representative, and is subjected to absolute divine control:

> The heart of a king is [like] canals of water in the hand of Yahweh, he leads it wherever he pleases. [Prov 21:1].

While the king is acknowledged to have power over life and death [Prov 16:14–15; 19:12; 20:2], his actual role in the book is surprisingly limited. The king is expected to be virtuous and self controlled, his main function being to serve as a juridical authority with the responsibility to uphold justice:

> A wise king winnows the wicked, runs over them the [threshing] wheel. [Prov 20:26]

> The king who judges the poor in truth, his throne will be established for ever. [Prov 29:14]

> [It is] not to kings, Lemuel, [it is] not to kings to drink wine, and to high officials beer is a woe.[37] Lest he drinks and forgets what is decreed, and he perverts justice of all who are poor … Open your mouth for one who is speechless,[38] for justice of all dumb[39] people. Open your

---

[36] 𝔐 עִם־שׁוֹנִים אַל־תִּתְעָרָב; 𝔊 μηθετέρῳ αὐτῶν ἀπειθήσῃς, *do not disobey either of them*, i.e., reading שְׁנֵיהֶם and עבר. This reading is quite plausible, although it could be the result of the translator's unfamiliarity with שׁוֹנִים. Thomas (1934) argued from Arabic for a separate root שׁנה with the meaning *exalted*, suggesting that this is in fact a warning against getting involved with people of high standing.

[37] 𝔐 K אוֹ, Q אֵי, emending to אוֹי.

[38] 𝔐 לְאָלֵם; 𝔊 λόγῳ θεοῦ, probably למלי אל, but the 𝔊 Vorlage seems to have been corrupted throughout this section of the book.

[39] 𝔐 חֲלוֹף; BHS proposes חֹלִי. I follow Thomas' (1965:277) rendering *dumb, incapable*, on the grounds of Arabic.

mouth to judge righteously, and to administer justice [to] the poor and underprivileged. [Prov 31:4–5, 8–9]

The king further serves as a military leader, but this is only mentioned in passing [Prov 30:27]. Outside of his military and juridical roles he has no other tangible function in the proverbial world and a certain degree of scepticism concerning his performance as a judiciary is evident:

Many seek the face of the ruler, but man's justice is from Yahweh. [Prov 29:26]

Thus, the image of the king in Proverbs is far from the strong totalitarian and semi-divine status of a typical ANE ruler. His impact on the life of the proverbial characters is marginal, in fact, save a single exception [Prov 29:4], the consequences of the king's actions are limited to him or people in his immediate vicinity.

Further more, there are no references to taxation or any other practical aspects of a centralised government. This is surprising if we are dealing here with a well instituted monarchy, for the taxation burden would have been significant and one would, therefore, expect the sages to offer some advice or comment in this matter, whether positive or negative. Further, there is very little material in the book that addresses the activities and customs of the court, with the notable exception of the instruction for king Lemuel [Prov 31:1ff.]. Most of the material that touches on the court can, in fact, be applied to virtually anyone, not just a courtier.[40] Thus, even though the number of courtly references is large enough not to be disregarded lightly, the frequently made assertion that the proverbial material originated at the court for the education of the courtier, is untenable.[41] Rather, the impression is given that the monarch has been grafted somewhat artificially on top of a depiction of a society that is largely decentralised and in which the king has a no real role to play.[42] Thus, I am of the view that the royal references

---

[40] In my view only Prov 14:35; 22:29; 23:1ff.; 25:5–6 have the courtier as the intended audience.

[41] See also Humphreys (1978); Whybray (1990:45–59); Golka (1993); Dell (1998).

[42] This becomes even more clear when the Proverbs of Solomon is compared to such a work as the Egyptian *Instruction for King Meri-ka-re*. This instruction of an Egyptian king to his son and successor addresses the issues that are specific to the royal setting, for instance how to deal with potential political opponents, how to deal with the nobility and the subjects, it speaks about the art of public relations, the importance of establishing and defending one's territory, what kind of punishments to use in what situation, and it contains information about political allegiances of different regions. In contrast, this type of advice is lacking in Proverbs.

are best understood as a result of a later courtly use and adaptation of a material that originated initially outside of the court.

To summarise, the world of the proverbial sages is a world of a small, tightly-knit community, in which each individual's behaviour has a great impact on the life of everyone else. The most essential socio-economic unit of this society is a family, which has a hierarchical, age-based, structure, and is co-responsible for the behaviour of its members. Beyond the family hierarchy, the proverbial society is not significantly centralised and its affairs are run mainly on the basis of a consensus of those who earned the respect of the community.[43] It should also be noted, that while the proverbial sages were striving for a better, if not entirely ideal, world, the world in which they found themselves was far from ideal. The repeated reassurances that the wicked will not prosper and will come to disaster indicated that in reality there were wicked in the proverbial world that did prosper and righteous who did not. Further, the emphasis on preservation of the family framework indicates that this arrangement might have been perceived as being under threat and that the book was shaped in a conscious attempt to avert dismantling of these traditional structures.

The Human World of Qoheleth

Qoheleth's Anthropology

As we take a closer look at the human world of Qoheleth, we will start with examinations of Qoheleth's anthropology. The relationship between God and human beings in Qoheleth is, similarly to Proverbs, that of the Creator with the created. Yet, Qoheleth's anthropology is low in contrast to Proverbs, even though it appears that he was familiar with high anthropological view in which human beings were considered superior to the rest of the creatures on the grounds that the human spirit, רוּחַ, is immortal. The following section of the book alludes to such a perspective:

> I thought to myself concerning human beings: God makes clear to them and shows them that they are animals. Indeed, as for the fate of human beings, and the fate of an animal—they have the same fate: as [is] death of this, so [is] death of the other and there is one breath to both. And there is no advantage to a person over an animal, for both are passing.

---

[43] Cf. Clements' (1993) conclusions that the primary focus of Proverbs is on family and city.

They both are on [their] way to the same place—both came from the dust and both are returning to the dust. Who knows? Is the breath of the human beings ascending above and the breath of the animals descending beneath to the earth? And I saw that there is nothing better than [if] a person rejoices in his deeds for this is his portion. For who shall take him to look at that which will be afterwards? [Qoh 3:18–22][44]

It is quite clear from this passage, as I have pointed out earlier, that Qoheleth himself does not subscribe to such opinions; in spite of the lack of a categorical denial his scepticism about the possibility of some meaningful afterlife is expressed subtly, yet clearly, by the rhetorical question of v. 21. Consequently, Qoheleth limits his enquiry to the here and now, and within this earthly realm, he can find no distinction between humans and other living creatures. In fact, he is convinced that it is the divine intention to demonstrate to humans that they are nothing more than earthly beasts, whose existence is fragile and without any genuine, lasting gain; the human being is just a הֶבֶל.

Thus, when Qoheleth finishes his deliberation with the statement that at the point of death the human spirit returns back to God from whom it came [Qoh 12:7], we need to keep in mind this larger picture of the finality of death that Qoheleth painted earlier in the book. In the context of the whole book, the spirit returning to God is not a quintessential human being freed of the earthly body moving onto a higher level of existence in a spiritual realm. Rather, the spirit is the raw life force that God gave all the living creatures, and which completed its 'service'. By returning the dust back to earth as it used to be, death restores the initial *status quo* and closes the profitless circle of existence.

I have already pointed out that Qoheleth thinks that when one dies depends at least to some extent on how one lives [Qoh 7:17], but the proverbial claims about wisdom leading to longevity are not shared by Qoheleth. In contrast to the proverbial sages, Qoheleth does not perceive life in terms of linear progress aided by wisdom, but rather as a rat-mill; no matter how much effort one makes and how fast one runs, life inadvertly returns to its very starting point. This difference of perspective projects itself into Qoheleth's system of values. In the proverbial world old age was a source of respect, longevity being a sign of wisdom, righteousness and, ultimately, of divine favour. These notions are foreign to Qoheleth:

---

[44] For textual notes see p. 112.

And remember your creator[45] in the days of your youth, before the bad days come, and years will approach when you say: 'I have no pleasure in them'. Before the sun and the light and the moon and the stars darken, and the clouds return after the rain. In the day when the keepers of the house tremble and warriors bend and the grinding girls cease [to grind], for they became few and the ones looking through the windows became darkened, and the doors into the street have been shut; when the sound of the grind-mill quietened. He will rise to the sound of birds, but all daughters of songs will grow silent. They also fear[46] height and [there is] terror in the path. And the almond tree blossoms and the locust drags itself along, and the caper-fruit bursts, for the person is going to his eternal home, and the mourners go around in the streets. Before the silver cord is torn,[47] and the gold bowl is crushed,[48] and pitcher is broken upon the spring and the wheel runs[49] into the well. And the dust returns[50] upon the earth as it used to be, and the spirit returns to God, who gave it. [Qoh 12.1–7]

While this final section of the book poses serious problems to the interpreter much of it being obscure, many of the poetic images reveal Qoheleth's view of ageing clearly; there is nothing desirable about being old. Longevity possesses no inherent positive value and can be more a curse then a blessing. If anything can be made of life, it is when one is young:

If a person begets a hundred [children] and lives many years, as many the days of his years may be, but his soul would not be satiate from the good things, and he even did not have a burial, I say: 'the miscarried one is better off than him'. For in absurdity he came and in darkness he will go and in darkness his name is covered. He did not see the sun either and did not get to know [anything], there is more peace to this one than the other. Even if he lives a thousand years twice, but does not enjoy himself, do not they both go to the same place? [Qoh 6:3–6][51]

---

[45] 𝔐 אֶת־בּוֹרְאֶיךָ. I follow Gordis' (1955a:340) suggestion that the י is a part of the suffix, with a III-א verb treated as III-י. Some wish to read בְּאֵרְךָ, *your well*, i.e., *your wife* (e.g. Crenshaw, 1988:184–5), but it is questionable, that if enjoyment of a female companion was intended here Qoheleth would use the verb זכר, which he never employs in sense *to enjoy*. Several emendations have been proposed (see Seow, 1997:351) but 𝔐 reading is supported by the versions and fits the context, in particular Qoh 11:9.

[46] 𝔔 יִרְאוּ, other mss יִרְאוּ; the subject of the verb is not clear, probably, indefinite. 𝔊, σ' ἀπὸ ὕψους ὄψονται, understanding the whole clause as referring to the birds mentioned previously.

[47] 𝔐 Q יֵרָתֵק, K ירחק; reading with 𝔊 ܢܬܦܣܩ, *broken off*, i.e., יִנָּתֵק, supported by the parallelism.

[48] 𝔐 וְתָרֻץ; reading Niphal with 𝔊.

[49] 𝔐 וְנָרֹץ; reading with 𝔊, 𝔖, 𝔗 וְיָרָץ.

[50] 𝔐 וְיָשֹׁב; reading Px with the versions in place of the 𝔐 juss.

[51] For textual notes see p. 113.

Young man, rejoice in your youth, and let your heart make you happy in your young days, and walk in the ways of your heart, and visions of your eyes, but know that concerning all of these God will bring you into judgement. Remove anger from your heart, make evil pass away from your body, for youth and <prime of life> are absurd. [Qoh 11:9–10][52]

This attitude represents a serious reversal of values when set against Proverbs, for youth equals inexperience, and experience is one of the greatest assets of the type of wisdom Proverbs represents. However, Qoheleth does not simply reverse the values. Even the advantage of youth is merely relative, for within the larger picture youth is passing, being unavoidably followed by old age.

If the proverbial human is labelled as *homo docilis* then Qoheleth's human being is ultimately *homo limitatus*:

And I set my heart (in order to seek and to investigate by wisdom) upon all that which happens under the heaven. It is a bad occupation God gave to humans to occupy/afflict[53] [themselves] with. I saw all the things that happen under the heaven, and behold, all this is absurd and striving after wind. What is crooked, cannot be straightened,[54] and a deficit cannot be counted.[55] [Qoh 1:13–15]

Indeed, what is there for a person in all his work and ambition of his heart, which he carries out under the sun? For all his days are painful and his business is sorrowful, and also at night his heart does not sleep—this also is absurd. [Qoh 2:22–23]

There is sickening evil which I saw under the sun—riches kept by their owner for their[56] destruction. And the riches perish in a bad business venture, and he begot a son, and there is nothing at all in his hand. Just as he came out of the womb of his mother naked, he will again go, just as he came; and he will take nothing [in exchange] for[57] his labour,

---

[52] For textual notes see p. 192.

[53] The question whether לַעֲנוֹת comes from the root ענה or ענן cannot be definitely answered. The modifying רַע in the previous clause suggests that the meaning here is negative, thus suggesting the former, while the use of עִנְיָן in the same clause points to the latter. Thus, it appears that this is a deliberate pun—the affliction and occupation are inseparable (see also note 59 on p. 74).

[54] Reading Niphal with apocopated ה, e.g. 𝔊 aor. pass.; Driver (1954:225) proposes to read Pu infc.; in any case passive sense is required by the context.

[55] Fox (1989:173) proposes to emend 𝔐 לְהִמָּנוֹת to לְהַמְלוֹת, *to be made up for*, on the grounds that 𝔐 is a truism. While this statement is undeniably trivial on the literal level, it is not pointless, because on the level of the metaphor it encapsulates a key element of Qoheleth's worldview, indeed, the main point of the whole book, i.e., the fact that this world does not produce profit.

[56] The ms sfx has עֹשֶׁר as its referent as Qoh 5:13 shows.

[57] בְּ *pretii*.

that he would carry[58] in his hand, [59]also this is sickening evil: exactly[60] as he came so he goes. And what advantage does he have, who works for wind? Also, all his days he [is] in darkness and mourning,[61] and great grief,[62] and sickness and anger.[63] [Qoh 5:12–16]

What humanity cannot achieve is by far more significant for Qoheleth than what it can, and his answer to the initial question 'what יִתְרוֹן?' is a resolute 'none!'; anything that he examines turns out to be הֶבֶל. The mere frequency of this term in the book says it all. It should, therefore, come as no surprise that Qoheleth views the entire human existence as a pitiful and sorrowful business.

The fundamental reason for the failure to achieve anything permanent lies in the severe limitations imposed on human intellectual capabilities, in the inability to really understand the way the world is. In addition to Qoh 3:10–14, which has already been discussed (p. 74), the following passages should be also noted:

All the things are wearisome—one is not able to describe [them]. The eye will not [ever] be satisfied by watching, nor will the ear be [ever] filled from hearing. [Qoh 1:8][64]

When I set my heart to know wisdom and to see the occupation which happens[65] upon the earth (indeed, neither during the day nor during the night [the heart][66] was seeing any sleep with its eyes[67]), then I saw

---

[58] Following 𝔐 reading Hiphil; 𝔊(𝔖, 𝔙) reads ἵνα πορευθῇ, שֶׁיֵּלֵךְ, i.e., Qal Px; the Hiphil fits the context better, as the notion of going has been expressed already in the verse.

[59] 𝔐 + *and*; I follow 4QQohᵃ.

[60] Reading כְּלְעֻמַּת with 𝔊 and 𝔖 in place of 𝔐 כָּל־עֻמַּת.

[61] 𝔐 יֹאכֵל בַּחֹשֶׁךְ; reading with 𝔊 ἐν σκότει καὶ πένθει, i.e., בְּחֹשֶׁךְ וְאֵבֶל. The confusion of ב and כ is common in the Aramaic script.

[62] Reading with 𝔊 (𝔖, 𝔗, 𝔙) וְכַעַס; 𝔐 וְכָעַס. Gordis (1955a:244) prefers 𝔐 on the grounds that if these were nouns the ב would have to be repeated with each one, but that is not necessarily the case (see WOC 11.4.2a).

[63] Reading with 𝔊; 𝔐 reads *he grieves greatly, and his sickness, and anger.* 𝔖 appears to have been corrupted offering a number of variant readings. Gordis (1955a:244) wishes to preserve 𝔐 חָלְיוֹ suggesting the sfx is elliptical for לֹ. However, in that case one would expect it with the final word of the clause. Delitzsch (1982b:301) understands the final two words as an exclamation, but the introductory ו speaks against that.

[64] For textual notes see p. 116.

[65] Concerning the translation of the verb see note 49 on p. 72.

[66] The whole clause introduced by כִּי is best understood as epexegetical, explaining the intensity of the heart's search. Gordis (1955a:298) thinks the sfx on בְּעֵינָיו is anticipatory referring to הָאָדָם in v. 17, but this is unlikely because v. 16 describes the search methodologically while v. 17 presents the results reached, with the two subordinate clauses in 16 and 17 respectively being mutually independent and formally unrelated.

[67] Ogden's (1987b:141) proposal *there was sleep in his eyes, [therefore] he was not seeing* is

[concerning] every activity of God, that a person is not able to find out [about] the activity which is happening under the sun, no matter how much[68] a person may work to search [it] out, yet, he cannot find [it] out, and even if the sage should say[69] that he knows, he cannot find [it] out. [Qoh 8:16–17]

Yet, it is not merely the inability to accomplish anything permanent that Qoheleth resents. Rather, it is the reality of a single fate for all, the fact that all are treated exactly the same, that appears to be the single most unpalatable characteristic of human existence. It stirs particularly strong emotions in Qoheleth:

Indeed, I set all this to my heart, and my heart saw[70] all this, that the righteous and the wise, and their deeds are in the hand of God. Whether love or hatred humans do not know, all that is before them is absurd because[71] for all there is the same fate, for the righteous and for the wicked, for the good and for the bad,[72] and for the clean and for the unclean, for the sacrificing one, and for the one who does not sacrifice - as the good so the sinner, as[73] the one who makes a vow so the one who is afraid [to make] a vow. This [is] the[74] evil in all that happens under

---

forced, requiring *sleep* to be understood as a metaphor which is somewhat unexpected in conjunction with *day and night*. Furthermore, the *not seeing* here can hardly refer to the search itself, as it is immediately followed by the claim *and I saw*.

[68] בְּשֶׁל אֲשֶׁר should mean *on account of which* (e.g. Jonah 1:12), but that does not make much sense in the context. Therefore, I am reading with 𝔊 ὅσα ἂν μοχθήσῃ ὁ ἄνθρωπος τοῦ ζητῆσαι; cf. also 𝔖.

[69] The Px is best interpreted as modal; to express an actual claim or intention Sx would be expected, cf. Qoh 7:23 (*pace* Fox, 1989:253, 56).

[70] Reading with 𝔊(𝔖) καί καρδία μου σὺν πᾶν εἶδεν τοῦτο, i.e., וְלִבִּי רָאָה אֶת־כָּל־זֶה in place of the 𝔐 וְלִבּוּר אֶת־כָּל־זֶה; the extra letters אה attested to by 𝔊 are easier to explain as a haplography in the 𝔐 on account of the similarity between ה and ת than a dittography in the Vorlage of 𝔊. Gordis (1955a:299) defends 𝔐 on the grounds that the repetition of *heart* in an immediate succession is unlikely, deriving בור from ברר, *to select*, but it should be noted the repetition does not pose any syntactic difficulties, nor does it make the flow of the text awkward.

[71] Reading הֶבֶל בַּאֲשֶׁר instead of 𝔐 הַכֹּל כַּאֲשֶׁר on the basis of 𝔊 ματαιότης ἐν τοῖς πᾶσιν (𝔖 conflates 𝔐 and 𝔊). Crenshaw (1988:159–60) and Gordis (1955a:300) prefer 𝔐, the former arguing for sense *everything is the same to everybody*, and the latter rendering *everything is like everything else*. Neither of these renderings is plausible, since כַּאֲשֶׁר does not mean *the same*, as Crenshaw's translation requires, and Gordis' solution ignores the preposition ל with the second כֹּל.

[72] Reading with 𝔊(𝔖, 𝔙) καὶ το κακῷ which is missing in 𝔐, but fits the list of pairs.

[73] Reading with 𝔊(𝔖, 𝔗, 𝔙) כַּנִּשְׁבָּע in place of 𝔐 הַנִּשְׁבָּע. The former is preferable because while the construction varies from pair to pair in the list, it is always identical for both elements in each pair.

[74] The article is lacking in Hebrew, but definiteness is required by the context. Fox (1989:258) suggests that it is a case of haplography of זֶה הָרָע, which is plausible, although Qoheleth's use of the article is irregular.

the sun, that there is the same fate to all, and even though the heart
of human beings is full of evil[75] and there is foolishness in their hearts
during their lives and afterwards[76] - join the dead! [Qoh 9:1–3]

The wise person has eyes in his head, while the fool walks in darkness.
But I also[77] came to know that the same chance happens to both of
them. And [so] I thought to myself: 'The same chance as that of the fool
happens also to me—for what gain[78] am I then wise?' And I thought to
myself, that also this is absurd. For there is no lasting remembrance for
the wise as well as[79] the fool. In those already imminent days, both will
be forgotten. But how can the wise be allowed[80] to die with the fool? And
I hated life, because what is happening under the sun, [pressed] bad[ly][81]
upon me. For all is absurd and striving after wind. [Qoh 2:14–17]

Here Qoheleth betrays how much he identifies with the sages who
came before him. The ideal of retributive justice, so crucial to the
proverbial wise men is very dear to him. Unfortunately, it remains
an ideal which is unfulfilled in his experience and he finds this reality
difficult to swallow.

Yet, in spite of the bleak picture of human existence that Qoheleth
paints, and even the strong emotions of dislike, he clings to life:

---

[75] Ogden (1987b:147) *painful thoughts*, but the parallel with *foolishness* suggests a more
active sense, since foolishness is not something that happens to a person, but something
one does.

[76] As there is no referent for the 3ms sfx in the context, אַחֲרָיו must be understood
here in a purely adverbial manner (Gordis, 1955a:301). 𝔊 ὀπίσω αὐτῶν; σ' τὰ δὲ
τελεύτετα αὐτῶν; these variations are not likely due to differences in the Vorlage.

[77] The position of the particle is unusual. It would seem that its primary referent
is not the act of knowing, but the persona of Qoheleth, as if Qoheleth's observation
associates him with others who had reached the same conclusion before him.

[78] Taking יֹתֵר as a substantive, referred to by the מַה of לָמָּה. It is also possible to
understand יֹתֵר adverbially: 'and why have I, then, become *especially* wise?' (Gordis,
1955a:212). However, a degree of wisdom does not seem to be the issue in the context—
the polarity is not *little wise : exceedingly wise*, but rather *foolish : wise*.

[79] Hebrew עִם, which some wish to interpret as comparative (e.g. Delitzsch,
1982b:247; Crenshaw, 1988:85). However, Qoheleth expresses the comparative regularly by the standard construction with מִן, and furthermore, the force of the preposition
must be the same as in 16b, since it connects wise and fools in both cases. On this latter
occasion the sense is undoubtedly associative—the point is not that the wise does not
have more remembrance than the fool, but that neither of them has any at all.

[80] The particle אֵיךְ followed by Px typically introduces rhetorical questions with
modal sense, cf. Hos 11:8 (in contrast exclamations introduced by אֵיךְ tend to use Sx).

[81] Gordis (1955a:213) suggests that רַע עָלַי means *it is worthless to me* on basis of טוֹב
עַל in Esth 3:9. However, there the idiom means *to please someone*, thus supporting the
present rendering.

Indeed, whoever is in the company[82] with all the living, there is hope[83] [for him]—indeed, [there is hope] for a living dog, who is better off than the dead lion. For the living know that they will die, but as for the dead, they know nothing, and they have no more any reward, because their memory has been forgotten. [Qoh 9:4–5]

The light is sweet and it is pleasant for eyes to see the sun. Indeed, if a person lives many years, let him rejoice in all of them, but let him remember the dark days, for they could be many, all that comes is absurd. [Qoh 11:7–8]

These two quotes should be supplemented by all the repeated calls to eat and drink and enjoy life scattered throughout the book, and together with the texts quoted earlier paint two diametrically contrasting views of life, on the one hand as pitiful, unjust and pointless existence, on the other hand as something that can and should be enjoyed. They stand in tension in the book, yet, they are not irreconcilable. As I have argued earlier, Qoheleth operates on two distinct levels; one which is abstract and all-encompassing on which he is asking about the meaning of life, and another which is concrete, the here and now. In the former there is no יִתְרוֹן, there is no higher meaning to life, human existence is not more than the process of dying. On the latter level there are ups and downs, and the ups can be exploited, and so, as we already observed, life can be worth living although it produces nothing of any genuine value.[84]

While he spends much time dealing with the nature of human existence, Qoheleth shows only limited interest in human character. Yet, the comments he makes bear a number of similarities with those we found in Proverbs. In harmony with the proverbial sages, Qoheleth considers the internal human reality as more important than the external. This is particularly well captured by the following sayings:

---

[82] Reading 𝔐 Q יְחֻבַּר, supported by versions. That the K יבחר is a mere scribal error (*pace* Crenshaw, 1988:160–1) is indicated by the fact that the object of בחר is not introduced by אֶל, which however is used with חבר (e.g. Gen 14:3). Placing a pause between בחר and אֶל, as the 𝔐 accents do, to avoid this problem, i.e., *whoever is chosen, there is hope to all living*, yields a poor sense.

[83] The MH sense of בְּטָחוֹן. Fox (1989:258) *something that can be relied on*, i.e., death, but the hope in vv. 4–5 is that of some reward that the dead do not possess anymore, and the following statement does not make sense if the certainty of death is in view here.

[84] A similar understanding of Qoheleth's quest was recently expressed by Christianson (1998:216–254).

> [A good][85] name is better than quality oil, and the day of death than the day of birth. It is better to go to a house of mourning than to go to a house of feasting because that is the end of every person, and the living one should ponder [it]. Sadness is better than laughter, for when the face is distressed, the mind will be well.[86] The mind of the wise is in the house of mourning, but the mind of fools is in the house of joy. [Qoh 7:1–4]

The second half of the first saying is puzzling, but it should most likely be understood in the light of the first colon—it cannot be said at birth what the person is like, only at the end of person's life can an accurate judgement be made. We can also note that similarly to Proverbs, Qoheleth views the difficult times as character building, they drive home to one the true realities of life.

Further, just as the proverbial wise men, Qoheleth observes that human beings have an inclination toward evil [Qoh 8:11; 9:3], that human appetite is insatiable [Qoh 6:7] and that human integrity is fragile [Qoh 7:7]. A widespread emotion in Qoheleth's world is envy:

> And I saw that all the fruit[87] and all the success of work [amounts to] man's envy towards his neighbour. [Qoh 4:4]

What is rendered here as *envy* is the Hebrew קִנְאָה, the jealousy that was considered by the proverbial sages the strongest emotion of all. For Qoheleth this emotion is not merely the strongest, it is also the most prevailing one; it is not merely applied to sexual relations, which is the case in Proverbs, but rather, it lurks in the background of everything that people do. Thus, Qoheleth's view of human nature is ultimately more negative than that of the proverbial sages,

I have pointed out in chapter 4 (p. 123) that Qoheleth apportions a certain degree of blame for human wickedness to God. However, the nature of Qoheleth's criticism needs to be appreciated. Qoheleth asserts that God is responsible for the evil perpetuated by people because by not putting into place strict and swift retributive justice he effectively encourages wickedness. Yet, Qoheleth does not lay any blame on God for the primary causes of evil, i.e., he does not assert that God made humans evil, rather the opposite:

---

[85] טוֹב functions predicatively in 1aa and attributively in 1ab. The attributive use in 1ab implies an additional gapped טוֹב with attributive sense in 1aa.

[86] I agree with Gordis (1955a:258) that the phrase should be understood in an intellectual sense, e.g., *understanding improves*.

[87] עָמָל here in the sense of the product of work (*pace* Fox, 1989:202).

All this I tested concerning Wisdom: I said, 'let me be wise', but she is far from me. [She] is distant from that which is, and very deep, who can find her?[88] In my heart I turned to get to know, to examine and to pursue wisdom, and [to get] an answer,[96] and [also] to get to know the wickedness of foolishness[89]—Folly is madness.[90] And I find more bitter[91] than death the woman, who[92] is a hunting net and whose heart is a mesh, whose hands are fetters. One who is pleasing to God will escape from her, but a sinner will be captured by her. 'Look! This is what I found', said Qoheleth[93] [adding] one to one to get [the] answer.[96] [94]'My soul sought again—and [again] I did not find: one man among a thousand I found, but a woman among all of these I did not find. Only, take a look at what I found, that God made mankind straight, but[95] they sought many answers'.[96] [Qoh 7:23–29]

Admittedly, this is one of the most challenging passages in the book, but it does contain a number of significant clues to its interpretation.

---

[88] See the discussion in the main text below.

[89] The construct relationship is indicated by the accents, and the phrase is so understood by ᵷ and ᵴ.

[90] The syntax of the final two words is somewhat obscure. Neither ᵷ nor ᵴ nor 𝔐 accents understand them as a construct chain and many Hebrew manuscripts, ᵷ and ᵴ supply a copula between them. In my view the article with סִכְלוּת, not attested in ᵷ (ᵴ has all three expressions in the colon definite), corresponds to the article used with חָכְמָה in v. 23. I prefer to read the whole construction as a clause commenting on the nature of folly. This fits with the fact that the statement about wisdom is preceded by a comment on the nature of wisdom in v. 24, and makes fluent transition into the following verse. The copula that introduces the phrase is epexegetical and is best left untranslated.

[91] Dahood (1958:308–309) renders *stronger*, but the parallel with *death* makes the common sense *bitter* very plausible here, cf. 1 Sam 15:32 (Crenshaw, 1988:146).

[92] Hebrew אֲשֶׁר־הִיא where הִיא functions as a gender-marker ensuring that the subject of the nominal clause is properly understood.

[93] 𝔐 אָמְרָה קֹהֶלֶת; reading with ᵷ ὁ Ἐκκλησιαστής, i.e., אָמַר הַקֹּהֶלֶת as in Qoh 12:8.

[94] The relative pronoun אֲשֶׁר resumes the direct speech interrupted by a parenthetical comment *said Qoheleth adding one to one to get [the result]*, and is best left untranslated. It is possible that *said Qoheleth*, the only occurrence of the 3rd person narration within the core of the book, was deemed necessary to indicate that what immediately follows is parenthetical. The suggested emendation of אֲשֶׁר to אִשָּׁה (e.g. Fox, 1989:242) is uncalled for.

[95] Disjunctive sense is preferable to simple co-ordination (*pace* Ogden, 1987b:124), for the B colon has to be the reason for the failure of the search of v. 22 and must, therefore, be understood in a negative sense.

[96] 𝔐 חִשְּׁבֹנוֹת is in my view incorrectly vocalised. I follow ᵷ and repoint to חֶשְׁבֹנוֹת. 𝔐 pointing could have been caused by nothing more than the daggesh placed incorrectly at some point, the vowels being subsequently adjusted to the new syllable division. The word חִשְּׁבֹנוֹת is otherwise found only in 2 Chr 26:15, where it refers to catapults, but such a sense is inappropriate in the present context. I chose the rendering *an answer*, for further discussion see the main text.

First of all, it is important that we appreciate that in v. 23 wisdom is not an instrument of Qoheleth's search, but its object. The same construction נִסָּה בְּ is found in Qoh 2:1, this time with reference to joy, and on this occasion the context shows beyond doubt that joy is the object of Qoheleth's enquiries, i.e., the idiom means *to test something, to inquire into something*. In the present passage Qoheleth is putting wisdom to the test in the same way he put enjoyment to the test in chapter 3. Consequently, the referent of the feminine pronoun *she* in the second half of v. 23 is wisdom, the object of the whole enquiry.[97]

The reference to wisdom continues in v. 24, where we should follow the versions and read מִשֶּׁהָיָה, *from that which is*, instead of the 𝔐 מַה־שֶּׁהָיָה, which makes poor sense and most likely arose by metathesis of the מ and the ה ending of the preceding feminine adjective (cf. 𝔊 μακρά). The preposition מִן then can be understood as comparative, which appears to be the case in 𝔊, but spatial interpretation is in my view preferable, cf. 𝔖 ܠܗ ܘܪܚܝܩܐ ܗܝ ܣܓܝ ܡܢ ܟܠ, *she is very far from all that which is*. The reference to wisdom then continues to the very end of the verse, as was correctly understood by 𝔖, even though the adjectives in 𝔐 and 𝔊 shift to masculine; such a shift of gender when the modified and the modifier are not in each other's proximity is found elsewhere in Qoheleth (see note 83 on p. 116).

A further peculiarity of this text is הַסִּכְלוּת in v. 25. The definite article makes this expression to stand out from what otherwise would appear to be a list of four synonyms, and I am inclined to think that its purpose is precisely to prevent v. 25b to be read as a list. More interestingly, a parallel and otherwise inexplicable definite article is found back in v. 23 in the expression בַּחָכְמָה, and I would like to suggest that it is this link between הַסִּכְלוּת and הַחָכְמָה that holds the interpretative key to this passage—we meet here the pair of the proverbial ladies, Wisdom and Folly.[98]

Qoheleth 'flirts' with both women, first with Wisdom, but finds her outside of his reach, deep and distant. Failing to befriend Wisdom, Qoheleth turns to Folly, but finds her to be a deadly snare, and any attempt to follow her an act of sheer madness. He then asserts that God

---

[97] The only other possible candidate for the referent of this pronoun is the feminine demonstrative זֹה which opens the verse (so Fox, 1989:239–40), but it should be noted, that in the final analysis this demonstrative also refers to wisdom, or more precisely, the different aspects of Qoheleth's scrutiny of wisdom.

[98] Cf. Seow (1997:271–72).

will protect those who please him from entrapment by Folly, and it is this statement that provides us with a point of departure for interpretation of vv. 27–29. What Qoheleth is looking for are individuals pleasing God. Having carried out an extensive search, he expresses his conclusion in v. 28; examining people around him one by one, he claims to have found hardly anyone, or more precisely one male and no females, of whom he could say that they were not trapped by Folly, i.e., that they were pleasing to God. Considering that the search of v. 27 will be flatly condemned by the sweeping judgement of v. 29, discussed below, v. 28 needs to be understood as a tongue-in-cheek statement, Qoheleth implying, with a healthy dose of self-mockery, that he is the only man not deluded by Folly, and so able to see the shortcomings of his comrades.

The negative picture of humanity painted in v. 28 raises the logical question of what is causing this sorry state of affairs. The answer to this is found in v. 29. It is not God, Qoheleth says, who is to blame, for he made people יָשָׁר, *upright*. Instead, the universal failure of the human race to please God and avoid the trappings of Folly stems from the search for חֶשְׁבֹּנוֹת (see p. 157 n. 96). Save the references to a place of that name, the word חֶשְׁבּוֹן appears only in Qoheleth in the Hebrew bible, and on three occasions in Ben Sira [9:15, 27:5f., 42:3]. The first occurrence in our book is in the passage under consideration in v. 25. Here חֶשְׁבּוֹן stands next to חָכְמָה. This parallel shows that the term is used by Qoheleth in line with the basic sense of the root חשׁב, which has cognitive connotations.[99] The precise semantic nuance is made clear when the word makes its second appearance in our passage in v. 27. On this occasion it is a part of the description of Qoheleth's own search for people pleasing God. This whole enquiry is portrayed by him using a metaphor of the mathematical process of addition. Adding one to one, Qoheleth is after the result of the 'calculation', the חֶשְׁבּוֹן, and indeed, once the result of his search is reached, Qoheleth reports it with a mathematical precision: one man

---

[99] Lohfink (1979:276) sees here a contrast between חֶשְׁבּוֹן, representing a hands-on inductive method of examining the world, and חָכְמָה, standing for the teach-and-learn approach of traditional wisdom, which Qoheleth is meant to be critiquing here. While I broadly agree with Lohfink's understanding of meaning of חֶשְׁבּוֹן (see the discussion in the main text), it should be noted that חָכְמָה does not stand in the book for the traditional wisdom, but rather, it simply refers to the search to understand the world and to benefit from such an understanding—Qoheleth's own quest, which is inductive, is also a quest for wisdom.

out of a thousand examined, and no women among the same number.
In other words, to search for חֶשְׁבּוֹן is to search for a precise, unambiguous and indisputable answer to the question at hand, and it is
the search for this type of answers, says Qoheleth, that is to blame
for the universal entrapment of humanity by the woman more bitter than death, Folly. The persistent human endeavour to fully understand, and thus control, the world around is at odds with the divine
will. The world of Qoheleth's God is intentionally ambivalent, preventing simple and clear-cut answers, and it is like that precisely so
that human beings could not get full control over it. God intended
not that humans understand everything, but rather that they fear him
[Qoh 3:10–14], and consequently humanity becomes displeasing to
God when it refuses to accept this. In other words, Qoheleth's quest
into wisdom and folly concluded that while being caught in the snares
of folly is worse than being dead, the alternative, the traditional wisdom ideal is unachievable, and insistence on it amounts to being at
odds with God.[100]

To summarise, Qoheleth's anthropology is of a low type, in which
human being, created by God, is de facto an animal. In contrast to the
Proverbial linear view of human life, Qoheleth's perceives human existence as moving around a circular trajectory, with death closing off the
cycle opened by birth. This is reflected in Qoheleth's devaluation of old
age, but also of wisdom. While the proverbial sages saw in humanity
great and unrealised potential, Qoheleth emphasises the severe, in his
view insurmountable, limitations that God imposed on human beings.
He shares with the proverbial wise many of the insights into the human
nature, including the belief that the natural human inklings are toward
evil and folly; yet, in contrast to the proverbial sages, he is sceptical
that it is possible to overcome these tendencies. The search for understanding, which in Proverbs was sanctioned and encouraged by God, is
not so black and white in Qoheleth, for the human desire to know can
ultimately lead to alienation from God, incurring his wrath. Thus, the
overall picture of human character and the nature of human existence
that Qoheleth paints is rather bleak. In spite of that Qoheleth clings to
life, and admonishes the reader to exploit all positive opportunities it
offers.

---

[100] One cannot avoid noticing certain similarities with the story of Gen 3, where the
innocent couple defied their maker in order to know in the way God knows and, thus,
became the object of his anger.

Qoheleth's Social Perspective

While Qoheleth builds largely on his personal experience, and much of his advice runs purely on an individual level, it should not obscure from us the fact that he does not think of humanity in strictly individual terms. On the contrary, humanity is to him a single, continuous flow of generations and it is precisely the character of this collective flow that determines the nature of individual human existence. This endless flow of humanity has two primary traits: (1) the nature of its existence does not change from one generation to the other, the human world is as it has been and will be as it is; (2) it is impossible to keep track of individuals within this flow; people are born, die and are forgotten. It matters no more what they were like, whether wise or fools, they cease to exist not only in the physical sense, but also as an element of the endless flow; human society viewed from a distance is anonymous.

The social nature of human existence is not found only on the abstract level, but Qoheleth thinks of human beings as social creatures in day-to-day existence. Loneliness is painful and undesirable; human beings need the support of others and indeed find satisfaction in sharing the passing reward of any success:

> And again I saw absurdity under the sun. There is one but he has no other—neither son nor brother—and there is no end to his work, nor is his eye satisfied [with] riches. And for whom do I work and deprive my soul of pleasure? Also this is absurd and it is an evil occupation. Two are better than one, because they have pleasant reward in their work. Indeed, if either one falls,[101] the one will raise his companion, but woe to him,[102] the [lonely] one when he falls—and there is no other to raise him up. Also, if the two lie down, then they are warm, but the one, how will he get warm? And if someone[103] attacks[104] one [of them], the two will stand against him, and a three-ply cord will not be easily torn. [Qoh 4:7–12]

This brings us finally to the examination of the socio-economic structures that the book reflects. I wish to suggest that Qoheleth points toward a well developed monarchic set up. The royal figure is much

---

[101] Partitive use of pl. (Crenshaw, 1988:111).

[102] Reading with 𝕲, 𝕾, 𝖁 and many manuscripts וְאִי לוֹ in place of 𝔏(𝕿) וְאִילוֹ. This could have been easily misunderstood by a scribe of a later period when the short i was also fully written.

[103] The subject of the verb is undetermined, the 3ms object sfx indicates that הָאֶחָד is the object of the verb.

[104] Such use of תקף has parallels in the Talmud (Gordis, 1955a:232).

more central to the life of Qoheleth's society than we found to be the case in Proverbs:

> Woe to you land, which is ruled by a servant and whose princes are used to feasting in the morning. Blessed are you land, which is ruled by a person of free descent and whose princes eat at [proper] time for the sake of[105] strength and not for the sake of drunkenness. In sluggishness the beam-work will collapse and in lowering of hands the house will leak.[106] They are making food for laughter and wine can make jolly life, but money is an answer to everything.[107] But not even in your thought[108] curse the king, and do not curse the rich in your bedroom, for a bird from heaven will carry [away] your voice and a winged creature will disclose[109] [your] word. [Qoh 10:16–20]

The king is portrayed here as a figure that ideally maintains the society in good order, likened to a house owner that makes sure the roof is sound. In other words, the character and conduct of the king and his courtiers is seen as having impact on the whole country. This is very different from what we observed in Proverbs, where the king's behaviour was largely related to his own fate and the fate of those in his immediate vicinity. The monarchy Qoheleth is familiar with reaches into the inmost private parts of people's lives, their bedrooms, and does not tolerate any dissent. The monarch is an absolute despot, answerable to no-one; this notion is found elsewhere in the book:

> Watch the mouth of king and concerning a divine oath, do not be hasty. Walk from his presence, do not stand in an evil matter, for he does whatever he pleases. Because the word of the king is powerful, and who will say to him: 'What are you doing?' [Qoh 8:2–4][110]

There is some evidence that the world in which Qoheleth lives experiences imperial exploits of mighty rulers. Consider the following verse:

> There was a small city and few men in it, and a great king came to it, and surrounded it, and built against it massive ramparts. [Qoh 9:14][111]

---

[105] Hebrew בְּ.

[106] Greenfield (1958:208–10) argues on the basis of evidence from Ugaritic for existence of a second root דלף, *to collapse*, which would make good sense here.

[107] Lit. *answers all.* Fox (1989:271) suggests *and money keeps them all occupied.*

[108] Thomas (1949) proposed to derive מַדָּע from ידע, *to be still*, on basis of Arabic, and render *even in your repose*, but the common meaning *thought* makes better sense here since the basic notion of the verse is *not even in the utmost privacy curse the powerful*.

[109] As Barton (1908:179) pointed out, 𝔐 pointing of the verbs as jussives is most likely incorrect.

[110] For textual notes see p. 198.

[111] For textual notes see p. 49.

It is not particularly significant whether Qoheleth had a specific historic occasion in mind or not. What is, however, important, is that for the story that follows this verse to serve Qoheleth's purposes, it must be compatible with the common experience of his day, for it is present experience that confirms or disproves what is and is not true in Qoheleth's epistemology. Now, great kings do not go about laying siege to insignificant cities to subdue them. Such work can be carried out by their military commanders. Mighty kings are only interested in mighty exploits. The only context in which a story of a mighty king personally supervising a siege of a small city is credible is that of a large-scale military campaign in which the taking of a small city is just one of many achievements, and its significance lies not in gaining control of the city *per se*, but rather in not spoiling the king's absolute and unchallenged victory. Qoheleth's world is one of such mighty campaigns where kings set out to make a name for themselves.

Furthermore, Qoheleth's world is not one of long-lived royal dynasties, but rather a world in which kings are overthrown by other kings. Yet, Qoheleth observes that while the rulers may change, the system remains the same, and those who welcome the new ruler hoping for a better future are soon disillusioned:

> Better is a poor lad who is wise, than an old king who is a fool who can no more take advice. For he came from prison to be a king, even though he was born poor in his kingdom. I saw the living (the ones walking under the sun) alongside the second lad,[112] who was to stand in his place. There was no end to all the people—to all those who were before them, but those who came later were not happy with him. Indeed, this also is absurd and striving after wind. [Qoh 4:13–16]

The king is not seen by Qoheleth as the upholder of justice; the social structures in his world are unjust and oppressive:

> And again I observed under the sun: the place of justice—wickedness [gets][113] there. And the place of the righteous—the wicked [gets] there.[114] [Qoh 3:16]

---

[112] As Fox (1989:207–8) pointed out, the shift to Px shows that Qoheleth has yet another person in mind who is still to appear on the scene.

[113] Note the locative ה on שָׁמָּה.

[114] Reading with 𝕲 and 𝕿 צַדִּיק and רֶשַׁע. This is in my judgement the better reading, since the theme of righteous and wicked is further developed in the following verse.

I saw all this and paid attention to every thing that happens under the sun: [there is] time when a person rules over a person to cause him evil.[115] [Qoh 8:9]

And I turned and I saw all the oppression which happens under the sun. And behold, the tear[s] of the oppressed, and they do not have a comforter, and from the hand of their oppressors [comes] power, and they do not have a comforter. And I congratulated the dead, who already died, over those still living. And more than both of them [I congratulated] the one who has not been yet, who has not seen the evil that happens under the sun. [Qoh 4:1–3][116]

The desperate tone of the last text suggests oppression on a scale that cannot be easily ignored. Qoheleth's examination of the way the society works leads him to the conclusion that the socio-economic structures are not just corrupt but are even intended to be an instrument of oppression:

Should you see oppression of the poor and denial of justice and righteousness in the province, do not be astonished by the matter. For a high one is keeping in check[117] a high one, and there are other high ones above them.[118] Profit [from] the land is behind all this; the king is served by the field.[119] The lover of money will not be satisfied [with] money,

---

[115] Reading with versions Hiphil with apocopated ה. 𝔐, 𝔙 read a noun, *to his evil.*

[116] For textual notes see p. 113.

[117] Fox (1989:213) understands the hierarchy pictured here as officials looking out for, and protecting each other, with the consequence that it is impossible to uproot corruption. However, Qoheleth is not so much concerned here with the pervasiveness and persistence of corruption, as with the reasons behind it.

[118] Ogden's (1987b:80–81) proposal that גָּבֹהַּ מֵעַל גָּבֹהַּ שֹׁמֵר means *more exalted keeper,* while the following plural has a superlative force, ignores the normal sense of מֵעַל as well as the fact that the plural sfx of עֲלֵיהֶם requires 7ba to have a plural, not singular, sense.

[119] There are four key issues in interpreting this verse. (1) the referent of בַּכֹּל; (2) the function of הוּא / הִיא; (3) the function of נֶעֱבָד; (4) the force of ל in לְשָׂדֶה. The suggested reading follows 𝔐 accents. There are three two-word phrases in the verse (a two-word phrase is linked by a conjunctive accent, Yeivin, 1980:221): (a) וְיִתְרוֹן אֶרֶץ; (b) בַּכֹּל הִיא; (c) מֶלֶךְ לְשָׂדֶה. Thus (b) needs to be translated *in all this* with the pronoun not referring to the following clause but to the preceding verse. According to the accents נֶעֱבָד is not modifying שָׂדֶה, but refers to the king. The ל then has its common instrumental force. On the other hand, if the ptc. is understood as modifying the field, the meaning of the ל, and consequently of the whole colon is obscure, e.g. the difficulties of the versions (in 𝔊 the king is the subject, tilling the field, yet, for that Qal ptc. would be required in Hebrew; 𝔊 βασιλεὺς τοῦ ἀργοῦ εἰργασμένου, implying the king *ruling over* the worked field, in which case one would expect עַל or בְּ, not ל in Hebrew). Although in the two other places where Niphal of עבד occurs in the OT it refers to land meaning *arable,* the data is too limited for any generally applicable conclusions. The proposed interpretation is fully in line with the typical uses of Niphal, and further supported

and whoever loves wealth will not [be satisfied with] crops[120]—also this is absurd. [Qoh 5:7–9]

The whole royal enterprise revolves around squeezing out profit from the land and, the second half of the concluding proverb appears to make an explicit reference to claiming taxes from the crops.

It was observed earlier that while slaves existed in the proverbial world, they had only a limited role. This does not seem to be the case in Qoheleth's environment. Apart from the abundance of slaves listed as a part of the Solomonic achievement, Qoheleth addresses himself to people who possess slaves, and slaves have a definite place in the way his society is structured:

> I acquired slaves, and maids, and I had slaves born[121] in the house. I also had greater possessions, cattle and sheep, than all those who were before me in Jerusalem. [Qoh 2:7]

> Also, do not pay attention to all the things that are said,[122] so that you may not hear your servant cursing you. For even your heart knows of many times when you also cursed others. [Qoh 7:21–22]

> There is an evil [which] I saw under the sun, like[123] an error that comes from the ruler. The fool[124] is put in many high positions but the rich

---

by the fact that in later Hebrew Niphal of עבד has a number of uses including *to be worshipped* (Jas), undoubtedly derived from a more generic *to be served*. Such an interpretation of v. 8 also fits the immediate context. The initial structure *province/officials* in 7a/7b implies supra structure *empire/sovereign*, which is in 8a/8b represented by the pair *land/king*—the provincial policies are a result of the overall royal policies.

[120] Gordis (1955a:241) wishes to revocalise לא תבואה to לא תבואה, *it will not come to him*. However, this fails to appreciate the poetics of the verse, where תבואה, i.e., the product of a field, establishes a link with שָׂדֶה in v. 8; 𝔐 is supported by 𝔊.

[121] Taking בְּנֵי־בַיִת as referring to the slaves that were born to the master, in contrast to those purchased. The singular form הָיָה probably agrees with the head of the construct, i.e. *the house* (Joü § 150i), or it is also possible that בְּנֵי־בַיִת are conceived of as a collective. A few manuscripts and 𝔊 read pl. Gordis (1955a:207) interprets the whole clause as concessive 'I bought … *although I already had* …'. But the construction of the clause is identical with the one that immediately follows which is clearly not concessive, being introduced by גַּם. In the light of that, the ו in 7a is best understood as a simple copula.

[122] Lit. *they say*, an impersonal plural with a passive function. Some 𝔊(𝔖) manuscripts + ἀσεβεῖς; 𝔐 is preferable in the context since quite clearly this verse is not about listening to the wicked, but about eavesdropping in general.

[123] Gordis (1955a:319) wishes to interpret the כ as asseverative, *indeed*, on the grounds that the verse is otherwise meaningless. Such assertion is untrue, and the examples of asseverative uses of כ he quotes, with the possible exception of Lam 1:20 and Neh 7:2, do not support such an interpretation.

[124] 𝔐 הַסֶּכֶל, *folly*, is used for poetic reasons (note the alliteration with בַשֵׁפֶל in the B colon) and is to be understood personally, cf. 𝔊 ὁ ἄφρων.

are made to sit low. I saw servants on horses and princes walking like
servants upon the ground. [Qoh 10:5–7]

The last passage quoted above raises the question of Qoheleth's personal attitude toward the social arrangement of his world. At first
glance, v. 7 seems to imply the view that the society has a certain built-
in and proper hierarchy, i.e., that certain classes of people are destined
to be rulers and others are not and should not be in such a position
(although the king may be ignorant of this natural order). Yet, the reference to the influential fool in v. 6, does suggest that Qoheleth thinks
that people should hold power on merit. Such a notion is expressed
more clearly elsewhere:

> And I said: 'Wisdom is better than strength, but wisdom of a poor person
> is despised, his words are not listened to, The quiet words of the wise are
> to be heeded more than the shouting of a ruler over fools.' [Qoh 9:16–
> 17][125]

> Better is a poor lad who is wise, than an old king who is a fool who can
> no more take advice. For he came from prison to be a king, even though
> he was born poor in his kingdom. [Qoh 4:13–14][126]

In the latter passage, Qoheleth reports a case of an overthrow of the
established order. An old king is replaced by a young man who is
poor. Here Qoheleth explicitly affirms that such a youth is preferable,
providing he is wise, in spite of the lack of any other formal creden-
tials. In the light of these, it is most likely that Qoh 10:7 is intended
to imply the precise opposite of what it is usually taken to mean,
i.e., that those who have the power through their pedigree or connec-
tions are not always worthy of being the rulers, while those who hold
the humble positions are sometimes the true princes, albeit unrecog-
nised.

Another characteristic of Qoheleth's world should not go unnoticed.
Family ties, so crucial to the proverbial worldview, have very little
significance for Qoheleth; he finds no sense of satisfaction in passing
the results of his labour onto an heir:

> And I hated all my accomplishment[s] which I am achieving[127] under
> the sun, which[128] I must leave to a person who will be after me. And who
> knows whether he will be wise or a fool. And he will rule over all the

---

[125] For textual notes see p. 190.
[126] For textual notes see p. 163.
[127] The form עָמֵל, found here and in Qoh 2:22, is best understood as a Qal participle.
[128] Possibly *because* (Crenshaw, 1988:87).

produce which I skilfully produced under the sun. Also this is absurd. [Qoh 2:18–19]

While there is no direct indication in this verse that Qoheleth has a relation in mind, this is very likely. This sentiment is reinforced by Qoheleth's explicit perception of there being no inherent benefit in having many descendants:

> If a person begets a hundred [children] and lives many years, as many the days of his years may be, but his soul would not be satiated from the good things, and he even did not have a burial, I say: 'the miscarried one is better off than him'. [Qoh 6:3][129]

It is quite clear from the examination of the socio-economic conditions reflected in the book, that it stems from a time of a much greater turmoil and wider spread economic activity than a principally tribal setting could account for. While I am personally somewhat reluctant to try to match these conditions to a very specific historical period, it has been argued by others that the socio-economic conditions of Qoheleth's world are best matched to the primitive market exchange, limited capital accumulation, and a strictly controlled economy of the Ptolemaic era (Harrison, 1997). Such conclusions are in my view not implausible, particularly when the probable linguistic date for the book is taken into account.

One final issue remains to be addressed and that is the book's attitude toward women. Qoheleth has been often labelled as a misogynist, mainly on the grounds of Qoh 7:26, 28.[130] In my view such a charge is based on misunderstanding of the passage, for I have argued earlier in this chapter (p. 157ff.) that *the woman more bitter than death* of Qoh 7:26 is not just any female, but she is the personified Folly so familiar to the reader of Proverbs, and that the statement of v. 28 is a tongue-in-cheek one, with Qoheleth being the single male out of a thousand, mocking the human search for simple answers to difficult questions. The overall claim made by this passage is not that women are dangerous and/or worse than men, but that humanity as a whole is entrapped by Folly, and displeasing to God on the account of wanting to be too clever. It should be further noted that for Qoheleth women are a part of the enjoyment of life, they not only figure in the list of the Solomonic

---

[129] For textual notes see p. 114.
[130] Recently Brenner (1993:201–202)

achievements, but, more importantly, a woman is a partner[131] in enjoying what life has got to offer in Qoh 9:9. At the same time, the latter text implies that Qoheleth does not expect women to be among his audience, the world of wisdom as he knows it, just as the proverbial world, is a male world.

Summary

Considering the anthropological views and the socio-economic conditions that the two books reflect, there are significant differences between them. The anthropology of Proverbs is high, human beings reflect their divine maker, and are endowed with powerful capabilities. While the human potential is not limitless, it is adequate for a person to be in control of one's life, and to be able to succeed and prosper. In contrast, Qoheleth perceives a human being as a mere animal whose limitations far outweigh the capabilities it possesses. The fundamental inability to understand the workings of the world prevents people from gaining control over it, and so stops them from achieving anything of a permanent value. The similarities in the two anthropological perspectives are largely limited to the views about basic human nature and tendencies, where both Proverbs and Qoheleth agree that humans are naturally inclined toward folly and evil, but the proverbial human being is capable of successfully curtailing this tendency, avoiding acting foolishly. In contrast, Qoheleth claims that all people are trapped by folly and ultimately displeasing to God.

The examination of the social arrangements that the two books point to suggests that they originated in two radically different worlds. One is a peaceful, and largely self-contained world of a community in a small village or town, where family and long-standing tradition are of the utmost importance. The king, when he appears, is more a symbol than a reality and his impact on day-to-day life is negligible. In contrast, in Qoheleth's society the king and the royal administrative structures are all important, and impact people's day-to-day lives. There is nothing cosy about the state, it is intrusive, unjust and oppressive. Further, it does not exhibit great stability, but rather it is plagued by imperial conflicts; kings come and go, yet, the system with its pitfalls, remains.

---

[131] She is not merely an entertaining object on a par with the food and drink; note the construction עִם־אִשָּׁה.

CHAPTER 6

LIVING WISELY

In the previous three chapters I examined the basic elements of the sages' perception of the world: the way in which they acquired knowledge about the world, their cosmological understanding, their key theological views, what they thought of human beings. In addition, I have examined the socio-economic conditions they found themselves in. It is now time to look at the conclusions the sages drew from their respective perceptions of the world, and examine the kind of practical behaviour that they were seeking to encourage on the basis of their understanding. Put differently, I will attempt to formulate what constitutes wise living from the point of view of the two books.

However, before I do so, I wish to come back to the point that was made in the previous chapter, namely, that the two books stem from diametrically different socio-economic conditions. Consequently, it should not come as a great surprise if the experience-based approaches to life that we find in the two books diverge from each other. The socio-economic divide makes it impossible to place the two paradigms side by side and then argue that one is superior to the other. One can question the validity of either, when setting them against their own socio-economic confines, but at the same time one must refrain from seeing in them two different sets of answers to identical problems, for they do not share the same daily experience. True, the two underlying methodologies are similar to each other and their goals are in most general terms identical. Yet, we have to appreciate that from this basic common strategy stem tactical procedures driven by the specifics of the daily reality, and thus of different nature; it is these tactical procedures that form the content of wisdom. The strategies can be compared, because they pursue non-historic ideals of prosperity and happiness; the tactics can be related to each other, but not compared in a competitive sense, because they are tied to matters fixed in time and space, starting with different initial conditions to which they address themselves. With this in mind, we can now turn to the sages' practical wisdom.

Wisdom of the Proverbial sages

It might be useful to open our consideration of what the proverbial sages considered as wise living with a review of the picture of the proverbial world uncovered so far. We saw that there are three basic elements to this world: cosmos, humanity and God. Of these three, the latter two are the dominant ones. The larger cosmos is more or less a medium manipulated by God in his dealings with humanity. On the one hand God reveals himself through the cosmos, on the other hand he uses it to shape human experience. The cosmos does not have any real autonomy and only very limited space is dedicated in Proverbs to deliberations about the cosmos *per se*. This is reflected in the practical advice of the sages, the vast majority of which is dedicated to relationships, God-human and human human, but primarily the latter.

We have seen that the God of the proverbial sages is first of all sovereign over the world, his creation, and he is also a just God. The main result of this is a stable and just order operating within the cosmos, one in which evil returns evil but good is repaid by good. The retributive element of the divine order leads to a process of 'natural selection', removing those who fail to comply with it. In addition to being just, the proverbial God is also favourably inclined to humans, allowing them to gain insight into the nature of the world and the order he imposes on it, essentially wishing them to achieve satisfaction in life. Thus, although he does not grant humans success and satisfaction in life *per se* he fully equips them to achieve it, and also provides an environment which creates a genuine opportunity to that end; the proverbial world is a good place to be. There is only one obstacle that prevents human beings from finding true happiness, their reluctance to accept unconditionally the divinely instituted order and to live in harmony with it. However, even though the proverbial human is naturally inclined to disregard this order, this natural tendency can be overcome from within if sufficient effort is made and self-discipline applied. It is perhaps worth pointing out that here lies one of the fundamental differences between proverbial and cultic Yahwism, for in the cult this problem is solved from outwith, through the atoning rituals.

The Place of God and Ethics in Proverbial Wisdom

The proverbial religious attitudes are summarised by the phrase *fear of Yahweh*; the very first statement of the book about wisdom and knowledge [Prov 1:7] is the assertion that it starts with this fear. This is not an isolated claim in the book, but it is reiterated elsewhere [Prov 9:10; 15:33]; altogether the phrase *fear of Yahweh* appears 14 times in Proverbs. The occurrence in Prov 2:1–5 is of a particular interest. On this occasion the relationship between wisdom and *fear of Yahweh* is reversed—those who find wisdom will come to understand *fear of Yahweh*. At the same time it is affirmed that it is God who gives wisdom and knowledge. In other words, the relationship between wisdom and *fear of Yahweh* is portrayed here as reciprocal, each one being the source and consequence of the other; wisdom promotes piety and piety promotes wisdom. Thus, *fear of Yahweh* is not only the beginning of proverbial wisdom, it is also its end; it is the one phrase that the sages choose to summarise their entire undertaking.

The single most elaborate depiction of the attitudes and conduct summed up by this phrase is found in the following passage:

> Trust in Yahweh with all your heart, and do not lean on your understanding, know him in all your ways, and he will straighten your paths. Do not be wise in your own eyes—fear Yahweh and turn away from evil. There will be healing to your body and refreshment to your bones. Honour Yahweh from your wealth and from the choicest [part] of all your produce—and your stores will be filled abundantly, and your presses will burst with new wine. [Prov 3:5–10][1]

Fear of Yahweh, is essentially the awareness of the superior status that God has and voluntary acceptance of its implications by subjection to the divine authority and demand.

As we saw in chapter 4, cult plays an extremely limited role in Proverbs. As a result, the relationship between God and humans is largely indirect, *fear of Yahweh* has to do primarily with turning away from evil:

> Fear of Yahweh is to hate evil … [Prov 8:13]

> The person who walks uprightly fears Yahweh, but one who twists his ways despises him. [Prov 14:2]

> In loyalty and truth guilt is atoned for, and in the fear of Yahweh [one] turns away from evil. [Prov 16:6]

> May not your mind envy the sinners, but rather [may it be] always in the fear[2] of Yahweh. [Prov 23:17]

---

[1] For textual notes see p. 67.

[2] 𝔐 בְּיִרְאַת; Toy (1899:438) proposes to emend to ירא את, which would render a better sense, but the suggested emendation has no textual support and it is difficult to account for the ב. While it is true that it could have been inserted after ירא את was

The notions of good and evil are dictated by the stable nature of the proverbial world, which leads to a fairly rigid code of proper behaviour. The divine order defines what should be done, i.e., what is good, and what should not be done, i.e., what is evil.[3] These are absolute in Proverbs and all pervasive; virtually every activity that the book is interested in can be classified under these two rubrics. Yet, it would be misleading to think of good and evil in the book as abstract theological categories; in Proverbs these are largely about what people do to other people as can be illustrated by the following example:

> Soul of a wicked person craves evil, his neighbour is given no mercy in his eyes. [Prov 21:10]

Consequently, it is justified to view the proverbial advice as a system of religiously motivated ethics. In the present shape of the text, this ethical thrust of the overall outlook is reinforced by the introduction to the whole book:

> Proverbs of Solomon, son of David, King of Israel
>
> —to know wisdom and discipline, to comprehend words of understanding
>
> —to obtain instruction of insight,[4] of righteousness and justice, and of that which is upright [Prov 1:1–3]

The listing of righteousness, uprightness and justice alongside wisdom, discipline and comprehension, as the qualities that the book is hoping to instil in its readers, makes it clear that the proverbial sages aim much higher than to impart mere technical skills. From the very start, the reader is left in no doubt that in addition to the ability to make sound judgements, and to understand other people and their points of view, proverbial wisdom is about knowing and being committed to doing that which is right, that which is good for others.

---

corrupted to יראת, it is more likely that יראת would have been restored to ירא את instead of adding a new consonant. Thomas (1965:273) proposes to take יְרְאַת as a feminine abstract noun used as a collective term for a concrete subject, but none of the examples from Proverbs given by Driver (1951b:196), which Thomas refers to, are convincing.

[3] This is made explicit on a number of occasions when the book speaks of certain types of behaviour as an abomination to God, e.g., Prov 3:32; 6:16–19; 11:1, 20; 12:22; 15:9, 26; 16:5; 17:15; 20:10, 23.

[4] Infa. used substantively (Delitzsch, 1982a:54–55).

The opening verses are not the only place where the connection between wisdom and ethics is explicitly expressed. The already mentioned Prov 2:1ff. portrays a tree-way link between wisdom, piety, and ethics:

> My son, if you accept my words, and treasure up my commands with you, [if you] make your ear to pay attention[5] to wisdom, if you stretch your heart to understanding, indeed, if you call for comprehension, give your voice to understanding, if you seek her like silver, and like treasure you search her out—
>
> —then you will understand fear of Yahweh, and you will find knowledge of God.[6] For Yahweh gives wisdom; knowledge and understanding [come] from his mouth. He treasures up success[7] to the upright, he is a shield to those who walk blamelessly. He guards the paths of justice, and keeps the path of his loyal ones
>
> —then you will understand righteousness and justice, and that which is upright, every good track. For wisdom will enter your heart, and knowledge will be pleasant to your soul. Discernment will watch over you, understanding will guard you. [Prov 2:1–11]

Wisdom here leads to both understanding what it means to fear Yahweh, and what is meant by righteousness and justice, with success and happiness being tied to these.

Similarly, Dame Wisdom asserts that she utters what is righteous and upright:

> To you men, I call, and to humanity my voice [is directed]. [You] immature, understand prudence! And you fools, get sense! Listen, because I speak <important things>, and [when] I open my lips, [out comes] that which is right. For my palate utters truth and wickedness is an abomination to my lips. All the words of my mouth are in righteousness, there is no twistedness, no crookedness among them. All of them are straight to the one who understands, and upright to those who seek knowledge. Accept my instruction rather than silver and knowledge in place of choice gold. ... My fruit is better than gold, and than chryso-

---

[5] The infc. is best understood as having a finite function, with the son being its subject (אָזְנֶךָ in this idiomatic construction is an object of the verb); cf. ⅁ ܘܬܪܟܢ ܐܕܢܟ, *and you incline you ear.*

[6] Considering 5a, the construct is best understood as denoting objective genitive.

[7] The meaning of 𝔐 תּוּשִׁיָּה is uncertain. ⅏ renders σωτηρία, ⅁ ܡܒܝܐ, *opinion*. Jas suggests *salvation, stability, wisdom*. Delitzsch (1982a:77) understands this as a Hiphil-based formation from ישׁה, *to advance*, i.e., *advancement*. This is not an implausible interpretation in the context. Bauer (1930:77) argued for derivation from יֵשׁ and a quasi-verbal root ישׁי. However, Delitzsch earlier rejected, in my view justifiably, such a possibility pointing out that such a formation is without analogy.

lite, and my produce [is better] than choice silver. I walk in the path of
righteousness and in the middle of tracks of judgement. To make those
who love me inherit property and I fill their storehouses. [Prov 8:4–10,
19–21][8]

It should be observed that it is the ethical qualities of the revelation
that Wisdom offers that are the source of its value; it is here where the
promise of success and prosperity is grounded. In contrast, her oppo-
nent Folly advocates life governed by immediate satisfaction without
ethical considerations:

> Woman Folly is bustling about silliness,[9] and knows nothing.[10] She sits at
> the doors of her house, upon a seat at the heights of the city, to call to
> the passers by, whose paths are upright. 'Who is immature, turn here!,'
> and she says to the one who lacks sense: 'Stolen waters are sweet, and
> bread of secret places is pleasant.' But he does not know that there are
> ghosts there, those she summoned [before] are in the depth of Sheol.
> [Prov 9:13–18]

Life, which puts that which is 'sweet' and 'pleasant' before that which
is right, the sages say, is grounded in ignorance, in knowing nothing
about the real world. In the final analysis it leads only to disaster, even
death.

The religio-ethical dimension of wisdom is also made explicit in the
introduction to the second sub-collection of Prov 10–24:

> Pay attention and listen to words of wise men,[11] and set your mind to
> my knowledge. For they are pleasant, if you keep them in your belly, they
> will be ready together[12] upon your lips. So that your trust would be in
> Yahweh, I will teach you today, also you. Have I not written to you three

---

[8] For textual notes see p. 58.

[9] BHS proposal that אֵשֶׁת is a dittography is unlikely considering the balance of the
two colons, and the fact that there is no feminine form for כְּסִיל, cf. אֵשֶׁת־חַיִל (Driver,
1951b:178–79).

[10] 𝔊 Γυνὴ ἄφρων καὶ θρασεῖα ἐνδεὴς ψωμοῦ γίνεται, ἣ οὐκ ἐπίσταται αἰσχύνην, *foolish
and bold woman lacks morsel, but does not know shame*, but that appears to be an interpolation
of a struggling translator. 𝔖 ܐܢܬܬܐ ܫܛܝܬܐ ܘܡܫܪܚܬܐ ܕܠܐ ܝܕܥܐ ܒܗܬܬܐ, *woman
folly is deceiving, she does not know shame*. Thomas (1953) proposed on the basis of Arabic to
read ידע in the sense *to be still*, however, the presence of an object requires a transitive
verb.

[11] See note 14 on p. 27.

[12] The BHS proposed emendation of 𝔐 יַחְדָּו to (כְּ)יָתֵד, *(like) a peg*, on the grounds
of Amen. 1:16 is to be rejected, for the Egyptian parallel is insufficient and the Hebrew
makes good sense (reference being made to both the words of the wise and of the
father). See also note 28 on p. 89.

[times],[13] in counsels and knowledge, sayings genuine[ly][14] true, so that you may bring back truth to those who sent[15] you? [Prov 22:17–21]

The wisdom and knowledge on offer is both profitable from a personal point of view, but also it inspires trust in God and honesty in dealing with one's superiors. Further, the opening sayings of this collection exhort one not to deprive the poor of justice, not to move boundary stones and not to take advantage of the weak, orphans and widows.

While the opening nine chapters of the book offer the most eloquent formulation of the *importance* of ethical conduct for those who aspire to succeed in life, their ethical content *per se* is limited, in line with the observation made in chapter 2, namely, that it is the sayings that contain most of the book's advice, i.e., the formulation of the book's wisdom and ethics. Yet, it needs to be pointed out that the ethical outlook of Prov 1–9, to the extent it can be formulated, does not deviate from that of the sayings in any noticeable manner.

---

[13] 𝔐 K שִׁלְשׁוֹם, *the day before yesterday*, is difficult, but not entirely impossible considering the temporal reference in the previous verse (see Whybray, 1994b). Maire (1995) argued that שׁלשׁום is the name of the son to whom the instruction is addressed, drawing attention to similarities with Ugaritic text *Teaching of Shube'awilum*. 𝔐 Q שָׁלִישִׁים, a term denoting certain high ranking officials in David's administration, could only be understood here as a majestic vocative, but that fits ill with the father-son discourse. 𝔊 τρισσῶς, *threefold*, is a guess. שָׁלִשׁ has been understood as referring to thirty sayings (cf. thirty chapters in Amen.), but since there are not thirty clearly defined sayings in the Hebrew composition, this is questionable. If the Hebrew text has been derived from Amenemope, which I think is probable, the editor took such a degree of freedom in adjusting the material to his own purposes, that it is unlikely that he would have felt compelled to retain the reference to thirty sayings (for a more extensive argument reaching similar conclusions see Whybray, 1994b). 𝔊 ܐܠܬ ܘܬܒ, *three times*, possibly reading simply שָׁלִשׁ. This could have been used to denote three times as a shortcut for שָׁלֹשׁ פְּעָמִים, and changed to שִׁלְשׁוֹם by a later scribe who misunderstood the idiom. While in my view none of these solutions is entirely satisfactory, I follow 𝔊.

[14] 𝔐 קֹשְׁטְ אִמְרֵי אֱמֶת, many commentators consider קֹשְׁט, common in Aramaic, as a late gloss, but as Cody (1980:419) points out, if omitted the altered text is unusually short for this section of the book. He suggests that אִמְרִים אֱמֶת might have belonged to 21a, and a note on the form was made in the margin which slipped into 21b by accident replacing some other expression. While ingenious, the suggestion is not particularly convincing.

[15] 𝔐 לְשֹׁלְחֶיךָ; 𝔊 τοῖς προβαλλομένοις σοι leading some to emend to the root שאל. However, Cody (1980:419) points out that προβαλλω in the middle voice with a dative does not mean *to ask*, but *to accuse*, and the choice of the verb probably reflects an Egyptian influence. Cody then renders *to teach you probity fitting you to return reports which inspire confidence in the man who sends you.*

I disagree with those scholars who see in the religious and ethical dimensions of Proverbs some kind of a later deformity. One may, for instance, quote McKane (1970:16) who states with implicit reference to Proverbs:

> There is a tendency for wisdom at a certain stage of its development to lose touch with mundane realities and to construct an ideal scheme of things ... marked by ... antithesis formulated in ethical terms ... this is ... the theory of a kind of Yahwistic piety.

Proverbs is not a book that contains occasional ethical terminology, the whole of Proverbs is essentially about ethics, the distinction between good and evil is truly all pervasive. The book contains no technical advice on conducting any common activity, be it agriculture, skilled work or trade. On the occasions where such daily activities are touched upon, the sages' concerns are confined to their ethical aspects. In no sense, thus, can the book as a whole, or any of its parts, be perceived as a manual for 'mundane realities' (to use McKane's terminology), for such realities are nowhere to be found in Proverbs. This cannot be overemphasised—one could not make a living by merely following the proverbial advice. This makes the assertion that the book contains earlier secular wisdom, of no ethical concern, alongside later religio-ethical wisdom wholly untenable.[16]

It might be objected at this point that the criticism of McKane's view of the proverbial tradition is misplaced since the present study is not concerned with scrutiny of the historical development of the material, but looks at the text from a primarily synchronic perspective, examining the overall composite picture that the book paints. This would be to miss the point of the criticism. The view that there are two strata of material in the book, one earlier and secular, without ethical or religious concerns, and other later, marked by both ethical and religious sentiments, stands and falls with the assertion that the religio-ethical layer can be extracted from the material, leaving behind a meaningful non-religio-ethical layer that offers sober, down-to-earth guidance to dealing with the mundane realities of life. However, the religio-ethical

---

[16] The view that the ethical element found in Proverbs was in fact an integral part of the wisdom perspective from early on finds support elsewhere as well. The antithesis righteous/wicked is found repeatedly in the Aramaic Ahikar, showing that this type of proverb is certainly not exclusively Yahwistic, and further, the only text with the occurrence of the noun $hkmh$ in known Western Semitic inscriptions contains reference to righteousness (Weeks, 1994:69–70).

thrust is so pervasive in the book, and that if it is removed, what is left is of no practical use; if the ethical dimension is distilled from Proverbs, the book has not only nothing whatsoever to suggest about how to live, but also loses any authority. Thus, even though this study is not looking into the diachronic development of the proverbial tradition, it shows that the distinction between religio-ethical and non-religio-ethical material cannot be used as the starting point for such a diachronic analysis.

There is no doubt, that wisdom of the type found in Proverbs did lose touch with reality at some stage. However, the nature of the causality is not that suggested by McKane, but rather its reversal; ethical concerns do not appear in wisdom as a result of losing touch with reality, but rather the loss of touch is caused by the proverbial ethics. At the heart of the tension lies a paradox: the value of experience present is denied on the grounds of experience past; that which numerous generations affirmed as true came to be perceived not as long-lasting but as truly timeless. This is due to the theological perspective from which such understanding of experience stems; the notion that there could be a discrepancy between divine character and the immediate human experience is foreign to the tradition represented by Proverbs. The whole proverbial attitude has been aptly summarised by Van Leeuwen (1992:34):

> The sages' stance is to maintain faith in God's justice ... [The] book of Job was inevitable, not because Proverbs was too simplistic, but because life's inequities, as reflected in Proverbs, drive faith to argue with the Deity.

The Nature of the Proverbial Ethos

The proverbial system of ethics is built around two pivotal notions, that of equal justice for all, and that of preservation of harmony in relationships. In a perfect world, these two principles would go hand in hand and would be to a large extent synonymous. However, in a real world where justice is always only an ideal aspired to, and the proverbial world is a real world with wicked people and injustices, these two notions stand in a partial tension. The process of accomplishing justice carries with it the unavoidable aggravation and alienation of the parties involved. Consequently, an ethical system based on these two ideals will have to resort to a compromise. In the case of Proverbs, emphasis is placed on justice for others and avoidance of conflict on one's own behalf. Thus, the reader is exhorted to treat others fairly and to see that others in the community are treated fairly, but nowhere do the sages encourage one, for instance, to start legal proceedings on one's own behalf. To the contrary:

> Fool's lips enter into argument, and his mouth asks for beating. [Prov 18:6]
>
> The beginning of strife is setting water[17] free, before the argument bursts out, drop it! [Prov 17:14]
>
> Do not come out quickly to argue your case,[18] lest what will you do at its end, when your opponent puts you to shame? [Prov 25:8]
>
> There is deceit in the heart of those who devise evil, but those who advise peace have joy. [Prov 12:20]

These proverbs are a warning against starting conflicts. A wise person avoids aggravating others and does not allow conflict to escalate; indeed, a wise person is a peacemaker.

In order to follow the proverbial advice and avoid conflict, it is necessary that a person understands what its root causes are. A number of sayings, therefore, deal with the question of how conflict arises and what perpetuates it:

> A perverse man causes disputes, and a slanderer alienates a friend. [Prov 16:28]
>
> Hatred stirs up strife, but love covers over all transgressions. [Prov 10:12]
>
> An angry man gets engaged in a strife, but a patient person appeases a dispute. [Prov 15:18]
>
> Charcoal to burning coals and wood to fire, and a quarrelsome man to make strife glow. [Prov 26:21]
>
> One who covers up transgression seeks love, but he who revels[19] in a matter, alienates a friend. [Prov 17:9]

---

[17] ⑥ λόγοις, probably reading מִלִּים, which destroys the poetic imagery; 𝔐 is preferable.

[18] Driver (1951b:190) proposed to render מָה as indefinite rather than interrogative, along the lines *lest you do something* ... but the object would normally be expected after the verb. Others propose, in conjunction with the suggestion to re-divide v. 7 and 8, to read רֹב in place of 𝔐 רָב, with the sense *do not reveal to many [people]* (e.g. Toy 1899:460). While such a reading is quite plausible, 𝔐 makes equally good sense and is supported by both ⑥ and Ⓢ.

[19] Rendering freely 𝔐 שֹׁנֶה, *repeats*; ⑥ μισεῖ, i.e., שֹׂנֵא, but the rest of the verse is clearly interpolated from the context, thus casting doubts on the textcritical value of the ⑥.

Emptiness[20] with insolence produces strife, as for mutual consultation, that is wisdom. [Prov 13:10]

Some conflicts are caused by third parties, sometimes through careless talk, sometimes quite intentionally for personal benefit. However, the prime source of conflict is, in the sages' view, lack of self-control. People who are irritable, or get carried away by negative emotions such as hate, cause trouble. In contrast, a wise person is self-controlled, and approaches life in a rational manner, seeking rational resolution. Further, within the tightly-knit proverbial world problems are to be approached in a collective manner; collective wisdom has the potential to overcome the negative bias of an individual and to approach any problem from a more neutral position.

While the sages prefer conflicts to be avoided or pacified before they gain serious proportions, they are aware that this is not always achievable. Although harmony in the community has a high priority, the ideal of justice for all cannot be abandoned because it reflects one of the basic tenets of the proverbial cosmology, that of divine retribution. Consequently, there is a need for certain formal means that can be used to resolve conflicts where the two parties cannot reach an acceptable solution by themselves. When a formal dispute cannot be avoided, Proverbs offers certain guidelines about how to deal with it. First of all, a personal vendetta is discouraged by the sages, even to the extent of prohibiting rejoicing at the misfortunes of one's enemies:

> Do not say: 'Let me recompense for evil!', wait for Yahweh and he will rescue you! [Prov 20:22]

> When your enemy falls, do not rejoice, and when he stumbles, do not let your heart exult. Lest Yahweh will see [it] and it will be evil in his sight, and he will turn his anger away from him. [Prov 24:17–18]

> If one who hates you is hungry, feed him with bread and if he is thirsty give him water to drink, for you are raking burning coals upon his head and Yahweh will recompense you. [Prov 25:21–22][21]

These proverbs show the unshakeable proverbial conviction that justice is not just a divinely inspired ideal, but that it is consistently enforced by God. Further, we can see here that the threshold that triggers divine involvement is very low, and even a desire for revenge can in itself constitute an offence against the divine standard. The third saying

---

[20] 𝔐 רַק, *only*, 𝔊 reading רַע; I follow McKane (1970:454) repointing to רֵק, *empty*.

[21] For textual notes see p. 106.

then suggests that avoidance of personal revenge and repaying good
for evil can have greater impact on the guilty party than retaliation
would accomplish. Again, confidence in the ultimate sufficiency of the
divine retributive order is quite clear here.

While all of these proverbs refer to, and emphasise, the cosmic
system of retributive justice upheld by God, this does not mean that the
sages principally objected to human-administered justice. The existence
of a formal juridical system is clearly detectable in Proverbs, even
though as far as the procedures are concerned, the information that
the book offers is limited. It was pointed out in the previous chapter
that formal conflicts were settled at the city gate by those respected in
the community, or even by the king. It appears that on these occasions
the verdicts were reached primarily by consideration of the facts when
both parties were allowed to put forward their point of view.

> Who begins the[22] dispute [seems] in the right, but then his neighbour
> comes and cross-examines him. [Prov 18:17]

However, sometimes a solution could be found by the use of a lot:

> Lot settles disputes, and separates between litigants.[23] [Prov 18:18]

This alternative is yet another sign of the sages' conviction of the
absolute divine control over the world.

Within the juridical process an important role is played by witnesses.
False testimony is considered a serious offence, as can be seen from the
number of sayings that condemn such behaviour [e.g. Prov 19:5]. In
addition, the proverbial sages do not possess the modern notion of the
right not to self-incriminate oneself. To the contrary, they expect the
guilty party to come clean:

> Whoever covers up his transgression will not prosper, but he who con-
> fesses and repents will be shown compassion. [Prov 28:13]

While the information concerning the juridical procedures is scarce, the
proverbial principles are simple and clear: to punish the guilty and to
justify the innocent:

> He who justifies a guilty person and condemns an innocent one—both
> of them are an abomination to Yahweh. [Prov 17:15]

---

[22] Heb. *his*.

[23] 𝔐 עֲצוּמִים, *mighty men*. I follow Driver's (1951:183) proposal to read עוֹצְמִים, *litigants*,
from *עצם , cf. Syriac ܥܨܡ, *to go to law*; the case for the existence of such a Hebrew
verb is strengthened by the use of עֲצֻמוֹת, *pleas*, in a legal context of Isa 41:21.

> To fine an innocent man is not right, or beat nobles[24] for [their] integri-
> ty.[25] [Prov 17:26]

> It is not good to show partiality to a guilty man in order to deprive an
> innocent person of justice. [Prov 18:5]

In contrast to our modern-day justice process where emphasis is placed
on not condemning the innocent, to let the guilty go unpunished is
equally wrong for the proverbial sages as condemning the innocent.
Both situations are unacceptable, for both fall short of the divine ideal.

Advice is offered not only to those who fulfil the function of the
arbiter, but also to the interested parties concerning how one should
argue one's case:

> Argue your case with your opponent, but do not reveal what someone
> else confided [in you]. Lest the one who hears will insult you, your bad
> reputation will not go away. [Prov 25:9–10]

Here the sages warn against betraying the confidence of third parties;
a mishandled dispute can seriously damage one's reputation. It would
appear from this instruction, that the sages were concerned that the
conflict does not spread beyond the two parties immediately involved
[cf. Prov 26:17]. Such a concern is not surprising, for nothing could be
more destructive to the proverbial society than a conflict that would
end up polarising the whole community.

The no-conflict policy of Proverbs is not concerned with actions
alone. It has been pointed out in the previous chapter that the inner
mental element of human existence is of a greater importance in the
proverbial perspective than external appearances. This is to some extent reflected in the emphasis on thought, and in particular on thought
expressed, i.e., speech. The spoken word is seen as having great power
which can be directed toward both good and bad ends. It is the key to
harmonious relationships and the ability to speak properly is, therefore,
of an immense value. Speech can mean the difference between success
and prosperity on the one hand and suffering on the other [e.g. Prov
12:19; 13:2; 18:7; 29:8]. The basic rule of sound speech in Proverbs is
'less is more'; garrulity is perceived as a sign of foolishness and a sure
way to get into trouble [e.g. Prov 10:19; 13:3].

---

[24] 𝔐(𝔊) נְדִיבִים‎; Toy (1899:353) wishes to take it, on the grounds of Arabic, in the
moral sense *righteous*. Such use is not attested in the OT, but cf. 𝔊 ܠܕ̈ܝܩܐ, *the righteous*.

[25] 𝔐 עַל־יֹשֶׁר‎ is difficult; McKane (1970:507) renders *improper* and Toy (1899:353)
reads בַּל־יָשָׁר‎ on the grounds of 𝔊 οὐδὲ ὅσιον, *not pure/sanctified*.

Sound speech comes as the result of reasoning, those who are quick to talk are bound to cause hurt. In contrast, the speech of wise people is soothing:

> Rash talking[26] is like stabbing with a sword, but the tongue of wise people is healing. [Prov 12:18]

What is said, in one way or another, has an impact on the speaker, the audience and also any people spoken about. It became apparent in the previous chapter that in the close-knit proverbial world reputation is a person's livelihood. It is, therefore, not at all surprising that those who ruin other people's reputations through malicious talk are disapproved of [e.g. Prov 11:9; 26:20], the reasons for that being captured in the following saying:

> Words of a slanderer are like greedily swallowed[27] [food] and they descend into deep chambers of [one's] bowels. [Prov 18:8]

The problem with slander is that it is unlikely to be simply ignored, people are eager to hear gossip, it takes root, and is impossible to undo.

We have observed in the preceding chapter that the proverbial society is largely made of equals, and this fact projects itself into the notion of preserving harmonious relationships with others. This principle does not apply merely to the relationships that are seen as potentially beneficial to a person, but also to situations where one may not get anything tangible out of such a harmony:

> Do not deny what is good to those to whom it belongs,[28] when your hand is capable to carry it out. Do not tell your neighbour: 'Go, come back, and tomorrow I will give [it to you]', while you have it with you. [Prov 3:27–28]

---

[26] In the light of the parallelism the ptc. is best understood impersonally.

[27] Hebrew כְּמִתְלַהֲמִים is difficult. The verse is missing in 𝕲 but in the identical proverb in Prov 26:22 𝕲 renders μαλακοί, *soft*; while 𝕾 is too free to be of real value. The translation adopted above, based on Arabic *lhm, to swallow avidly*, appears to be the best option (see Toy 1899:359–60).

[28] 𝔐 אַל־תִּמְנַע־טוֹב מִבְּעָלָיו; 𝕾 ܐܠܐ ܬܟܠܐ ܠܚܒܪܟ ܐ, *do not refuse to do good*, i.e., מִבְּעָלָיו was either omitted, or the translator read לִמְעַבֵד. 𝕲 μὴ ἀπόσχῃ εὖ ποιεῖν ἐνδεῆ, *do not withhold good, doing short of [your power?]*, cf. τῆς δυνάμεως ἐνδεᾶ πρᾶξαι, *to act short of real power* (L&S). Toy (1899:79) rejected 𝔐 on the grounds that בַּעַל always denotes the one who controls something, and בַּעַל טוֹב cannot, therefore, refer to one to whom good is done. However, the construction *owner of* is primarily a syntactical means of forming expressions of characterisation from nouns, i.e., A is characterised by / associated with X, but not necessarily implying that A is in control, dispenses or employs X. Consider *owner of dreams*, i.e., one to whom dreams happen [Gen 37:19]; an *owner of affairs*, i.e., one

> There is a person who scatters and still accumulates, and [another] withholding from what is right only to have lack. [Prov 11:24]

> He who gives to the poor does not have lack, but he who shuts his eyes, [receives] many curses. [Prov 28:27]

> She opens the palm of her hand to the poor, and her hands stretch forward to the underprivileged. [Prov 31:20]

The proverbial sages considered it wise to be helpful when one can, to be generous and to have compassion for the poor.

Within the body of the proverbial material that is concerned with preservation of harmony among human beings, there is one group of texts that deserves particular attention. As it was pointed out in the previous chapter, the central socio-economic unit of the proverbial world is the family. In order to ensure the prosperity of the larger community it is necessary to preserve the coherence of the family unit:

> He who maltreats [his] father and drives away [his] mother is a disgraceful son and behaves shamefully. [Prov 19:26][29]

> He who steals from his father and mother and says that it is not a crime, he is a companion to the man who destroys. [Prov 28:24]

The concern with preservation of the family unity within a particular generation can be seen mainly in the material that deals with the question of adultery and prostitution. This topic is most emphatically developed in Prov 5:1–23, 6:24–35 both of which are worth quoting at length:

> My son, pay attention to my wisdom ... For the lips of adulteress[30] drip honey, and her palate is smoother than oil. But her ends are bitter like wormwood, sharp like a two-edged sword. Her feet descend to death,

---

who is involved in a matter without having a full control over it [Exod 24:14)]; an *owner of hair*, i.e., a hairy man [2 Kgs 1:8]; *owners of horses* [2 Sam 1:6] implying control, but not ownership, since these are the possession of the king; in the case of *owner of tongue* [Qoh 10:11] possession is clearly not the issue at all. Further, בַּעַל itself can denote rightful ownership rather than present control [Gen 20:3]. Thus, while admittedly there is no other use of the construction that would be parallel to בַּעַל טוֹב, there is nothing to warrant a conclusion that it cannot express both an actual and desirable state. Since the construction of the type אִישׁ טוֹב refers unequivocally to a person who does good, this could be the only succinct way available to the author to express the desirable, yet unreal, ownership, with the semantic ambiguity being resolved by the context.

[29] For textual notes see p. 141.

[30] The context, particularly the external threat to which the involvement with the *strange/other* woman leads, shows quite clearly that she is a woman of *another man* (*pace* McKane, 1970:314, who considers the woman to be a prostitute).

her steps are grasping Sheol. The path of life she does not watch,[31] her paths are unsteady—she does not know. ... Distance your way from her, do not draw near to the door of her house, lest you give your strength to others and your years[32] to one who is cruel. Lest strangers are sated from your strength, and [the product of] your pain [is found] in the house of a stranger. Then you will groan[33] in your end, in the destruction of your flesh and body, and you will say: '... I came so near to a total disaster, in the midst of the assembly and congregation.' Drink water from your cistern, and the trickling water from the midst of your well [or] they will spill out [water] from your spring into the street, streams of water into the squares. Let them be to you alone, and do not share them with strangers. May your well be blessed, so that you rejoice in the wife of your youth. A doe in heat and a graceful mountain goat, her breasts, may they satisfy you all the time, may her love have you in its power always. Why should you my son be led astray by an adulteress, and embrace the lap of a strange woman. For the eyes of Yahweh are fixed [on] the ways of man, and all his paths he watches. The guilt of the wicked will ensnare him, and he will be tied by the ropes of his sin. He will die, because there was no discipline, and in much folly he will go astray.[34] [Prov 5:1–23]

For a command is a lamp and teaching is a light, and the rebukes of instruction are the path of life—to keep you from the evil[35] woman, from the smooth tongue of[36] the adulterous woman. Do not desire her beauty in your heart and do not let her take you by her eyes. Because of a prostitute [you will be reduced] to a loaf of bread, but a wife of [another] man will hunt down your precious life.[37] Can a man rake fire into his lap without scorching his clothes? If one walks on burning coal, will not his

---

[31] 𝔐 פֶּן־תְּפַלֵּס; I follow here KBL-3 Akkadian-based proposal for פלס II, *to observe, to examine*; both 𝔊 and 𝔖 understood this in the sense *she does not walk in the path of life*.

[32] McKane (1970:316) proposes Arabic derivation for שׁנה, rendering *dignity*, but such a meaning is unattested in Hebrew and the emendation is unnecessary as 𝔐 makes good sense.

[33] 𝔐; נָהַמְתָּ; 𝔊(𝔖) μεταμεληθήσῃ, *you will repent/regret*, possibly reading נֶחַמְתָּ, which fits well the context.

[34] 𝔊 ἀπώλετο, *was destroyed*, for which BHS suggests יִסָּפֶה in the Vorlage, but more likely this is a guess on behalf of the translator who did not know שׁגה (note that he does not render it in either Prov 7:19–20).

[35] 𝔐 רָע; 𝔊 ὑπάνδρου, *married*, i.e., רֵעַ; 𝔐 supported by 𝔖, but both readings are plausible.

[36] Reading as a construct, cf. 𝔖.

[37] Since a prostitute is not exactly synonymous with a wife of another man, I am inclined to agree with McKane (1970:329–30) and Toy (1899:136–37) that the וְ is adversative here; the prostitute represents a serious threat, but the wife of another man spells total disaster. McKane prefers to render נֶפֶשׁ יְקָרָה as *man of means*, on the grounds that the resulting parallelism is better. However, one would expect אִישׁ rather than נֶפֶשׁ to be used in such a construction.

feet burn? So anyone who enters to the wife of his neighbour will not escape punishment, anyone who touches her. They are not[38] in the habit of despising a thief if he steals to satisfy his appetite because he suffers hunger. But [if] he is found, he will have to make a sevenfold restitution, he will have to give all the possessions of his house. He who commits adultery with a woman lacks sense, he who does so, is destroying his life. Beating and disgrace he will find, his dishonour will not be wiped out. Since jealousy [drives] the husband's anger, he will have no compassion in the day of revenge. He will not accept any satisfaction and will not consent no matter how big the gift. [Prov 6:23–35]

The passion with which the father admonishes the son here is striking; the only other occasions of such a passionate language are found in the admonitions to pursue Dame Wisdom. This strong rhetoric shows that this issue is perceived by the speaker as of the utmost importance.

Notably, the urgency with which the father speaks stems here from practical economic concerns rather than abstract morality. This is most obvious in the latter passage in the contrast between involvement with a prostitute and committing adultery. Both of these are perceived in negative terms, yet, the consequences of the latter are seen as much more serious, and it is against adultery that the passage is primarily aimed. The central issue here is not the morality of sexual intercourse outside of marriage, but rather the socio-economic impact of illicit sexual behaviour. Both passages speak of adultery as necessarily resulting in disgrace and destruction. The husband's resources are channelled to some other household, strangers take over and enjoy what he worked hard for. What is, however, even more interesting, is the imagery of spilled water we find in the former text. There is little doubt that the well here is a metaphor for the wife, i.e., it is the wife's resources that are in some sense squandered, let out into the open, into the public domain—it is apparent that both the husband and the wife are seriously effected. While the sexual overtones of the imagery of giving out strength and spilled water are unmistakable, the reference here is to the entirety of the couple's being; what is dissolving and flowing out is not merely their sexual bond, but their entire existence. Adultery breaks

---

[38] Toy (1899:139) emends to a positive statement, on the grounds that there is no sign of this sort of leniency in the OT and that the thief here is a man of property. Yet, property cannot always provide food, and there is no leniency in the formal treatment of the thief, only in human attitude to him (note the habitual use of Px throughout this verse—the text does not envisage a man who is momentarily hungry, but who suffers hunger as a chronic condition). McKane (1970:220) prefers to render the verse as a question, but this type of question is regularly introduced by הֲלֹא (e.g. Prov 8:1).

apart the family framework and in Proverbs there is no prosperous life outside of it.

While the former passage relates the primary impact on the family of the adulterer, the latter passage also brings into the discussion the damage caused to the husband of the adulterous woman. The comparison with the hungry thief here illuminates the mechanism of the economic disaster depicted in the previous passage. Two major factors are involved in the adulterer's downfall. First, he, in contrast to the hungry thief, comes to be despised by the wider community, and second, the damage that he caused to the other man is perceived as so grievous, that in practical terms restitution cannot be made; the offended husband will pursue the other man to a complete destruction, with the tacit support of the community.

The concern about the impact of adultery and prostitution is not limited to the first nine chapters of the book, although it finds its most forcible formulation there. A similar perspective is found in the following sayings:

> My son, give me your mind, let your eyes guard my ways. For a prostitute[39] is a deep pit, and a foreign woman is a narrow well. Also, she is like a robber lying in ambush, and she adds [to] the unfaithful among men. [Prov 23:26–28]

> A man who loves wisdom makes his father happy, but a companion of prostitutes squanders wealth. [Prov 29:3]

> This is the way of a woman committing adultery: she eats and wipes her mouth, and she says, 'I have not committed wickedness'. [Prov 30:20]

Again, involvement with a prostitute or another man's wife is seen as a cause of disaster, as wasting of wealth and resources.

On the issue of marriage, it can be further observed that the expression אֵשֶׁת נְעוּרֶךָ in Prov 5:18 accompanied by בְּכָל־עֵת and תָּמִיד in v. 19 implies that a marriage is a long-term relationship for which no endpoint is envisaged. A similar perspective is implied by several sayings portraying a marriage that is not satisfactory from the husband's point of view:

> A woman of valour is a crown of her husband, but like rot in one's bones is one who brings shame. [Prov 12:4]

---

[39] זוֹנָה ;זֹנָה ﬡ ἀλλότριος, i.e., זָרָה (McKane, 1970:390). Note, however, that in ﬡ the topic is not a woman, but a house. Thus the whole verse has a rather different thrust.

> A foolish son is a destruction to his father, and a contentious wife is a continuous dripping. [Prov 19:13][40]

> It is better to dwell in a desolate land, than [to have] a contentious wife and grief. [Prov 21:19]

> It is better to dwell in the corner of a roof, than [to have] a house in common[41] with a quarrelsome wife. [Prov 25:24]

> Continuous dripping[42] on a rainy day, and a quarrelsome wife are alike. [Prov 27:15]

All of these verses paint such a state of affairs as most undesirable, yet, they also imply permanency of such an arrangement; the concept of divorce seems to be foreign to Proverbs. This is notable since provision for divorce is made in, for instance, the legal OT traditions. This fact further underlines the importance that the stability of the family framework has for the proverbial world. Divorce undermines the coherence of the family and also of the broader community by causing damage to relationships between the wider families that are related through such a terminated marriage. We have seen so far that the proverbial views concerning marriage are driven by economic concerns, it is more than likely that also the absence of divorce from Proverbs has its roots here, probably in matters of ownership of land.

Beyond the basic principles of juridical justice and family-centred ethics, Proverbs presents the reader with rather clearly defined work and business ethics. While wisdom is portrayed in Proverbs as the ultimate source of wealth and success, this is not to be understood in some abstract manner:

> The sluggard's appetite desires and nothing happens, but the soul of the diligent people will fatten. [Prov 13:4]

> Who is idle in his own business is a brother to one who destroys what belongs to him. [Prov 18:9]

Wealth does not come through mere shrewdness or intellectual speculation, but through hard work. Thus, diligence is one of the prime proverbial virtues, while laziness is despised.

Furthermore, wisdom is not a guide as to how to get rich quickly. Rather, prosperity comes gradually as a result of persistent endeavour

---

[40] For textual notes see p. 142.

[41] Albright's (1955:11) suggestion that וּבֵית חָבֵר means *brewery* is unconvincing, as the regular sense fits the context better.

[42] For discussion of the verb טרד see Greenfield (1958:210–12).

and skill; there are no shortcuts and the proverbial emphasis on justice projects itself forcibly into the arena of commerce and related activities [e.g. Prov 11:1; 13:11; 20:10; 21:6; 22:29; 28:20]. It becomes apparent from the numerous sayings that while success and prosperity are the aim and the driving force behind the proverbial wisdom, the ethical ideal of justice and fairness is more important to the sages than these; the following proverb expresses it in the clearest of terms:

> Better is little in righteousness than great produce in injustice. [Prov 16:8]

In addition to open dishonesty, such as short measures, certain other business practices are perceived as unethical in Proverbs. These include speculation with food and charging interest:

> People curse a person who withholds grain, but there is blessing for the head of one who sells. [Prov 11:26]

> He who amasses wealth through interest and usury, gathers it for someone else, one gracious to the poor. [Prov 28:8]

Further, under the category of work ethics falls the responsibility to pay due attention to livestock:

> A righteous person knows the needs[43] of his animal, but the bowels of wicked people are cruel. [Prov 12:10]

This is not just a piece of practical advice on farming, but rather it is an extension of the ethical considerations beyond the confines of inter-human relationships, and fits in with the observation made earlier concerning the coherence of the proverbial world and the applicability of the divine order to it in its entirety.

One other issue that belongs under the ethics category is that of using bribes. This is an area where the sages' views are somewhat ambiguous. Sometimes a bribe appears as a useful tool, sometimes it is condemned. For McKane (1970:18) this is one of the indications that the early wisdom was secular without ethical concerns, thus approving of bribes, while only in the later wisdom the attitude has changed. However, there is another possible explanation of this seeming tension. It can be observed that bribery is condemned only where it is intended to manipulate the process of justice. On the occasions where the view of it seems to be positive, it is used to other ends, such as to improve one's social standing, or to pacify an enemy:

---

[43] The Hebrew נֶפֶשׁ encapsulates the tangible experience of life.

A wicked person takes a gift under the table,[44] in order to stretch justice. [Prov 17:23]

A man's gift makes room for him, it lets him rest before the great. [Prov 18:16]

A gift in concealment covers anger, and a present under the table[45] [covers][46] a great rage. [Prov 21:14]

It is, therefore, possible, that these verses do not witness to a diachronic change in an attitude, but rather to an ethical perspective on use of gifts different than that of the modern western society. That this is likely is confirmed by the conformity of this attitude to the basic tenets of the proverbial ethics, upholding of justice and promoting of harmonious relationships. A gift as a means of perverting justice is unacceptable, but a gift as a means of building and strengthening relationships with others is not only legitimate, but also desirable.

Wisdom of Qoheleth

Fundamentals of Qoheleth's Wisdom

It is quite easy to overlook the fact that Qoheleth's aim is at least in principle very much the same as that of the proverbial sages; they are all interested in the question of how to make the most of life. The reason why this principal similarity may go easily unnoticed, lies in the fact that Qoheleth's understanding of the world is very different from that of the proverbial wise men. I have argued in chapter 4 that the basic characteristic of Qoheleth's world is an overall equilibrium between the positive and the negative events and experiences in life, and that this equilibrium means that no permanent and lasting gain can be made in life. However, I have also pointed out that the paired positive and negative events are not synchronic, i.e., there are temporary situations of gain, as well as temporary situations of loss. The occurrences and disappearances of these states do not happen according to any predictable pattern, they are governed by chance:

---

[44] Lit. *from lap*, i.e., secretly.

[45] Lit. *in the lap*, i.e., secretly.

[46] ⅏ took this as antithetical (Toy 1899:404), construing the B colon as a nominal sentence, but it is quite clear that the two lines are synonymous with the verb being gapped in the B colon.

And again I saw under the sun, that the race is not to the swift and the
battle is not to the mighty, and neither is bread to the wise, nor riches to
the intelligent, nor is favour to the knowledgeable, for time and chance[47]
may happen to[48] all of them. For a person also does not know his time:
like fish that are caught in an evil net, and like birds caught in the snare,
so human beings are trapped[49] at an evil time as it suddenly falls upon
them. [Qoh 9:11–12]

Because human effort and insight cannot predict and/or control changing fortune, the only hope of getting something positive out of life lies
in fully exploiting the good times while coping with the bad times. It is
within this context that Qoheleth understands wisdom:

And I saw that wisdom has an advantage over stupidity, like the advantage of light over darkness. The wise person has eyes in his head, while
the fool walks in darkness. But I also came to know that the same chance
happens to both of them. [Qoh 2:13–14][50]

And I said: 'Wisdom is better than strength, but wisdom of a poor person
is despised, his words are not listened to.' The quiet words of the wise are
to be heeded more than the shouting[51] of a ruler over fools. Wisdom is
better than weapons, but one sinner destroys much good. Dead flies[52]
cause a cup[53] of aromatic[54] oil to stink, and a little folly abounds[55] over
wisdom. [Qoh 9:16-10:1]

Wisdom has some relative, but no absolute, value; it has a potential
but this potential can be easily thwarted. Consequently, *wisdom* means

---

[47] Fox (1989:260) sees here a hendiadys, *time of accident*, but in the light of the very
particular use of עֵת in Qoh 3:1–9 discussed earlier the וְ is better seen as a regular
copula.

[48] For the same syntax of יִקְרֶה אֶת־ see Qoh 2:14.

[49] יוּקָשִׁים is an unusual form, possibly an old form of Qal pass. ptc., or Pu ptc. that
lost the מ prefix through haplography.

[50] For textual notes see p. 154.

[51] זְעָקָה is always used of a cry under adverse circumstances as Ogden (1987b:162)
pointed out, although his assertion that it is specifically a cry for help is not justified (cf.
Esth 4:3).

[52] Lit. *flies of death*, an attributive genitive, cf. ⵂ; Fox (1989:264–5) suggests re-dividing
the consonants זבוב ימות rendering *a fly dies and spoils* ..., but that is unnecessary.

[53] Reading גְּבִיעַ, *cup*, with ⵂ; ⵂ σκευασία, *dressing*; יָבִיעַ is omitted by σ', ⵉ, ⵛ. This
could indicate dittography with יַבְאִישׁ, but in the light of ⵂ and ⵂ, it is more probable
that the omission is due to the difficulties with the understanding of the word.

[54] 𝔐 רוֹקֵחַ; I am reading with ⵂ ἡδύσματος, *spicy*, i.e., רֹקַח, cf. ⵂ ⵏⵎⵙⵙⵂ, *pleasant,
sweet*.

[55] Emending 𝔐 מִכָּבוֹד to מַכְבִּיר, cf. BHS. This is the easiest way to supply a
contextually meaningful verb to the clause. It is not necessary to emend further to
create a feminine form of the ptc, since a masculine form of a verb is not unusual when
the feminine subject follows it (see Jou §150b and note 83 on p. 115).

something quite different in Qoheleth than it does in Proverbs. The proverbial sages aspired to excellence and wisdom was ultimately a perfect tool producing impeccable results if adopted wholeheartedly. In contrast, for Qoheleth wisdom is a tool that can only improve one's odds and even that cannot be guaranteed.

What then are the practical aspects of Qoheleth's wisdom? The most noticeable element of it is the call to enjoy life repeated throughout the book. It finds its fullest expression in the following passage:

> Go! Eat your bread with joy, and drink your wine in enjoyment of heart, for God has already paid off[56] your deeds. Let your clothes always be white, and may there not be shortage of oil upon your head. Enjoy life with a woman whom you love all the days of your absurd existence, which[57] he gave to you under the sun, all your absurd days, for that is your share in life, and in the work which you carry out under the sun. Whatever you may be able to do, do it with your vigour,[58] for there is no doing or devising or knowledge or wisdom in Sheol, where you are [already][59] going. [Qoh 9:7–10]

Qoheleth's emphasis on enjoyment has often been understood as hedonistic, advocating a superficial *carpe diem* approach to life, in which only the present matters, and the future should be ignored. Yet, the intention of these calls, and the real nature of the attitude from which they spring, is rather different. First of all, the reference to eating and drinking cannot be taken in a limited literal manner, and even less so as an encouragement of a lazy lifestyle. What Qoheleth has in mind is not a life of idleness and orgies, but rather the phrase *eat and drink* represents personal satisfaction in a broader sense, and what is most important, one that comes as the result of work. This is made quite clear in v. 10 of the quoted passage: the call to enjoyment is a call to act, to apply intelligence, knowledge and wisdom, and then to enjoy what comes out as a result of such an activity, providing anything does. The satisfaction

---

[56] I am taking this as רצה II, *to pay off, restitute* [e.g. Lev 26:41, 43], as this makes good sense in the context where the enjoyment is the only reward for one's work. However, the context does not make reading רצה I impossible (cf. KBL-3).

[57] אֲשֶׁר understood as referring to *days of your absurd existence*. Against understanding אִשָּׁה as the referent (Ogden, 1987b:153) speaks the presence of the qualifying *under the sun*, and the repetition of *all your absurd days*.

[58] I follow 𝔊 understanding בְּכֹחֲךָ as an adverbial modifier for עֲשֵׂה, *pace* 𝔐 accents, which link it with עֲשׂוֹת. This appears to be a slightly better reading, as בְּכֹחֲךָ conveys a notion that is already implicitly present in the idiom מָצָא יָד.

[59] The ptc. underlines that this is an activity that is presently underway.

derived from one's endeavour is the best one can hope for, it is the best that life can offer.

That Qoheleth's attitude is not that of a carefree hedonism is further shown by the material in the book that encourages the contemplation of more serious and less enjoyable matters:

> It is better to go to a house of mourning than to go to a house of feasting because that is the end of every person, and the living one should ponder [it]. Sadness is better than laughter, for when the face is distressed, the mind will be well. The mind of the wise is in the house of mourning, but the mind of fools is in the house of joy. [Qoh 7:2–4][60]

> The light is sweet and it is pleasant for eyes to see the sun. Indeed, if a person lives many years, let him rejoice in all of them, but let him remember the dark days, for they could be many, all that comes is absurd. Young man rejoice in your youth, and let your heart make you happy in your young days, and walk in the ways of your heart,[61] and visions of your eyes, but know that concerning all of these God will bring you into judgement. Remove anger[62] from your heart, make evil pass away from your body, for youth and <prime of life>[63] are absurd. And remember your creator in the days of your youth, before the bad days come, and years will approach when you say: 'I have no pleasure in them.' [Qoh 11:7-12:1]

The emphasis on enjoying the product of one's work is only a particular example of a more general principle that characterises Qoheleth's wisdom, that of seizing the day. More light is thrown on this issue by the advice of the concluding part of the book:

> If the clouds are full of water, it will rain upon the land, and whether a tree[64] may fall to the south, or to the north, the tree will be on the place where it fell. He who watches for wind, may never sow, and he who observes the clouds may never harvest. Just as you do not know

---

[60] For textual notes see p. 156.

[61] Some 𝕲 manuscripts + ἄμωμος *blamelessly*, as well as supplying a negative in the following clause; this is almost certainly an intentional change narrowing the scope of possible interpretation.

[62] In the light of the parallelism with רָעָה in the B colon this would appear to be a more appropriate rendering for כַּעַס than *anxiety*.

[63] The Hebrew שַׁחֲרוּת is obscure, but the overall sense seems clear. Gordis (1955a:337) points out possibly related Arabic *šariḥ, youth*, but I find more plausible Ibn Ezra's explanation that the word has been coined from שַׁחַר, *dawn*, and formed along the same pattern as יַלְדוּת (see Rottzoll, 1999:236–37).

[64] Barton (1908:182–3) thinks that עֵץ in v. 3 refers to a divination stick tossed in the air on the basis of Hos 4:12. However, it is not at all implied by Hos 4:12, that the talk is about a stick tossed into the air, and furthermore, in the present case the nature-imagery of the A colon suggests a similar sense for the B colon.

what the path of the breath [is] in[65] the bones in the womb of a pregnant [woman],[66] so you cannot know the activity of God who does[67] all these. In the morning sow your seed, and do not rest your hand until[68] the evening, for you do not know, which of these will succeed, this or that, or whether both of them will be equally good. [Qoh 11:3–6]

Qoheleth is not just concerned that one seizes the opportunity to enjoy oneself, but more generally, that one seizes the moment for anything one may be doing. This principle of grasping the opportunity is derived from considerations about what the future holds, and there is nothing superficial about it. Qoheleth's world offers only limited windows of opportunity. Conditions and ability to carry something out come and go; the singular certainty in life is that anything positive will come to an end, while at the same time any change of conditions for the better cannot be guaranteed. The way to overcome this is to know at any time what one can realistically accomplish and carry it out while it is possible.

However, such an approach is not without potential pitfalls, precisely because one is never certain what will come next. It is important to grasp that Qoheleth does not advise ignoring this uncertainty. Rather, one has to know the potential problems and be prepared to take a calculated risk. This element is expressed by the contrast between vv. 3 and 4 of our passage. There are some problematic situations that are obvious. If the sky is covered in clouds pregnant with rain, then it will rain and one has to adjust the farming activity accordingly, and a tree that has fallen is not going to move itself. On the other hand the farmer

---

[65] Reading with many manuscripts and 𝔖 𝔙 בְּ instead of כְ found in 𝔏.

[66] There are several ways of reading the second half of the first colon. הַמְלֵאָה can either form a construct chain with בְּבֶטֶן, i.e., *in the womb of a pregnant woman*, or, after slight repointing, it could be an attributive modifier for בְּבֶטֶן, i.e., *the pregnant womb*, it could further be an attributive modifier for הָרוּחַ, *the filling spirit*. The vocalisation speaks against the second option, while the accents support the first interpretation in which case the main verb in the clause is gapped. Irrespective of the preferred interpretation, the overall sense is similar.

[67] Habitual use of Px. It would be possible to render the verb as modal, *who may do anything*, which would fit the preceding verses, but in the immediate context the habitual interpretation is better since the unknowability, and therefore, unpredictability, of divine action has been already asserted.

[68] Terminative temporal use of לְ, cf. Exod 34:2; Deut 16:4 (see WOC 11.2.10c). Crenshaw (1988:181) and Fox (1989:276) prefer to render *in*, in the light of the following *this or that*, which they take to refer to *morning* and *evening* respectively. However, if that was the case, one would expect the same preposition to be used in both cases, and further, *this or that* is better understood as referring to a sample of the seeds rather than morning and evening.

who waits for ideal conditions for sowing or worries too much whether
the weather may not adversely change in the near future, affecting his
harvest, may never grow or harvest anything. A balance needs to be
struck between avoiding the risk and missing the chance.

It should be further observed that Qoheleth's advice is not simply to
take the risk, but also to organise one's business in such a manner as to
minimise the potential mishaps. The farmer who cannot be certain that
the conditions are entirely satisfactory to allow his sowing to succeed
must make a double effort to beat the odds; life is not about taking
what comes when it comes, but about being prepared for what may
come. This perspective is behind the initial verses of Qoh 11:

> Send[69] your bread upon waters, for in many days you may find it. Give
> portion to seven, and even to eight, for you do not know what evil may
> come upon the land. [Qoh 11:1–2]

The precise meaning of these lines, and in particular of v. 1 has been
disputed.[70] However, what remains quite clear, irrespective of the details, is the fact that these verses encourage an attitude of foresight in
one's life, they are about considering what the future may bring and
taking steps to be prepared. This ability to assess risk and be prepared
accordingly is, alongside the *seize the day* principle, the second critical
part of what Qoheleth perceives as wisdom. To express it differently,

---

[69] The image is of placing bread upon water, not throwing it into it (Fox, 1989:275).

[70] There are two common lines of interpretation: (1) These are commercial meta-
phors, v. 1 refers to investing into overseas trade, v. 2 has a similar meaning as the
English *do not keep all your eggs in one basket*; (2) these verses have charitable actions in
mind. Both of these approaches have their stronger and weaker points. In the former
case, the thematic link with what follows is obvious. The objection has been made that
v. 1 can hardly refer to investment since in such a case one would expect a greater
return than the principal investment (e.g. Fox, 1989:273–5), but the basic theme of
the unit is not how to make a profit, but how to limit losses, and moving a portion
of one's property abroad serves as an insurance against localised crisis. At the same
time, it is questionable that the imagery of casting bread on water, an activity with little
obvious purpose, and little predictable outcome, can serve as a metaphor for a purpose-
conscious business strategy. As for the latter line of interpretation, its main weakness
is the fact that the following verses are not really concerned with charity as such,
and Qoheleth's previous conclusions were that righteousness (within which charitable
actions fall) does not make any material difference to a person's life. At the same time,
the language of casting into water in connection with charitable behaviour is found
in Ptahotep 333–49, and the Instruction of Onchsheshonqy 19.1.10 (Fox, 1989:273–5;
Gemser, 1960:126). Further, v. 1 resembles an Arabic proverb with charity in mind,
although there is a chance that it might be dependent on our text (Barton, 1908:112;
Ogden, 1987b:184). In my view the precise meaning cannot be satisfactorily determined
at present.

Qoheleth's wisdom is not deterministic, as the wisdom of the proverbial sages is, but probabilistic. It is about relating the present to the possible future in a probable way, and yet, being prepared for the unforeseen.

This character of Qoheleth's wisdom is further seen in the following series of proverbs:

> He who digs a pit, may fall[71] into it, and he who breaks through a stone wall may be bitten by a snake. He who quarries stones, may be hurt by them, he who splits trees, may be endangered[72] by them.

> When someone has blunted the axe[73] and he does not sharpen[74] [it] first,[75] then one will have to exert strength repeatedly,[76] but wisdom makes advantage possible.[77]

---

[71] The proverb is not the same as the English 'who digs a pit falls into it', for such gnomic statements are formed in BH using Sx (see WOC 30.5.1c). Rather, the Px forms used in vv. 8–9 express potential, as is quite clear from the two proverbs in v. 9; the concern of these sayings is with awareness of hazards that stem from the very nature of an activity a person is involved in.

[72] The sense of סכן in MH (see Jas), cf. ⅚ κινδυνεύσει *will take risk (with them)*. ⅀ ܐܠܐ, *to become weary, tired*.

[73] As Schoors (155) pointed out Piel is rarely intransitive, it is therefore best to take the subject as unspecified, referred to by הוא in the following clause. Fox (1989:268) argues that the antecedent for הוא is the man from v. 9, however, vv. 8–11 seem to contain proverbs that make a similar point, but are otherwise unrelated.

[74] Some oriental manuscripts read לו instead of לא of 𝔏. ⅀, ⅚ do not have an explicit negative, but neither reflects לו, and in both cases negative is implied by the verb (⅀ ܗܠ, *to trouble*; ⅚ ταράσσειν, *to stir*); 𝔙 follows 𝔐. קלל is difficult, I follow KBL-3.

[75] I follow Seow (1997:317) who understands פָּנִים adverbially; others prefer to emend to לפנים, e.g. Driver's (1954:232), Gordis (1955a:322–3).

[76] The plural form חֲיָלִים denotes a repeated action, or intensity (see WOC 7.4.2c).

[77] The B colon is difficult, and its interpretation depends both on the reading adopted (𝔐 K הכשיר / 𝔐 Q הכשר / ⅚ הכשירי; note that there is no Q in 𝔏) and the parsing of that reading—3ms Hiphil Sx, Hiphil infc., Hiphil infa., a determined sg. noun or a determined pl. cs. noun. In the context of the disadvantage caused by the axe's bluntness, the expected sense is that wisdom produces advantage, and so it appears best to read הכשר and parse as Hiphil infa. in the sense *to enable, to prepare ground for* (see Jas), with wisdom being the subject, i.e., *wisdom makes advantage possible*. Gordis (1955a:323) reads K in the sense *to prepare*, rendering the B colon: *it is an advantage to prepare one's skill beforehand*, but it is unlikely that wisdom would be spoken of in the sense of preparing it—wisdom is acquired through long-term training and experience, it is a state of being, not a routine to be carried out. Fox (1989:268) is reading הַכָּשִׁיר in light of Aramaic כָּשְׁרָא, *the skilled man*, which finds some support in ⅚ τοῦ ἀνδρείου σοφία, although it should be noted that σοφία is not rendering הכשיר but translates חָכְמָה.

> If the snake bites before[78] the snake-charming, then the enchanter[79] brings no advantage.[80] [Qoh 10:8–11]

Wisdom is about knowing the risks, using intelligence rather than brute force and avoiding potential problems, rather than solving them; it makes little difference whether one can charm a snake to stop it from biting or not when the snake has bitten already. What matters is not only the possession of a skill, but also its deployment at the proper time. The ability to combine these, i.e., knowledge and timing, is wisdom:

> ... the heart of a wise person knows time and procedure. Indeed, for every matter there is a time and a procedure ... [Qoh 8:5–6][81]

While the probabilistic nature of Qoheleth's approach is rather different from the deterministic wisdom of the proverbial sages, some aspects of Qoheleth's approach to life are remarkably similar to theirs. In general, in spite of the severe limits of wisdom, Qoheleth abhors the fool and his conduct:

> It is better to listen to the rebuke of a wise person, than to be listening to the song of fools. For like the sound of thorns under the pot, so is laughter of the fool. And this also is absurd. For[82] oppression[83] will make the wise foolish and a gift[84] corrupts[85] the heart. [Qoh 7:5–7]

---

[78] I follow here Ogden (1987b:171).

[79] Idiomatic use of בַּעַל denoting occupation. The significance of eloquent speech for enchanting can be seen in Ps 58:6 (Barton, 1908:177).

[80] Lit. *the enchanter has no advantage*. Crenshaw (1988:173) observes the phonetic qualities of the verse, note in particular the repeated occurrence of שׁ, as if imitating the sounds of a snake.

[81] For textual notes see p. 198.

[82] Schoors (1981) understands the כִי as purely emphatic, but there is a clear logical relationship with the previous verse, since this verse explains the reasons for the הֶבֶל judgement that precedes it.

[83] 𝔐 עֹשֶׁק; 𝔊 συκοφαντία, *slander*, but the root can have the overtones of extortion, see L&S; 𝔖 ܡܣܝܢܐ, *slander*, but note that this could be an internal Syriac error (or correction toward 𝔊) from ܡܣܝܢܐ, *oppression*. Driver (1954:229–30) proposes the existence of root עשׁק II, *to slander*, on the basis of the versions and Aramaic. Admittedly such a rendering fits the context well but the evidence of the versions is questionable and the internal evidence for such a root in Hebrew is lacking.

[84] 𝔐 מַתָּנָה; not present in 𝔊 but attested by 𝔖. Driver (1954:229–30) proposes to derive מַתָּנָה from מתן, with the ה possibly being a personal suffix, rendering *and it destroys a/his stout heart*, but attestation of this root in Hebrew is dubious.

[85] 𝔐 וִיאַבֵּד; 4QQohᵃ יעוה, from עוה *to be guilty* (Qal), *to pervert* (Pi), which might reflect an audible error. The gender disagreement is most likely due to the separation of the verb from the subject by the object (see note 83 on p. 115).

Yet, the demarcation line between the fools and wise is very thin and fragile. The clear-cut and tangible division of people into the two camps so familiar from Proverbs is nowhere to be seen; in Qoheleth's experience it takes relatively little to turn a wise man into a fool.

It was also noted earlier that the enjoyment which Qoheleth encourages stems from work. It is, therefore, not too surprising that Qoheleth also shares the proverbial view that laziness is self-destructive:

> In sluggishness the beam-work will collapse and in lowering of hands the house will leak. [Qoh 10:18][86]

Further, Qoheleth shares with the proverbial sages the attitude toward speech:

> The words of the mouth of a wise person are grace[ful], but the lips of a fool engulf him.[87] The beginning of the words of his mouth are folly and the end of his mouth is bad madness. But the fool multiplies words; [88]one[89] does not know what will[90] come [next] and what will be afterwards.[91] Who can tell him? [Qoh 10:12–14]

Speech is powerful. The wise person channels the power in a positive direction, the fool has no control over what he says and causes harm, principally to himself.

The advice that Qoheleth offers is general and conceptual rather than specific, even the verses quoted above from Qoh 11 that talk about the farmer are clearly not aimed at the farmer *per se* but are illustrations. There is only one group of guidelines that are context-

---

[86] For textual notes see p. 162.

[87] The suffix is ambiguous, and could refer to the fool, the wise person, or the graceful words of the wise. The latter option (e.g. Ogden, 1987b:173) seems least likely, since, as the following verse indicates, the concern here is with what comes out of the fool's mouth. The middle option cannot be completely ruled out, but the proposed reading best fits the context, which does not appear to be concerned with the fool's impact on others, but rather on himself.

[88] Many manuscripts + ו. The B colon is best taken as yet another comment by Qoheleth on the fool; it is unlikely that it should be understood as direct speech uttered by the fool concerning the general state of things, because such a comment has been previously made by Qoheleth himself, and Qoheleth emphatically denies being a fool.

[89] הָאָדָם is here unlikely to denote species (i.e., mankind), or to refer to the fool himself (in such a case no noun would have been necessary). It is best understood as referring to the man that serves the fool as an audience.

[90] 𝔏 מַה־שֶׁיִּהְיֶה; a few manuscripts, 𝔊, 𝔖 appear to have read מַה־שֶׁהָיָה, but the difference could be only interpretative, due to the past-future passages elsewhere in the book. In the immediate context 𝔏 is preferable.

[91] Gordis (1955a:324) *after his lifetime*, but that does not fit the context very well, since the B colon appears to be a comment concerning the fool's speech.

specific. I suggested in the previous chapter that the monarchy was an intimate reality for Qoheleth, and this is expressed in instructions for those who interact with the king:

> Watch the mouth[92] of the king and concerning a divine oath, do not be hasty.[93] Walk from his presence, do not stand in an evil thing, for he does whatever he pleases. Because the word of the king is powerful, and who will say to him: 'What are you doing?'. Who obeys an order will not experience any bad thing, and the heart of a wise person[94] knows time and[95] procedure. [Qoh 8:2–5]

> If the spirit of the ruler rises against you, do not leave your place, for calmness[96] can appease great sins. [Qoh 10:4]

> … not even in your thought curse the king, and do not curse the rich in your bedroom, for a bird from heaven will carry [away] your voice and a winged creature will disclose [your] word [Qoh 10:20][97]

Interestingly enough, this advice has nothing to do with the factual aspects of the court, it has no partisan slant (in the political sense), and reveals nothing of what the courtier's duties would have been and how they should or might have been approached. Nor does it show how to exploit one's position at the court to one's benefit. Instead, what Qoheleth offers are simple guidelines on how to survive being a courtier. The key to this is unquestionable loyalty; the kings Qoheleth knew tolerated no dissent. Such a loyalty needed to be accompanied by shrewdness, understanding what would be acceptable at any given moment (which is just a variant on the basic concept of wisdom as skill and timing). But even the loyal and shrewd courtier could not obviously

---

[92] Reading with versions אֶת־ instead of 𝔐 אֲנִי. Gordis (1955a:287) proposes that אֲנִי should be understood as standing for *I declare*. This is possible, but the resulting sense is virtually identical to that of the versions.

[93] I follow 𝔊, σ', 𝔖 in ending the clause after תִּבָּהֵל in v. 3. This is necessary due to the presence of the conjunction ו before עַל דִּבְרַת which indicates that that עַל דִּבְרַת שְׁבוּעַת אֱלֹהִים does not modify what precedes, and, thus, requires subject and predicate to form its own independent clause.

[94] Possibly *wise heart* (Crenshaw, 1988:151).

[95] Several manuscripts and 𝔊 omit the copula, i.e., *time of judgement*, but 𝔏 is preferable in the light of v. 6.

[96] So KBL-2 for מַרְפֵּא here and in Prov 14:30; 15:4. Although this sense is unlikely in Prov 14:30, the use of the verb רפה in Judg 8:3 suggests that this meaning is within the semantic range of the root, in spite of the fact that there is no evidence that the word was so used in MH (Barton, 1908:176). Fox's (1989:266) rendering *ability to soothe anger* would seem to capture the thrust of the verse.

[97] For textual notes see p. 162.

avoid the king's anger, those who wished to stay alive needed to be able to face the king calmly and appease the royal rage.

In face of the fact that these texts contain very little of any deeper insight, in contrast to the profundity of Qoheleth's comments elsewhere, it is hard to avoid the impression that Qoheleth did not consider being close to the king as something that one should desire and pursue. While in Proverbs skill and mastery bring one in front of the king, there appears to be little space for real wisdom at the court of Qoheleth's world, where fools can be easily placed in positions of power. It can be concluded from this that while the sages of Qoheleth's time played a role at the court, it was not the court and their place at it that gave them their identity; the sage would have been used as a political advisor, but Qoheleth is far from equating the sage with a politician and wisdom with political science.

The Place of God and Ethics in Qoheleth's Wisdom

In the above rehearsal of the key elements of Qoheleth's wisdom, nothing has been said of God and/or ethical considerations. In Proverbs these two were inseparably linked and encapsulated in the hallmark phrase of proverbial wisdom, *fear of Yahweh*. This phrase *per se* is missing from Qoheleth, yet, he speaks of fearing God on four separate occasions [Qoh 3:14; 5:6; 7:18; 8:12–13]. He means by this an acknowledgement of the qualitatively different planes on which God and humanity operate and acceptance of the divine superiority. The resulting attitude is that of respect, which means refraining from attempts to manipulate and/or deceive the deity. Thus, Qoheleth urges the reader to avoid false and void religiosity, such as making religious commitments that one cannot, or does not intend, to keep, or offering sacrifices that are a mere cover for disregard for God; Qoheleth's God favours obedience over sacrifice. In spite of the fact that Qoheleth spends only limited space addressing the question of how humans should relate to God (he is much more interested in how God relates to humans), his religious attitude is not tokenistic. While the motivation for fearing God in the book is avoidance of his wrath, it is obvious that this requires a genuine attitude—religious tokenism is a mark of fools.

Qoheleth perceives a link between fearing God and avoidance of evil, but this is much weaker than in Proverbs, and in general ethical considerations play only a very limited role in the book. The reason for this is concisely summarised in the following passage:

> Since the sentence of the evil deed is not carried out quickly, therefore, the heart of human beings which is within them is full to do evil — because a sinner does evil a hundred [times], yet, his [life] is prolonged— although I know that it should be well with the fearers of God, those who keep fearing him. And it should not be well with the wicked, and [his] days should not be prolonged like a shadow, because he did not fear God. There is absurdity which happens upon the earth, that there are righteous men to whom it happens as if they were wicked and there are wicked men, to whom it happens as if they were righteous. I said that also this is absurd. [Qoh 8:11–14][98]

Whether one is righteous or wicked does not, in Qoheleth's experience, make any noticeable difference to one's quality of life. Therefore, ethics does not enter into the equation he is seeking a solution to. Yet, it would be misleading to say that Qoheleth does not care about ethical issues, or that he advocates situation ethics. The book is not about ethics, but neither does it seek to legitimise behaviour without ethical norms. It is evident from the above quoted passage that Qoheleth had a clear concept of good and evil. He implied that wickedness deserves to be punished, although it is not, suggesting that he did not see wickedness as an acceptable way of life.

What Qoheleth does not say, though, is what constitutes good and evil. In the proverbial material it is clearly implied that the differentiation between wisdom and folly, righteousness and wickedness, good and evil, is ultimately dictated by divine standards; good is what God approves of, evil is what he abhors. Such an implied definition of good and evil is missing from Qoheleth, for when he declares that the world is crooked by divine design and that bad things that should happen to the wicked happen to the righteous and vice versa, he is criticising the divine standards, and so implying that his definition of right and wrong is independent of what God seems to consider right and wrong. Yet, nowhere in the book we find any discussion of where he derives his standards from. This would seem to suggest that his perception of right and wrong is arrived at in the same manner as his entire worldview is constructed, through his personal experience and observation. The clearest indication that this is the case is found in the following passage:

> Also, do not pay attention to all the things that are said, so that you may not hear your servant cursing you. For even your heart knows of many times when you also cursed others. [Qoh 7:21–22][99]

---

[98] For textual notes see p. 71.
[99] For textual notes see p. 165.

Although the primary concern of this instruction is contained in the former verse, v. 22 reveals an important attitude: Qoheleth warns the reader not to treat others any more harshly than one treats oneself. The self serves Qoheleth as a mirror reminding him of the fact that there is no-one who is so righteous as to be without any blemish; self-honesty and humility foster an attitude of tolerance.[100]

The following passage is also of considerable interest for the question of Qoheleth's ethical stance:

> Both[101] these I saw during the days of my absurd [existence]: there is a righteous person who perishes in his righteousness and there is this wicked person who prolongs his days in his evil. Do not overdo it as a righteous person,[102] and do not conduct yourself wisely[103] beyond a measure, why should you ruin[104] yourself? Do not behave exceedingly wickedly, and do not be foolish, why die prematurely? It would be good if your hand lays hold of this, and does not let go of that, for one who fears God will go out[105] with both of them. Wisdom is more powerful[106]

---

[100] In fact the attitude of honesty and humility is the principal hallmark of Qoheleth's approach to life and his writing. It shows on the intellectual level when, in spite of his wisdom roots, he finds (and acknowledges) that wisdom lacks true power; it shows in his cosmological perspective when he accepts the apparent realities of life, no matter how unpalatable implications they might have; it shows on the anthropological level, when he is unable to affirm any higher ontological status for a human than for a beast; it shows on the sociological level when he urges one not to be surprised when witnessing the cruelty that one human being causes another; it shows on the theological level, when he assesses the relative positions of God and humanity urging deep respect for God and his power.

[101] 𝔐 אֶת־הַכֹּל; as the rest of the verse indicates, the author has two realities in mind (Fox, 1989:233).

[102] Whybray (1978) proposes to interpret the periphrastic construction *do not be self-righteous*, but there is no indication that the righteous in the preceding verse is only a would-be one. Ogden (1987b:115) suggests that הַרְבֵּה modifies the verb and not the adjective צַדִּיק, but the adjective cannot be separated from the auxiliary verb in a periphrastic construction.

[103] This appears to be a benefactive reflexive use of Hithpael (WOC 26.2e), similar to Exod 1:10.

[104] Px Hithpael with apocopated ת. Fox (1989:235) renders *why should you be shocked*, because wisdom is not a source of physical destruction. However, the surrounding context is explicitly concerned with destruction.

[105] 𝔐 supported by 𝔊. 𝔖 ܢܕܒܩ, *to cling to*, but this appears to be an internal 𝔊 error from ܢܕܦܩ, *to go out*. Delitzsch (1982b:326) points out a MH idiom, where יצא means *to satisfy one's duty*.

[106] 𝔐 תָּעֹז; 4QQohᵃ, 𝔊 תעזר; either could be the result of a simple scribal error. 𝔐 is the more difficult reading, as the verb is intransitive, but it could have the sense, *the wise [considers] wisdom more powerful...* Also 𝔐 reading fits well the parallel with the B colon (*power : rulers*), the association of rulers with help is not really obvious. Fox (1989:232) points out that עזז can be used as a synonym of עזר.

to the wise than ten rulers,[107] who are in the city. Surely, there is no
righteous person in the land, who would do what is good, and would not
sin. [Qoh 7:15–20]

This text has been often interpreted as a formulation of the golden
mean rule: be a little righteous and a little wicked, a little wise and a
little foolish—everything in moderation.[108] I am not convinced that this
is the correct understanding of the text. The זֶה - זֶה construction of v.
18 suggests that in vv. 16–17, Qoheleth has only two types of activity
in mind and that there is a semantic redundancy present among the
four imperatives. The golden mean proponents take this as a reference
to the two verses respectively, each setting a limit on one side of the
golden mean. Yet, this is unlikely. While these verses together display a
carefully constructed semantic and syntactic chiasm, each one of them
is constructed in an asymmetrical manner, which makes it impossible
to understand the two colons within each verse as synonymous, and,
thus, to see them as a single command expressed twofold. Also, I have
already pointed out that wisdom and righteousness are not synonymous
in Qoheleth in the way they are in Proverbs, and this fact further
undermines such an understanding of v. 16. In addition, the passage
quoted previously [Qoh 8:11–14] shows that Qoheleth considers being
wicked as an equivalent to not fearing God, making it most unlikely
that he would encourage those who fear God to aspire to a little
wickedness alongside of a little righteousness.

    In my view the synonymity, needed to reduce the redundancy of
the four commands into two notions, is not to be found within the
individual verses, but between them; v. 17 is a negatively formulated
expression of the same notion as found in v. 16, and v. 18 then refers
to the two separate commands in v. 16 (and their negated equivalents
in v. 17). A closer scrutiny of the text supports such an understanding.
The A colons use as a modifier of the commands הַרְבֵּה (Qoheleth's
basic word for much/many and antonym to מְעַט), but 16b uses יוֹתֵר
(a term which denotes excess beyond a limit[109]), and the command
in 17b has no qualifier at all. Thus rather than suggesting be a little
wise and a little foolish, Qoheleth's bias expressed by the B colons is

---

[107] Fox (1989:232) suggests to re-divide the consonants מעשר השליטם, *riches of the rulers*,
but in the lack of textual evidence 𝔐, which is not obscure on this point, is preferable.

[108] For a comprehensive survey of approaches to interpreting this passage see Brindle
(1985).

[109] The semantic difference between the הַרְבֵּה and יוֹתֵר can be seen, for instance, in
Qoh 12:12.

unequivocally toward wisdom; behave wisely up to a point (the value of wisdom is never unlimited in the book), but do not be a fool at all. Further, it can be observed that colons 16b and 17a use simple verbal constructions אַל־תִּרְשַׁע / אַל־תִּתְחַכַּם, but 16a and 17b use periphrastic constructions אַל־תְּהִי סָכָל / אַל־תְּהִי צַדִּיק. The main difference between these two types of clause is that the former refers to a person's conduct, the latter to a person's identity; the two תְּהִי constructions describe the primary identity of the person who follows Qoheleth's advice, a righteous person who is not a fool. The qualifier in 16a captures the fact that no person has the potential to be perfect, the righteous identity Qoheleth has in mind is from this world, not an absolute ideal. What he means is explicated by 17a, and amounts to not behaving excessively wickedly. This has to be understood in the context of the observation made in the previous chapter that in Qoheleth's world human beings have a natural tendency to be wicked. Therefore, Qoheleth is calling for consciously curtailing this tendency, rather than allowing oneself a degree of wickedness. That it is wisdom and a realistic degree of righteousness Qoheleth has in mind in v. 18 is affirmed by vv. 19–20, further elaborating on the value of wisdom, and limits that there are to human righteousness.[110] These two qualities are to be held onto in spite of the limited capabilities of the former and the limited achievability of the latter. The degree of movement between certain boundaries that the adverbial qualifiers imply is not that of what is permissible, i.e., the golden mean, but rather what is achievable in the real world. The desired position is not found halfway between righteousness and wickedness, wisdom and folly, but rather off-centre; in principle one is supposed to be righteous and not to be a fool.

What the reader is left with is a tension between wisdom and ethics. On the one hand Qoheleth is forced to admit that ethics do not make any perceptible difference to how successful one is and, thus, have no genuine place in wisdom, while on the other hand he is unwilling to take this to the necessary conclusion and entirely abandon ethical norms as of no value. It might be tempting to try to ascribe this tension to the activity of some pious editor, but the conflict between

---

[110] It was suggested that v. 19 has been misplaced, e.g. Fox (1989:232) places it after v. 12, but this is done exclusively on the grounds of lack of links with the context. Concerning v. 20, it should be observed that it cannot be understood as an assertion that there are no righteous people at all, for Qoheleth already said that he knows of righteous who suffer a fate they do not deserve.

what Qoheleth thinks should be happening and what he experiences
permeates the entire book, making such a solution unconvincing. It is
much more likely that the tension is one between Qoheleth's experience
and his intuition, between his experience and his wisdom heritage.

The book is often understood as a critique of traditional wisdom,
such as that found in Proverbs. This is true only to a point. Qoheleth
indeed struggles with the claims that resemble those found in Proverbs,
and repudiates them questioning the optimistic beliefs in the power of
wisdom and divine retributive justice. Yet, he does not do this from a
stance of someone who despises wisdom, indeed as we have just seen,
he is reluctant to completely abandon traditional wisdom values. Terminology such as *attack on traditional wisdom,* that is sometimes applied to
Qoheleth, does injustice to the book, for it gives emotional colouring to
Qoheleth's relationship with traditional wisdom that it does not have;
to see in Qoheleth a clash of differing ideologies is to misunderstand
the book. Rather, I am inclined to see Qoheleth with Fox (1987:154) as
appropriating and extending wisdom; Qoheleth is not about winning
an argument with the sages of the past, but about the search for truth
in the present.

Wisdom and the Epilogue of Qoheleth

As we examined the different elements of the worldview of Qoheleth,
we observed that the epilogist's perspective diverges repeatedly from the
views found in the core of the book. This is no less true of the epilogist's
opinion of how a person should live; even thought the contribution of
the epilogue is only brief, a very clear picture of what constitutes true
wisdom emerges:

> The words of the wise are like spikes and like nails set in place [by]
> collectors, given by one shepherd. Above these, my son, be warned:
> there is no end to producing many books, and much reading tires the
> body. End of [the] matter, [of] everything heard, fear God and keep his
> commandments, for this perfects a human being. For every deed God
> will bring into judgement, concerning everything hidden, whether good,
> or bad. [Qoh 12:11–14][111]

While, as noted earlier (p. 78), all the notions forming the epilogist's
perspective are derived from the core of the book, the selection and
emphasis are such that the reader is led in a rather different direction

---

[111] For textual notes see p. 78.

than Qoheleth was heading. The epilogist focuses essentially on three of Qoheleth's ideas: limits of wisdom, fearing God and divine judgement.

Qoheleth reiterates again and again that wisdom has serious limits. Yet, the point he is making is not that wisdom and knowledge are entirely useless, but only that they are powerless when it comes to defeating the fundamental flaws of human existence; one should not expect wisdom to deliver the impossible. In contrast, the epilogist presents the limits of wisdom in such a way that he undermines the value of intellectual undertaking *per se*; for him the limits of knowing have been reached and anything worthwhile knowing has been recorded. Verses 11–12 suggest that he has a fixed body of material in mind which contains this knowledge; the sages are no more independent thinkers, they have been reduced to collectors. Thus, while Qoheleth urges the reader to acknowledge the limits of knowing, the epilogist effectively prescribes what these limits are.

The second idea that the epilogist takes over from Qoheleth is the notion of fearing God. It was observed above that in contrast to Proverbs, Qoheleth's fearing of God has stronger cultic overtones, with the emphasis being on not abusing the cult and manipulating God. The epilogist takes this emphasis further. For him fear of God is expressed in obedience to divine commandments, i.e., direct divine revelation.[112] This concept of fearing God is closely tied to the third of Qoheleth's notions found in the epilogue, that of divine judgement. In Qoheleth proper the divine judgement operates largely on a cosmological level through the bipolarity of life's events preventing genuine gain. At the same time Qoheleth observed that wickedness is not punished and righteousness is not rewarded on an individual basis, and his personal preference for righteousness is not, in spite of his association of righteousness with fearing God, so much grounded in a sense of religious obligation as in his own wisdom roots. In contrast, the epilogist expects a different kind of judgement than the cosmic neutrality. Similarly to the proverbial sages, he believes in judgement that operates on an individual level, and in fact on the plain of individual actions.

As a result of the selective treatment of Qoheleth's ideas the following picture emerges in the epilogue: in the light of human limits, the only thing that really matters in human life is the acceptance of divine

---

[112] The copula in Qoh 12:13 is probably best understood as epexegetical, i.e., fear God *by* obeying his commandments.

authority *and* of the divine command; human beings are held accountable for the response they show to these. In other words, true wisdom,
the epilogist argues, is piety and piety alone.[113] At first sight this may
seem very much like the proverbial notion of *fear of Yahweh*, but in reality
it is not. From the point of view of the epilogue the value of the words
of the wise rests solely on the divine origins of the collections that the
speaker has in mind—just as in Proverbs, the sages' wisdom has divine
origins. Yet, here the divine inspiration is not applied to the *process* of
acquiring wisdom, as it was in Proverbs, but rather to some limited
and further unspecified *body of material*. Thus, the separation between
experience past and experience present, that started with the proverbial emphasis on cumulative collective experience, has reached a new,
and a logically necessary stage; the past wisdom, or more specifically
some of it, became sacrosanct and was perceived no more as inspired
experience, but simply as revealed command.

Summary

While there are some points of contact between the concepts of wisdom in Proverbs and Qoheleth, in general these are radically different. Proverbial wisdom is essentially a system of ethics and it is largely
about dealing with people. Being wise is the same as being righteous,
being wicked amounts to foolishness. The authority of proverbial wisdom stems from inseparable unity between human experience, divine
sovereignty and just divine character. In contrast, Qoheleth's wisdom
is void of ethical consideration. While Qoheleth does not advocate life
without ethics, his concept of wisdom *per se* is thoroughly pragmatic
and his approach to life is probabilistic, looking for ways to handle
the unpredictability of the phenomenon of life. The authority of his
advice rests squarely on validation by experience. He maintains the
notion of divine sovereignty, but in the light of his experience lets go of
the proverbial conviction that God deals justly with individual humans.
The brief entry of the epilogist brings in yet another perspective, one
in which wisdom amounts to piety, and its authority stems from divine
revelation alone, leaving little, if any, space for experience and intellectual endeavour.

---

[113] This identification of wisdom with piety in my opinion needs to be taken into
consideration when dealing with Qoh 12:11 suggesting that *one shepherd* is a reference to
God.

The former two concepts of wisdom are not incompatible or even irreconcilable, precisely because Qoheleth's wisdom applies equally to the righteous and to the wicked. Anyone who wishes to follow Qoheleth's advice still has to make the choice whether to accept or reject the proverbial ethics (or some other ethical system). The epilogist's viewpoint is more difficult to merge with the other two. This is not because wisdom of the proverbial sages or Qoheleth would exclude piety, in fact the command to fear and obey God is inherent to both. The problem is that piety in these two cases exists in the context of independent intellectual inquiry, which the epilogist more or less rejects. His piety is entirely cult driven and the revelatory process is all encompassing—in the 21st century, we would label this a fundamentalist viewpoint.

PROVERBS AND QOHELETH
IN AN HISTORICAL CONTEXT

The worldviews represented by the two books and pieced together in the preceding chapters raise certain questions of an historical nature which have not been addressed so far, mainly because they do not lie at the heart of the present work. Yet, since the study has a direct bearing on these questions, at least a few brief comments are appropriate.

I am convinced that the origins of Prov 1–9 are very closely tied together with the rest of the book. I have pointed out that the principal function of Prov 1–9 is to motivate the reader to take the sayings that follow seriously, while containing only limited practical advice. In my view this imbalance is such that the opening section of the book is not capable of a genuinely independent existence, for it speaks of the significance of acquiring wisdom without largely defining what constitutes such wise living. These observations strongly suggest that Prov 1–9 was composed[1] specifically as a foreword to the sayings that follow it. In other words, it is not possible to do justice to the material of Prov 1–9 when it is treated as a wisdom text in its right; such a treatment can throw important light on the composition and the internal dynamics of the text, but not on its overall function and aims.

It was noted in chapter 4 that the theological perspective expressed in the Wisdom speeches of Prov 1–9 serves as a backbone to the proverbial paradigm, on the one hand fitting exactly the needs of this paradigm, on the other hand failing to provide theologically satisfactory answers to the problem of the origins of Folly and its power over humanity. This led us to the conclusion that the theological perspective was derived from the wisdom paradigm itself, or in other words, that the theological perspective is subservient to it. The significance of this emerges when it is held together with the observations mentioned in the previous paragraph, namely, that the proverbial concept of wisdom

---

[1] By *composed* I do not mean here necessarily the production of an entirely original composition, for the inner makeup of this material is rather complex (see for instance Whybray, 1994a), but rather the editorial activity that formed it into its present shape.

is mostly formulated in the sayings of Prov 10–31. This implies that the theo-cosmological framework we find in Prov 1–9 is principally derived from the worldview of the sayings in Prov 10–31; it is not an external framework imposed on it, and it does not represent a tradition radically different from that of Prov 10–31.[2] This casts very serious doubt on the claims that Prov 1–9 has to be much later than the other parts of the book, because it contains much more developed theological perspective—it does not, it is merely formulated in a more eloquent manner. Consequently, the arguments for the feasibility of more ancient origins of this section of the book made by several scholars in the past, should, I think, be reconsidered afresh.[3]

In chapter 4 it was observed that the use of the personal name יהוה appears to be mainly apologetic, trying to identify the sages' God with Yahweh. This, it was argued, would seem to suggest that the origins of the proverbial wisdom come from the time when the mainstream religious perception of Yahweh was as a tribal God. Thus, it is likely that the perspective that Proverbs represents originates before the exile, and it is most likely that the book attests to early stages of conscious interaction of wisdom with the cult. In contrast, Qoheleth's systematic reference to God as אֱלֹהִים, yet, accompanied by a strictly monotheistic perspective, suggests that Qoheleth is writing at a time when Yahweh is no more seen as a tribal deity, but as the only God, i.e., in a time when what initially appeared to be the perspective reserved to the wisdom sages became widespread. Considering the point made above concerning the relationship between Prov 1–9 and the rest of Proverbs, this in my view decreases the probability that Prov 1–9 was written in an historical proximity to Qoheleth. Further, these observations suggest that in fact the shift from tribal to global theological perspective was influenced by the wisdom enterprise, giving some credence to Sheppard's (1980:13) claim that rather than speaking of theologisation of wisdom, we should speak of 'wisdomisation' of theology, at least concerning one stage in the development of the relationship between the two.

While dealing with the epistemology of the two books in chapter 3 we noted a critical epistemological shift between the outlook of

---

[2] Compare the conclusion reached by Kassis (1999:275) that distinct stages of religious development cannot be discerned in the present shape of the book.

[3] See Kayatz's (1966) work on the affinity of Prov 1–9 with ancient Egyptian wisdom, Lang's (1986) observations about possible rooting of the Dame Wisdom figure in an ancient Hebrew goddess, and Kitchen's (1977) comparative work on the development of wisdom forms in the ANE.

Qoheleth proper and Proverbs on the one hand, and the epilogue to Qoheleth on the other hand. The difference in these perspectives led us to the conclusion that the perspective of the epilogist is not a wisdom perspective but a cultic one; the epilogist is not a sage, but a theologian. Thus, the epilogue attests to a stage in the development of the relationship between wisdom and the cult, where the theologian regains the control. In the emerging worldview that the epilogist represents, the human quest for understanding, so central to wisdom, loses its autonomy, and ultimately significance. While it might be an exaggeration to say that this is due to Qoheleth alone, there is little doubt that it is the result of the state of affairs that Qoheleth witnesses to, namely, wisdom failing to provide the absolute, black and white, answers that human beings always desired and probably always will. The epilogist's answer to this is to theologise wisdom in a manner it had not been before, and it is this form in which it is found in the later wisdom writings such as Ben Sira.[4]

In chapter 5 we observed a major difference between the socio-economic structures that are reflected in Proverbs and Qoheleth. I have argued that the world of Proverbs is one of a decentralised economy revolving around a small local community, where each individual has its place and the success of the community depends on its members working and living together in harmony. The family is the most significant and in principle the highest formal hierarchical structure of the proverbial society. We have observed that while kingship appears in Proverbs on numerous occasions, the king is not a truly meaningful part of the book's world. In contrast Qoheleth's world is one of large empires, where the proverbial equality has been replaced by a hierarchy in which only those at the very top benefit from the produce of the land. Thus, the world that Qoheleth portrays fits the Hellenistic period extremely well. The question of matching Proverbs to a historical period is more difficult. First of all, I am inclined to reject the possibility that the proverbial world is a fictional one, i.e., that it was created without the conviction that it depicts the real world out there.

---

[4] Cf. Dell (1994b:313). It is worth noting that this oscillating relationship between wisdom and theology is not peculiar to ancient Israel, for precisely the same phenomenon can be observed in more modern theological development, such as the shift from the medieval scholasticism to the liberal theology springing from the enlightenment, and again the renewed 'cultic' emphasis of neo-orthodoxy after the disillusionment of the First World War. It is this type of phenomenological pattern that hides behind Qoheleth's claim that there is nothing new under the sun.

For this the concerns of the book are too down-to-earth, and the aims
it strives to achieve too practical; there is a clear conviction in the book
that this is not just the world as it should be, but as it really is. Thus,
I think we need to look for an historical setting that would reasonably
match the world that the book outlines.[5]

It is my view, that the proverbial perspective is unlikely to have
originated in the Hellenistic, or more generally post-exilic period, for
the forces that would have been a part of a large emporium (be it Persia
or Greece), caused by centralised rule and taxation accompanied by
extensive international trade (that are seen at work in Qoheleth), do not
fit the proverbial state of affairs. Further, the period of the Babylonian
exile is also an improbable setting. While one may want to argue that
the closed-off community pictured here is that of the exiles, trying
to preserve their own identity, it is unlikely that an effort to instruct
the young generation in such a manner as to differentiate themselves
from the society of the captors would have systematically avoided any
reference to the entity of Israel, the preservation of which would have
been the primary concern of the authors of the material, if such an
identification was to be correct. It is much more likely, that this feature
of the material stems from a time when the national identity was not
the real issue.

Placing the origins of the proverbial perspective as a whole into the
pre-exilic monarchy is in my view not fully satisfactory either. While
the degree of centralisation would have been lesser than during the
imperial period after the exile, the socio-economic structures would
have been of a larger scale than the proverbial material depicts. In
particular, taxation was already very severe under Solomon,[6] and it is
precisely the unbearable level of taxation that is reported in 1 Kgs 12 as
the reason for the break-up of the monarchy. Further, the system where
land was considered strictly tribal/family property was breaking down
during the monarchy.[7] Therefore, there would have been the possibility

---

[5] At this stage a distinction has to be made between the proverbial outlook on the
one hand, and the tangible expression of it that we find in the present shape of the
book, for the date assigned to the two can be significantly different if, for instance, the
book was composed as a retrospective return to a distant past in an attempt to restore
some of its values. It is the outlook that I wish to concentrate on at the present.

[6] While the historical value of the account of Solomon's rule can be questioned, I
am prepared to give at least some credence to the assertions of 1 Kgs 4–5, concerning
the erection of the Jerusalem temple in the early monarchy, which project would have
required major resources.

[7] Consider for instance the purchase of land by David from Araunah [2 Sam

to purchase land allowing for some degree of movement from one small community to another. In addition, the Solomonic building projects must have had a far reaching impact on the social arrangements of the time, for they required a huge number of labourers and, thus, on the one hand would have hindered the family-based farming and agriculture, and on the other hand meant large scale movement of population. Yet, there is no hint in Proverbs of such an upheaval taking place and the rather superficial integration of the royal references into the socio-economic structures of the proverbial world makes origins in a well established pre-exilic monarchy unlikely.

I am, therefore, inclined to think that we have to look for the origins of the proverbial outlook in the pre-monarchic and the early monarchic periods. Family-based, rather than nation-based identity and socio-economic independence of small family units, such as seen in the patriarchal narratives or depicted in the book of Ruth, combined with the closed nature of these family-based communities, fits the proverbial profile best and it is my view that the book needs to be interpreted against that background.[8] Once this perspective is accepted, some of the persistently criticised naiveté of the book disappears, for in such a setting the wicked would indeed more often than not suffer and the righteous prosper, simply due to the economic forces at work in such a small and interdependent community.

At the same time, it has to be appreciated that the text as we find it in the book today is a literary product rather than a mere recording of an earlier oral tradition, one unlikely to have originated in what is basically a rural setting. I wish to suggest that the wisdom tradition and ideals originating in the pre-monarchic era continued to be cultivated and adhered to even when the monarchy came into place; a monarch can be put on the throne overnight, but a change in the society's daily practices and structures develops only gradually. The early royal advisors would have been grounded in the pre-monarchic wisdom and would have adjusted their understanding only gradually, as the monarchy was

---

24:18ff.] or the story of Naboth's vineyard [1 Kgs 21].

[8] The suggestion that wisdom roots are in such a setting is not entirely new. However, in the past this has been generally argued on the basis of comparing Proverbs to proverbial material from contemporary tribal cultures, namely in Africa (e.g. Golka, 1993; Westermann, 1995). Such an approach is connected with certain methodological problems, namely the possibility of direct influence of the biblical tradition on the material to which it is being compared. In contrast, I have attempted to show that Proverbs itself provides ample clues to such a primary setting of the material.

taking root. Initially, there would have been very little that needed to be adapted to the new conditions, for the king could easily be fitted into the proverbial paradigm as a representative and defender of the rule of the divine order over chaos. Such a development would be logical and matches the proverbial picture well. I am, therefore, inclined to think that we should look for the literary beginnings of the book during the early monarchy.[9] As the monarchy settled in and developed, the increasing socio-economic changes would have meant that the harmonious life pictured by the ancient sages would have been more and more remote from daily reality, and so would have become an ideal from a distant past, yet, a heritage passionately held onto by successive generations of wise men, for I have explained that the nature of the role of God in the proverbial epistemology is such that it makes it difficult, if not entirely impossible, to adapt the paradigm to any significant degree of change.

However, eventually the picture of the world that it portrayed would have become untenable even to those who stood firmly within the wisdom tradition, as Qoheleth's evaluation of the traditional wisdom understanding of the world shows. We have, therefore, to ask what it was that caused the book to survive and eventually be included in the Hebrew bible. In this respect the later trend toward the theologisation of wisdom, pointed out above, would have helped, providing a new point of reference for reading the book, affirming the validity of its perspective not on the grounds of experience, but the affinity of its ethical stance with the ethos of the prophetic and legal traditions. However, it is possible that there is yet another, and more practical, factor at play here. In my view it is quite possible that the proverbial world and values have been intentionally resurrected during a much later time than the one from which they stem, a time when the nation lost the ultimate control over the socio-economic superstructures and when the importance of the family for preservation of the nation and its heritage became increasingly clear.[10] The book then would not have been seen as depicting the world that was, but the world that could have and ultimately should have been, a world worth striving for, offering

---

[9] If my analysis is correct, it might also be necessary to review the modern critical evaluation of the traditional association of Proverbs with Solomon, for this could be closer to reality than is normally allowed.

[10] A similar concept of the world, with emphasis on the family, can be found in the Mishna, see for instance Neusner (1998).

hope by pointing back to a time when the righteous prospered and the joy of the wicked was quickly snuffed out.

This brings us to the question of the *Sitz im Leben* of Proverbs and Qoheleth. As for the latter book, the information on which the judgment can be formed is scanty. The comments of the epilogist suggest a didactic setting. At the same time, it was observed in chapter 4 that although Qoheleth's perspective is strictly monotheistic, he does not engage in apologetic with polytheistic views. Considering the Hellenistic environment in which he found himself, this silence makes it quite likely that the book was not intended for wide use but rather was addressing a smaller group for which this was not an issue that needed to be discussed. It is possible to speculate from this that in fact the book is a kind of an 'academic paper', however, the data is too limited to allow a convincing case to be built.

The *Sitz im Leben* of Proverbs has been widely debated. Usually the setting suggested for the material is a formal school (Kovacs, 1974; Shupak, 1987), the royal court (Fox, 1996b), or a life of a small village or town based community (Golka, 1993; Westermann, 1995). If the understanding of the origins of the book proposed above is adopted, then each of these settings is applicable to the book at a particular stage in its transmission. The book is clearly meant as didactic material, and the perspective it expresses shows that the education it was intended to aid initially revolved around the family. At the same time, it was observed in chapter 2, that formal education on a commercial basis was not only known, but also seen as an element, if not a particular stage, in the educational process. Later, as the court became the centre of wisdom, the material came to be used in this new setting, and probably for purposes that were not entirely identical with the initial intention, such as education of the courtiers. Finally, if my suggestion about later re-appropriation of the book under the threat of loss of national identity is correct, the book would have changed its *Sitz im Leben* yet again, for since it would have been seen as a tool in restoring the world from a distant past, a world no more in existence, it would have needed to be used in a much wider context than merely education of youngsters. Consequently, the book *per se* cannot be assigned exclusively to any particular setting.[11] The brief proverbial forms elude the form-critical category of *Sitz im Leben*, which has proved so useful in analysing other

---

[11] A similar conclusion was reached by Fontaine (1993) and Kassis (1999).

genres of the OT. This, I wish to suggest, is due to their flexibility, which allows them to be adapted to new conditions without losing their cutting edge. Thus Van Leeuwen's (1988) thesis that the *Sitz im Leben* is replaced in Proverbs by *Sitz im Buch* may need to be revised, for it appears that proverbial forms have no inherent *Sitz im Leben* in the first place.

CONCLUSIONS

The Two Worlds

Having examined the 'dissected' pieces of the worldviews behind the two books it is time to take a step back and look again at the whole. What have we learned about the sages who produced these books, about the world they lived in, about the issues they struggled with? First of all, it was observed that the enterprise which these books witness to is concerned with understanding of the place of humanity in the world, understanding of what shapes human experience and what can be done to influence it. This entire enterprise has one specific end in view, to make the most of being, or as we may put it nowadays, to improve one's quality of life.

We have observed that the sages' search for understanding is paradigmatic, in the sense that it does not operate with absolute and precise truths, but only reasonable approximations of the reality that are sufficient for its purposes. The fundamental reason for this approach lies in the conviction, traceable in both texts, that there are limits to human knowledge, albeit these limits differ between the two books. For the proverbial sages that which one can know greatly outweighs that which is inaccessible; Qoheleth, in contrast, perceives the impact of that which is beyond the reach of the human intellect as far more important than what a human being can comprehend.

This issue is closely related to the process of acquiring knowledge. In the case of both books the primary source of knowledge is observation. Both texts share the view that human experience is essentially uniform across the ages, but they draw radically different conclusions from this initial premise. The proverbial sages give priority to collective experience, to observations that have been confirmed again and again by successive generations, assuming that the present and future can be understood from knowing the past. Qoheleth, on the other hand, relies largely on first-hand data. For him the uniformity of human experience means that the key to understanding the future lies not in the past, but in the verifiable present.

We saw that God is an important part of the epistemological process in both books, yet, his role is radically different in each case. The God of the proverbial sages walks along with them in their quest to understand the world and their place in it, encourages their enquiry, and ultimately speaks to them through their experience. Qoheleth's God, in stark contrast, is largely silent, if not actively obstructive. He does not have any genuine interest in humanity gaining deeper insights into the nature of the world and his plans with it; human ignorance guards his position and human respect for him.

It was further noted that the epistemological perspective of the epilogue is different from either that of Proverbs or Qoheleth, for in the epilogue information about the world that matters comes from direct revelation. The epilogist's epistemology is centred around the cult, the value of the human search for understanding of the world is depreciated by him, and the emphasis is put on the limits of the wisdom search. The seeming resemblance of this emphasis to that of Qoheleth himself is only superficial, for while Qoheleth principally believed that the world is ultimately unknowable in the sense that there is more to be known than humans can possibly comprehend, the epilogist was convinced that everything worth knowing had already been revealed, emptying the search for more knowledge of meaning.

One thing that Qoheleth and the proverbial sages have in common is their lack of belief in a meaningful afterlife; their interest is in the here and now, their paradigms are built around, and meant to be applied to, this world alone. The dead reside in Sheol, an undesirable place of oblivion, a place from which there is no return and which offers no opportunities to exercise wisdom. Beyond these commonalities the two cosmologies differ.

The proverbial world is highly regular and predictable. This is because God has a tight grip on it and makes sure that human actions are accompanied by appropriate, i.e., just, consequences. Yet, we have detected in the book that it is not an ideal world, that in fact, the sages were aware that sometimes the wicked prosper and the righteous do not. While this is always implied to be only a minor and temporary setback, it does raise the question of who is responsible. The sages are reluctant to put the blame on God, for the proverbial God is never on the side of the fools, never condoning their ploys. At the same time, the sages are unwilling to even contemplate the possibility that the divine grip on the world might not be as firm as they assume.

As a result, forces of chaos are always tacitly present in the proverbial cosmos and their battle with forces of order is vividly portrayed in the imagery of the two women, Wisdom and Folly. The origin and place of these forces in the proverbial cosmos are never really spelled out. We have concluded from this that the theo-cosmological framework is derived from, and subservient to, the larger picture of the world arrived at through observation. The proverbial Yahwism is quite different from the Yahwism of the cult, and in the light of that it is unlikely that the religious layer of the proverbial worldview has been imported from the cult. Rather, an attempt is made to present the proverbial theological perspective so as not to look too divergent from it. The central instrument in this is the concept of *fear of Yahweh* which is sufficiently specific from the wisdom perspective to describe how humans should live in God's world, and at the same time, it is also sufficiently vague from the cultic perspective so as not to clash with the theology of the cult.

Qoheleth's world is also predictable, but in an entirely different sense than applied to Proverbs. The predictability lies in the fact that the world never produces any long-term benefit for human beings, the positive is always in the end paired up with the negative cancelling it out; death reverses everything, whether good or bad. This feature of the world is an intentional divine design; it is to inspire fear of God. Qoheleth wishes that his God would be more like the one of the proverbial sages, blessing the righteous and punishing the wicked, but he finds no tangible evidence of that; the divine judgement does not appear to entail anything more than the reality of death.

There is no hint of the tacit dualism we detected in Proverbs, no struggle between Wisdom and Folly, order and chaos; Qoheleth's God is entirely in control, an absolute ruler, accountable to no-one. He is neither positively inclined to humans, nor is he perceived as a tyrant; he stands at a distance. Yet, Qoheleth advises to respect him fully, not by foolish and shallow rituals, but by accepting and revering his qualitative superiority. We also saw that the epilogist shares Qoheleth's view about the absolute sovereignty of God, yet, in contrast to Qoheleth, he believes that God is involved in human existence more directly, and presumably, in a more positive manner, via the cult.

This brings us to the view of human beings and human society that the two books have. In both cases humanity is understood as divine creation. However, proverbial anthropology is quite high, humans were created in the image of God and were endowed with a number of skills, and in particular with a powerful reasoning capacity. In contrast, a human being is very much an animal for Qoheleth; he is unable to affirm any significant difference between the two. Further, any capabilities that God gave to humans are severely crippled. This perspective would appear to be shared by the epilogist, who, as we have already noted, takes the implications of the inability to understand further than Qoheleth himself does.

It was also noted that both Proverbs and Qoheleth agree that the natural human inclination is toward folly and evil, but again behind the agreement lies a rather different understanding. The proverbial sages are optimistic about the power of wisdom and discipline to overcome this natural tendency. In contrast, Qoheleth expresses explicitly the view that righteousness is merely an ideal which is unachievable.

The social perspectives, and the social structures that we have detected in the two books are strikingly different. The proverbial world is one of a small community of neighbours and relatives who are mutually dependent on each other for their prosperity and even mere survival. The basic structure in this world is the family with age-based hierarchy, but in essence the individual members of the community are perceived as equals, irrespective of their economic condition—even the poor are perceived as having a place in the community and are to be treated with compassion and respect. The principal concern of the proverbial sages, lurking in the background of most of what the book has to say, is to preserve the community's coherence. This should not be obscured from us by the fact that the form of address and the motivation centres around an individual; the proverbial worldview is at its very heart communal.

Qoheleth's world could not be more different. It is a world where power is centralised, a world of large empires, military campaigns, fast changing administrations. The mutual interdependence of near neighbours is nowhere to be seen, the sense that the poor still have a valid place in the society is gone. It is a world with no hint of equality, a world where hierarchy is everything and the structures of which are geared to serve those at its very top. It is a world of no privacy where the ears of the powerful stretch as far as people's bedrooms.

In the light of these differences, it should not be at all surprising that the two concepts of wise behaviour are diametrically different. We have seen that in Proverbs being wise and being righteous are two sides of the same coin, for in the divinely upheld order of the world righteousness is the prerequisite of success. In contrast, Qoheleth's wisdom is void of ethical considerations, for whether one is righteous or wicked makes little impact on one's prospects of success. True, Qoheleth shows preference for righteousness, but from the point of view of the wisdom quest he is unable to affirm it as an integral part of being wise. In Qoheleth's world success is always only temporary and wisdom is about ways that might prolong its life-span or avoid total disasters, yet, only in terms of probabilities rather than certainties. Consequently wisdom, a priceless commodity in Proverbs, has only limited value for Qoheleth. It is better than folly but in the end it cannot deliver what Qoheleth would like it to, and what the Proverbial sages believed it did. The epilogist is prepared to take Qoheleth's analysis even further, essentially rejecting the continuation of the wisdom enterprise as meaningful; the sages already know all they possibly can and need to. For the epilogist the way to success is not via human understanding, but lies in obedience to the divine command.

The principal difference between the perspectives of Proverbs, Qoheleth and of the epilogue can be formulated differently again, in the terms of the Joban problem, i.e., the tension at the heart of the Joban dialogues, between human experience, the sovereignty of God and divine justice. In Proverbs, this problem does not exist; experience, God's sovereignty and divine justice are in mutual harmony. However, the problem emerges as soon as the type of paradigm that is found in Proverbs, and adhered to by Job's friends, has to deal with experience that does not fit into it; the proverbial paradigm is not capable of coping with situations such as that found in Job. This is due to the vicious epistemological circle pointed out earlier in this study, which means that the sages cannot give up either of these three notions and still hold onto their paradigm; a brand new paradigm is needed. Thus, Qoheleth insists on the validity of experience and the sovereignty of God, but abandons the notion that God deals justly with humanity. In contrast, the epilogist holds onto the sovereignty of God and the notion of divine justice, but devalues experience. The former solution is that of a reverent sage, the latter is that of a theologian.[1]

What overall conclusions then should be drawn from our observations? The first implication, and probably one of the most important, concerns the fact that the nature of the relationship between the two books is much more complex than is sometimes acknowledged. Putting aside for the moment the complications introduced by the epilogue to

---

[1] In contrast, Job challenges both divine justice and sovereignty, while the narrative frame of Job offers a solution in the divine, rather than earthly domain.

Qoheleth, Proverbs and Qoheleth proper cannot be perceived as voices singing slightly different variations of the same basic tune in harmony with each other. Yet, painting them as two voices in a head-on conflict with each other is equally unsatisfactory.

On the one hand, we have seen that there are major differences between the two perspectives concerning the nature of the cosmos and God and the relationship between the two, and this prevents the conclusion that the two voices are at least in principle variations on an identical theme. On the other hand, it was argued that there are significant similarities between the two books in the object of their quest and methods they employ in their search for answers; both books are an expression of a quest for understanding of the place of humanity in the world with the view to facilitating success, and both of them use observation as the starting point of their quest. Further, both Qoheleth and the proverbial sages perceive knowledge and understanding as the keys to achieving the goal. Thus, these two books clearly stem from the same tradition of thought, one which I have argued can be characterised as *a quest for self-understanding in terms of relationships with things, people and the Creator, and self-realisation in the context of these relationships, based on a primarily empirical epistemology and a paradigmatic approach to understanding.* Further, while in many important respects Qoheleth disagrees with the perspective of the proverbial sages, it is quite clear that he wishes to hold onto certain ideals firmly rooted in the proverbial world, even though he is not able to justify them in a manner that he would find satisfactory.

This already complex picture is further complicated by the third voice, that of the epilogue. While the perspectives of Proverbs and Qoheleth proper originate in the same tradition, we are forced to conclude that the views of the epilogist do not stem from the same background and presuppositions. The epilogist is not a sage, he is a theologian whose primary interest is in the cult and the revelation that it provides. His concern is that the human quest for understanding is acknowledged to be truly limited in what it can achieve, and this fact is pressed to its full implications, i.e., that the wisdom quest needs to be subjected to the understanding that comes from the cult. In this respect the epilogist is not unlike the modern-day theologian with his or her preference for the cultic and prophetic material, and what we are witnessing here is probably one of the earliest attested attempts to bring together the two different traditions; to the credit of the epilogist, his approach would seem to have become the later norm.

When the two methodologies and the two perceptions of the world are brought together, another important point emerges. What we have seen are two basically empirical epistemologies accompanied by the conviction that the world is immutable, yet, they arrive at radically different conclusions about the nature of the world. In my opinion, there is only one feasible explanation for this, namely that the differences between Proverbs and Qoheleth have to be sought not in different initial premises, but in different experience. This is confirmed by the observations about the social structures reflected in the books. The proverbial sages find themselves in a world that operates on different economic principles and is governed by different social arrangements than the society in which Qoheleth is located. While the different perspectives are influenced by other issues, such as a different audience, it is my view that the different socio-economic structures detected were the principal formative factors in the process through which the two different worldviews were arrived at.

The fundamental problem with these books lies not in the fact that the worlds of the sages differed, but in their inability to shake off the premise of uniformity of human experience through time, on which both epistemologies rest. It is this premise that is largely responsible for the impossibility of reconciling these books with each other, for they continue to speak of *the World*, without ever considering that they may know merely *a world*, the one of their own. If the present conclusions about the principal socio-economic roots of the differences are correct, it is pointless to compare the two perspectives asking which one is better, more realistic and accurate. They both speak of what they know and experience, trying to come to grips with their individual worlds; trying to make the two to conform to one another is merely an extension of the same fallacy the sages fell for, the belief that the human world does not change.

I pointed out at the start of the present inquiry, that the query about the nature of the world that hides behind Proverbs and Qoheleth is closely related to the widely debated question of what constitutes wisdom. I believe that the results of the present examination of Proverbs and Qoheleth lend some support to the suggestion I made at the outset, namely, that the key question in attempting to come to grips with wisdom is not that of forms, vocabulary or elementary subjects, but rather one of overall aims and methodology. Applying this approach to Proverbs and Qoheleth allowed us to see a very tangible and profound link between Proverbs and Qoheleth proper, and yet, we were

able to do so without ignoring the significant differences between these
two books. At the same time, this method enabled us to spot a principal difference between Proverbs and Qoheleth proper on the one hand,
and the epilogue of Qoheleth on the other, in spite of the superficial
similarities that the epilogue might have with either book.

The principal divergence of the epilogue from the other two bodies
of text is symptomatic of the wider gap between these texts and much of
the OT material, suggesting that the present approach has the potential
to cast further light on our understanding of the wisdom phenomenon
in the wider OT context. For instance, it might be fruitful in coming to
grips with material such as Job, which, although traditionally perceived
as a wisdom text, fails to fit into a narrow definition of wisdom based
on forms, content and *Sitz im Leben*.[2]

Further, the significance of the tension created by the epilogue for
our understanding of the biblical wisdom tradition has not yet been, in
my view, fully appreciated. The noticeable shift of perspective between
Proverbs and Qoheleth arises, I argued, as a result of a socio-economic
change, i.e., it is a response of the empirical methodology to new
conditions, and can, therefore, be seen as an internal development of
the tradition. However, what the epilogue represents is rather different,
for it amounts to putting another tradition and its methodology in
control of the original quest, so that for all practical purposes the
epistemology ceases to be empirical; in other words, this is not merely
an internal development of the tradition. I suspect that in fact this is
what is happening in the later wisdom texts,[3] such as Ben Sira and
Wisdom of Solomon, and that an examination of these works with focus
on their aims and methods might reveal that the affinity of these texts
with books like Proverbs and Qoheleth is in fact much weaker that a
form-critical analysis might suggest.

Wisdom Theology Revisited

It was acknowledged in the Introduction that the present enquiry had
been motivated largely by theological concerns about the place of the
two books, and wisdom material in general, in the OT canon; questions
that have to do with a community of faith and the use it makes, can
make, and perhaps should make, of these texts. Yet, these questions

---

[2] Dell (1991).
[3] See Hayman (1991a).

have not so far been touched upon at all. This, as explained at the beginning, has been a deliberate decision stemming from the conviction that before these texts are responsibly placed into a larger theological framework of a canon/community of faith, their individual voices have to be heard and their individual points of view considered carefully. It is only when the theologian allows the autonomous voices to be heard that he or she can step into the dialogue in which these voices are engaged (and have been long before he or she entered the scene); only then can the theologian perhaps seek more systematic answers to the questions they raise and struggle with. While it has been obvious from the very beginning that the scope and physical limits of this work would not allow engagement in this type of dialogue with the two books, it is only appropriate to make a few limited comments along these lines in these final paragraphs; these should be perceived more as suggestions for further work than an attempt to resolve the issues.

It was the author's sincere, and with hindsight naïve, hope that a detailed examination of the perspectives of the two books might offer some simple solution to the tension between them that the successive generations of their readers perceive in them, or at least instinctively sense. While I believe that the outcome of the examination offers a suitable starting point for further considerations of the place and significance of the voices of the sages in the OT, and in this sense represents a step forward in dealing with the broader theological implications of wisdom literature for OT theology, it does not offer an easy way out of the difficulties that the OT theologian faces with respect to wisdom material, as was outlined in the Introduction.

The observations made in the present work, and summarised in the previous section, confirm what has now been acknowledged for some time, namely, that wisdom is not about timeless truths, but it is the product of its own time and circumstances. Thus, simply understanding Proverbs and Qoheleth as two different analyses of the same reality is not possible, for they deal with two distinct realities. On the level of the worldviews these books represent, and it is the worldviews that are the theologian's principal raw material, there are differences between them that cannot be easily disregarded, indeed, differences that in my view cannot be reconciled. The world of Proverbs is one in which justice operates with a high degree of reliability, a world in which integrity, diligence and wisdom lead to success. In contrast, in Qoheleth's world none of these virtues guarantees anything, justice is at best as often done as it is not, and the only thing that can be taken for granted is the reality of death with all its implications.

When I said that the two worldviews cannot be reconciled, I meant more precisely that they cannot be reconciled on their own terms. In reality, the theologian will always find ways to reconcile perspectives he or she considers as needing to be upheld; the whole notion of a canon dictates so much. A number of options are open to such a theologian. For one, he or she can conclude that while Qoheleth makes a valid point, the validity of the proverbial perspective, and in particular of the proverbial ethics, does not stem from the assertion that it leads to success and prosperity, but from the fact that it is divinely revealed truth. Such an approach is, I think, in the spirit of Proverbs, for success is used in Proverbs as a motivation rather than justification; when the choice between wisdom and material prosperity is to be made, wisdom wins. What, however, such a theologian has to ask him- or her-self, is whether relegating Qoheleth merely to the position of a warning against excessive optimism concerning wisdom's potential does justice to the latter book; I think not.

Another obvious option is open to the theologian: to declare the epilogue of Qoheleth to be the normative voice prescribing how the book should be understood and effectively emptying the material of any serious force. At least two points have to be raised here in response to such an approach. First, it is unlikely that the epilogue was ever intended to be an outright nullification of Qoheleth proper. It does soften the edges of the book, but it shows too much respect for the person of Qoheleth and is too brief to be seen as a complete rebuttal; its primary purpose is to draw conclusions of its own from the results of Qoheleth's enquiry. Further, such an understanding of the relationship between Qoheleth proper and the epilogue fails to fully appreciate the perspective the epilogue itself represents, for as I have argued the epilogist's world revolves around a cult-centred view of God and as such his perspective is not at all a wisdom perspective in terms of the definition laid down earlier. Re-reading Qoheleth purely in the terms of the epilogue may seem to eliminate the tension between Proverbs and Qoheleth, but this is not the result of making Qoheleth more like Proverbs, but rather transforming Qoheleth into a non-wisdom text. Further, if the point of the epilogue is pressed, the theological value of wisdom texts in general, not just Qoheleth, is undermined because the epilogist's solution takes away from them the axis around which they revolve, the quest for understanding itself. The wisdom tradition becomes merely wisdom texts, and I have argued that this is an inadequate way of perceiving wisdom, for wisdom is about a quest of the human intellect, not about mere possession of information.

The theologian can adopt yet a different approach, by integrating the two books into a broader theological framework that circumvents their differences. The typical example of such a solution is the introduction of the concept of life after death as a mediator between the two. While this concept is external to both, it can be done without much violence to the two books; Qoheleth never resolutely denied such a possibility, limiting his claims strictly to the here and now, and Proverbs does not contemplate the option at all. By extending the proverbial retribution beyond the grave the most obvious tension between the two books is at least muted if not removed. Is such a solution adequate? Not really, since, just as all the solutions outlined above, it deals with the symptoms, not the cause.

The tension within the wisdom tradition is usually analysed in terms of the question of retribution, i.e., whether the world is or is not just. While this is the most obvious clash point in the dialogue of the OT wisdom texts, it is not really the heart of the problem. The real issue that the theologian has to address is not what the books have to say about the world, but what they have to say about God himself, because, as I have argued, in both books the perceptions of the world are inseparable from the views about God. It is precisely for this reason the epilogist, who is a theologian at heart, felt it necessary to make himself heard. His worries are not about what Qoheleth has to say about life, but what he implies about God; his concern is not to stop one identifying with the reality that Qoheleth describes, but to stop one losing faith in God on account of this reality.

In my view, a completely new approach is required from the biblical theologian, a simple synchronic treatment of these texts is unsatisfactory. A possible answer may lie in a dialectical approach, considering not only the differences and similarities between the two books, but the changes that lie at the heart of them; I personally am inclined to think that the formative influence of external environment on the wisdom perspective is possibly of a greater theological significance than the particular perspectives of Proverbs and Qoheleth *per se*.

Quite clearly, further work is needed by those interested in biblical wisdom. In spite of the significant advances that have been made in this relatively young field of biblical studies, our overall understanding of the background of the wisdom material in the OT, its true extent, and its impact on the intellectual and theological formation of ancient Israel, is still rather limited. Should one feel daunted by the enormity of the task ahead, a consolation can be found in the fact that such a quest continues a fine tradition, for there is no end to making many books about wisdom.

APPENDIX

Distribution of Verbal Forms in Qoheleth

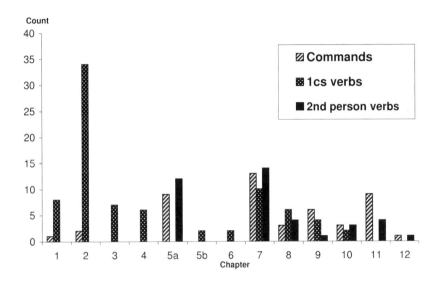

SELECTED BIBLIOGRAPHY

Albright, W. F.
    1955   'Some Canaanite-Phoenician Sources of Hebrew Wisdom', in Rowley, Noth, Thomas (eds), 1955: 1–15.

Aletti, J. N.
    1976   'Proverbes 8:22–31: étude de structure', *Biblica 57*: 25–37.
    1977   'Seduction et parole an Proverbes I-IX', *VT 27*: 129–44.

Andrew, M. E.
    1978   'Variety of Expressions in Proverbs 23:29–35', *VT 28*: 102–103.

Armstrong, J. F.
    1983   'Ecclesiastes in Old Testament Theology', *Princeton Seminary Bulletin 4*: 16–25.

Austin, J. L.
    1962   *How to Do Things With Words* (The William James Lectures; Oxford: Clarendon Press).

Barr, J.
    1969   *Biblical Words for Time* (Studies in Biblical Theology, First Series 33; London: SCM).

Bartolomew, C. G.
    1998   *Reading Ecclesiastes: Old Testament Exegesis and Hermeneutical Theory* (Analecta Biblica 139; Roma: Editrice pontificio instituto biblico).

Barton, G. A.
    1908   *A Critical and Exegetical Commentary on the Book of Ecclesiastes* (ITC; Edinburgh: T & T Clark).

Barton, S C (ed.)
    1999   *Where Shall Wisdom Be Found?: Wisdom in the Bible, the Church and the Contemporary World* (Edinburgh: T & T Clark).

Bauer, H.
    1930   'Die hebraischen Eigennamen als sprachliche Erkenntnisquelle', *ZAW 48*: 73–80.

Beentjes, P. C.
    1997   *The Book of Ben Sira in Hebrew* (SVT 68; Leiden: Brill).

Berlin, A.
    1985   *The Dynamics of Bibilical Parallelism* (Bloomington, IN: Indiana University Press).

Bewer, J. A.
    1948   'Two Suggestions on Prov 30:31 and Zech 9:16', *JBL 67*: 61–62.

Blenkinsopp, J.
    1991   'The Social Context of the "Outsider Woman" in Proverbs 1–9', *Biblica 72*: 457–73.
    1995   'Ecclesiastes 3:1–15: Another Interpretation', *JSOT 66*: 55–64.

Bloomfield, M.
    1984   'The Tradition and Style of Biblical Wisdom Literature', in Hirsch, Aschkenasy (eds), *Biblical Patterns in Modern Literature* (Brown Judaic Studies 77; Chico, CA: Scholars Press): 19–30.

Boer, P. A. H., de
    1955   'The Counsellor', in Rowley, Noth, Thomas (eds), 1955: 42–71.

Boström, L.
    1990   *The God of the Sages: The Portrayal of God in the Book of Proverbs* (ConBOT;
            Stockholm: Almqvist & Wiksell International).
Bratcher, R. G.
    1983   'A Translator's Note on Proverbs 11:30', *Bible Translator 34*: 337–38.
Brenner, A. D.
    1993   'Some Observations on the Figurations of Woman in Wisdom Literature', in
            McKay, 1993: 192–208.
Brindle, W. A.
    1985   'Righteousness and Wickedness in Ecclesiastes 7:15–18', *Andrews University
            Seminary Studies 23*: 243–57.
Brown, F.; Driver, S. R.; Briggs, C. A.
    1979   *The New Brown - Driver - Briggs - Gesenius Hebrew and English Lexicon* (Peabody,
            MA: Hendrickson).
Brueggemann, W. A.
    1990   'The Social Significance of Solomon as a Patron of Wisdom', in Gammie,
            Perdue (eds), 1990: 117–32.
    1997   *Theology of the Old Testament* (Minneapolis. Fortress Press).
Bryce, G. E.
    1972a   'Another Wisdom-book in Proverbs', *JBL 91*: 145–57.
Burkes, S.
    1999   *Death in Qoheleth and Egyptian Biographies of the Late Period* (SBLDS 170; Atlanta,
            GA: Society of Biblical Literature).
Burney, C. F.
    1926   'Christ as the APXH of Creation', *JTS 27*: 160–77.
Burns, J. B.
    1989   'Some Personifications of Death in the Old Testament', *IBS*: 23–34.
    1995   'Proverbs 7:6–27: Vignettes from the Cycle of Astarte and Adonis', *SJOT 9*:
            20–36.
Camp, C. V.
    1987   'Woman Wisdom as Root Metaphor: A Theological Consideration', in
            Hoglund, Huwiler, Glass, 1987: 45–76.
Carasik, M.
    1994   'Who were the "men of Hezekiah" (Proverbs XXV 1)?', *VT 44*: 289–300.
Carny, P.
    1992   'Theodicy in the Book of Qohelet', in Reventlow, Hoffman (eds), *Justice and
            Righteousness* (JSOTSup 137; Sheffield: Sheffield Academic Press): 71–81.
Cathcart, K. J.
    1970   'Proverbs 30:4 and Ugaritic Hpn, "garment"', *CBQ 32*: 418–20.
Ceresko, A. R.
    1982   'The Function of Antanaclasis (ms' "to find"//ms' "to reach, overtake,
            grasp") in Hebrew Poetry, Especially in the Book of Qoheleth', *CBQ 44*:
            551–69.
Childs, B. S.
    1979   *Introduction to the Old Testament as Scripture* (Philadelphia: Fortress Press).
    1985   *Old Testament Theology* (London: SCM).
    1992   *Biblical Theology of the Old and New Testaments* (London: SCM).
Christianson, E. S.
    1998   *A Time to Tell: Narrative Strategies in Ecclesiastes* (JSOTSup 280; Sheffield:
            Sheffield Academic Press).
Classen, W. T.
    1983   'Speaker-Orientated Functions of kî in Biblical Hebrew', *JNSL*: 29–46.

Clemens, D. M.
1994 'The Law of Sin and Death: Ecclesiastes and Genesis 1–3', *Themelios 19*: 5–8.
Clements, R. E.
1990 *Wisdom for a Changing World: Wisdom in Old Testament* (Berkeley Lectures 2; Berkeley, CA: BIBAL Press).
1992 *Wisdom in Theology* (Carlisle: The Paternoster Press).
1993 'The Good Neighbour in the Book of Proverbs', in McKay, 1993: 209–28.
Clifford, R. J.
1975 'Proverbs 9: A Suggested Ugaritic Parallel', *VT 25*: 298–306.
Clines, D. J. A.
1989 'The Wisdom Books', in Bigger (ed), *Creating the Old Testament* (Oxford: Blackwell): 269–94.
Cody, A..
1980 'Notes on Proverbs 22:21 and 22:23b', *Biblica 61*: 418–26.
Cohen, A.
1945 *Proverbs* (Hindhead, Surrey: The Soncio Press).
Collins, J. J.
1980 'Proverbial Wisdom and the Yahwist Vision', *Semeia 17*: 1–17.
1998 *Jewish Wisdom in the Hellenistic Age* (Edinburgh: T & T Clark).
Cook, J.
1994 'אִשָּׁה זָרָה (Proverbs 1–9 Septuagint): A Metaphor for Foreign Wisdom?', *ZAW 106*: 458–76.
1997 *The Septuagint of Proverbs—Jewish and/or Hellenistic Proverbs?: Concerning the Hellenistic Colouring of LXX Proverbs* (SVT 49; Leiden: Brill).
Crenshaw, J. L.
1969 'Method in Determining Wisdom Influence Upon "historical" Literature', *JBL 88*: 129–42.
1974 'Wisdom', in Hayes (ed.), *Old Testament Form Criticism* (San Antonio: Trinity University Press): 225–64.
1978 'The Shadow of Death in Qoheleth', in Gammie et al. (eds), 1978: 205–16.
1980a 'Impossible Questions, Sayings, and Tasks', *Semeia 17*: 19–34.
1980b 'The Birth of Skepticism in Ancient Israel: Studies on God's Control of Human Events', in Crenshaw, Sandmel (eds), *The Divine Helmsman* (New York: KTAV): 1–19.
1981 *Old Testament Wisdom, An Introduction* (London: SCM).
1985 'Education in Ancient Israel', *JBL 104*: 601–15.
1985 'The Wisdom Literature', in Knight, Tucker (eds), *The Hebrew Bible* (The Bible and Its Modern Interpreters 1; Chico, CA: Scholars Press): 369–407.
1986 'The Expression mî yôdēaʿ in the Hebrew Bible', *VT 36*: 274–88.
1988 *Ecclesiastes: A Commentary* (Old Testament Library; London: SCM).
1989 'Clanging Symbols', in Knight, Peters (eds), *Justice and the Holy*: 51–64.
1990 'The Sage in Proverbs', in Gammie, Perdue (eds), 1990: 205–16.
Crüsemann, F.
1984 'The Unchangeable World: The "Crisis of Wisdom" in Koheleth', in Schottroff, Stegemann (eds), *God of the Lowly: Socio-Historical Interpretations of the Bible* (New York: Orbis Books): 57–77.
Dahood, M. J.
1960 'Immortality in Proverbs 12:28', *Biblica 41*: 176–81.
1968a 'Proverbs 8:22–31: Translation and Commentary', *CBQ 30*: 512–21.
1968b 'Scriptio Defectiva in Qoheleth 4:10a', *Biblica 49*: 243.
1968c 'Hebrew-Ugaritic Lexicography VI', *Biblica 49*: 355–69.

1973   'Honey That Drips: Notes on Proverbs 5:2–3', *Biblica 54*: 65–66.
1975   'Archaic Genitive Ending in Proverbs 31:6', *Biblica 56*: 241.
1982a   'Philological Observations on Five Biblical Texts', *Biblica 63*: 390–94.
1982b   'The Hapax Charak in Proverbs 12:27', *Biblica 63*: 60–62.

Daube, D.
1985   'A Quartet of Beasties in the Book of Proverbs', *JTS ns 36*: 380–86.

Davies, E. W.
1980   'The Meaning of qesem in Prov 16:10', *Biblica 61*: 554–56.

Davies, G. I.
1995   'Where There Schools in Ancient Israel?', Day, Gordon, Williamson (eds),
        1995: 199–209.

Day, J.
1995   'Foreign Semitic Influence on the Wisdom of Israel and Its Appropriation in
        the Book of Proverbs', in Day et al. (eds), 1995: 55–70.

Day, J.; Gordon, R. P.; Williamson, H. G. M. (eds)
1995   *Wisdom in Ancient Israel: Essays in Honour of J.A. Emerton* (Cambridge: Cam-
        bridge University Press).

Delitzsch, F., Easton, M. G. (tr.)
1982a   *A Biblical Commentary on the Proverbs of Solomon* (Grand Rapids, MI: Eerdmans).
1982b   *Commentary on the Song of Songs and Ecclesiastes* (Grand Rapids, MI: Eerdmans).

Dell, K. J.
1991   *The Book of Job as Sceptical Literature* (BZAW 197; Berlin: Walter de Gruyter).
1994a   '"Green" Ideas in the Wisdom Tradition', *SJT 47 Number 4*: 421–51.
1994b   'Ecclesiastes as Wisdom: Consulting Early Interpreters', *VT 44*: 301–29.
1997   'On the Development of Wisdom in Israel', in Emerton et al. (eds), *Congress
        Volume: Cambridge, 1996* (SVT 66; Leiden: Brill): 135–51.
1998   'The King in the Wisdom Literature', in Day (ed), *King and Messiah in Israel
        and the Ancient Near East* (JSOTSup 270; Sheffield: Sheffield Academic Press):
        163–186.

D'Hamonville, D.-M.
2000   *La Bible d'Alexandrie, 17, Les Proverbes* (Paris: Cerf).

Dressler, H. H. P.
1988   'The Lesson of Proverbs 26:23', in Eslinger and Taylor (eds), *Ascribe to the Lord*
        (Sheffield: JSOT): 117–25.

Driver, G. R.
1931   'Problems in Proverbs', *ZAW 50*: 141–48.
1934   'Hebrew Notes', *ZAW 52*: 51–56.
1951a   'Hebrew Notes', *VT 1*: 241–50.
1951b   'Problems in the Hebrew Text of Proverbs', *Biblica 32*: 173–97.
1954   'Problems and Solutions', *VT 4*: 225–45.
1955   'Proverbs 19:26', *TZ 11*: 373–74.

Eaton, M. A.
1983   *Ecclesiastes: An Introduction and Commentary* (Tyndale Old Testament Commen-
        taries; Leicester: IVP).

Eichrodt, W.; Baker, J A (tr.)
1967   *Theology of the Old Testament* (Old Testament Library; London: SCM).

Ellermeier, F.
1963   'Das Verbum חוּשׁ in Koh 2:25', *ZAW 75*: 197–217.

Elliger, K.; Rudolph, W. (eds)
1990   *Biblia Hebraica Stuttgartensia* (Stuttgart: Deutsche Bibelgesellschaft).

Emerton, J. A.
1964   'Note on Proverbs 12:26', *ZAW 76*: 191–93.

1968 ‘Note on the Hebrew Text of Proverbs 1:22–3’, *JTS ns 19*: 609–14.
1979 ‘A Note on Proverbs 2:18’, *JTS ns 30*: 153–58.
1984 ‘The Meaning of Proverbs 13:2’, *JTS ns 35*: 91–95.
1988 ‘The Interpretation of Proverbs 21:28’, *ZAW 100 supp.*: 161–70.

Fiddes, P. S.
1996 ‘Where Shall Wisdom Be Found?’, in Barton, Reimer, *After the Exile* (Macon, GA: Mercer University Press): 171–90.

Fisch, H.
1988 *Poetry with a Purpose: Biblical Poetics and Interpretation* (Indiana Studies in Biblical Literature; Bloomington, IN: Indiana University Press).

Fontaine, C. R.
1993 ‘Wisdom in Proverbs’, in Perdue et al. (eds), 1993: 99–114.

Fox, M. V.
1968 ‘Aspects of the Religion of the Book of Proverbs’, *HUCA 39*: 55–69.
1977 ‘Frame-narrative and Composition in the Book of Qohelet’, *HUCA 48*: 83–106.
1986 ‘The Meaning of hebel for Qohelet’, *JBL 105*: 409–27.
1987 ‘Qohelet’s Epistemology’, *HUCA 58*: 137–56.
1988b ‘Qohelet 1:4’, *JSOT 40*: 109.
1989 *Qohelet and His Contradictions* (JSOTSup 71; Sheffield: Almond Press).
1993 ‘Wisdom in Qoheleth’, in Perdue et al. (eds), 1993: 115–31.
1994 ‘The Pedagogy of Proverbs 2’, *JBL 113*: 233–43.
1996a ‘Amon Again’, *JBL 115*: 699–702.
1996b ‘The Social Location of the Book of Proverbs’, in Fox et al. (eds), *Texts, Temples, and Traditions* (Winona Lake, IN: Eisenbrauns): 227–39.
1997 ‘What the Book of Proverbs is About’, in Emerton, *Congress Volume: Cambridge, 1996* (SVT 66; Leiden: Brill): 153–67.

Franklyn, P.
1983 ‘The Sayings of Agur in Proverbs 30: Piety or Scepticism?’, *ZAW 95*: 238–52.

Franzmann, M.
1991 ‘The Wheel in Proverbs 20:26 and Ode of Solomon 23:11–16’, *VT 41*: 121–22.

Fredericks, D. C.
1988 *Qoheleth’s Language: Re-evaluating Its Nature and Date* (Ancient Near Eastern Texts and Studies 3; Lewiston, NY: Edwin Mellen).

Gammie, J. G.; Brueggemann, W. A.; Humphreys, W. L. et al. (eds)
1978 *Israelite Wisdom: Theological and Literary Essays in Honor of Samuel Terrien* (New York: Union Theological Seminary).

Gammie, J. G.; Perdue, L. G. (eds)
1990 *The Sage in Israel and Ancient Near East* (Winona Lake, IN: Eisenbrauns).

Garrett, D. A.
1990 ‘Votive Prostitution Again: A Comparison of Proverbs 7:13–14 and 21:28–29’, *JBL 109*: 681–82.

Geller, S. A.
‘“Where is Wisdom”: A Literary Study of Job 28 in Its Settings’, in Neusner, Levine, Frerichs, *Judaic Perspectives on Ancient Israel* (Philadelphia: Fortress Press): 155–88.

Gemser, B.
1955 *The rîb- or Controversy-Pattern in Hebrew Mentality*, in Rowley, Noth, Thomas (eds), 1955: 120–37.
1960 ‘The Instructions of Onchsheshonqy and Biblical Wisdom Literature’, in *Congress Volume: Oxford, 1959* (SVT 7; Leiden: Brill): 102–28.

Gilbert, M.
    1979   'Le discours de la Sagesse en Proverbes, 8: Sturcture et coherence', in Gilbert
            (ed.), 1979: 202–18.
Gilbert, M. (ed.)
    1979   *La Sagesse De L'Ancien Testament* (BETL 51; Paris: Gembloux: J Duculot).
Ginsberg, H. L.
    1955   'The Structure and Contents of the Book of Koheleth', in Rowley, Noth,
            Thomas (eds), 1955: 138–49.
Glück, J. J.
    1964   'Proverbs 30:15a', *VT 14*: 367–70.
Goldingay, J. E.
    1977   'Proverbs V and IX', *RB 84*: 80–93.
    1994   'The Arrangement of Sayings in Proverbs 10–15', *JSOT 61*: 75–83.
Golka, F. W.
    1983   'Die israelitische Weisheitsschule oder "des Kaisers neue Kleider"', *VT 33*:
            257–70.
    1986   'Die Königs- und Hofsprüche und der Ursprung der israelitischen Weisheit',
            VT 36. 13 36).
    1993   *The Leopard's Spots: Biblical and African Wisdom in Proverbs* (Edinburgh: T & T
            Clark).
Good, E. M.
    1978   'The Unfilled Sea: Style and Meaning in Eccl. 1:2–11', in Gammie et al.
            (eds), 1978: 59–73.
Gordis, R.
    1943   'The Heptad as an Element of Biblical and Rabbinic Style', *JBL 62*: 17–26.
    1955   *Koheleth - the Man and His World* (Texts and Studies of the Jewish Theological
            Seminary of America 19; New York: Bloch).
Gottlieb, C.
    1991   'The Words of the Exceedingly Wise: Proverbs 30–31', in Younger et al (eds),
            The Biblical Canon in Comparative Perspective (Scripture in Context IV; Lewiston,
            NY: Edwin Mellen): 277–98.
Gottwald, N. K.
    1980   *The Tribes of Yahweh: A Sociology of the Religion of Liberated Israel 1250–1050 B.C.E.*
            (London: SMC).
Greenfield, J. C.
    1958   'Lexicographical Notes 1', *HUCA 29*: 203–28.
    1985   'The Seven Pillars of Wisdom (Prov 9:1): A Mistranslation', *JQR 76*: 13–20.
Grossberg, D.
    1994   'Two Kinds of Sexual Relationships in the Hebrew Bible', *Hebrew Studies 35*:
            7–25.
Gunneweg, A. H. J.
    1993   *Biblische Theologie des Alten Testaments: Eine Religionsgeschichte Israels in biblisch-
            theologischer Sicht* (Stuttgart: Kohlhammer).
Habel, N. C.
    1972   'Symbolism of Wisdom in Proverbs 1–9', *Interpretation 26*: 131–157.
    1984   'The Role of Elihu in the Design of the Book of Job', in Ahlstrom, Barrick
            and Spencer, *In the Shelter of Elyon: Essays on Ancient Palestinian Life and Literature*
            (JSOTSup 31; Sheffield: JSOT): 81–98.

Hadley, J. M.
    1995   'Wisdom and the Goddess', in Day et al. (eds), 1995: 234–43.
Harrington, D. J.
    1996   *Wisdom Texts From Qumran* (The Literature of the Dead Sea Scrolls; London: Routledge).
    1997   'Two Early Jewish Approaches to Wisdom: Sirach and Qumran Sapiential Work A', *JSP 16*: 25–38.
Harris, R. L.; Archer, G. L.; Waltke, B. K.
    1980   *Theological Wordbook of the Old Testament* (Chicago, ILL: Moody Press).
Harris, S. L.
    1995   *Proverbs 1–9: Study of Inner-Biblical Interpretation* (SBLDS 150; Atlanta, GA: Scholars Press).
    1996   '"Figure" and "Riddle": Prov 1:8–19 and Inner-biblical Interpretation', *Biblical Research 41*.
Harrison, C. R., jr.
    1997   'Qoheleth among the Sociologists', *BibInt 5*: 160–80.
Hasel, G.
    1991   *Old Testament Theology: Basic Issues in the Current Debate* (Grand Rapids, MI: Eerdmans).
Hawkins, T. R.
    1996   'The Wife of Noble Character in Proverbs 31:10–31', *BSac 153*: 12–23.
Hayman, A. P.
    1991a 'Qoheleth and the Book of Creation', *JSOT 50*: 93–111.
    1991b 'Monotheism: A Misused Word in Jewish Studies', *JJS 42*: 1–15.
    1993   'Qohelet, the Rabbis and the Wisdom Text from the Cairo Geniza', in Auld (ed.), *Understanding Poets and Prophets*: 149–65.
Healey, J. F.
    1989   'Models of Behavior: Matt 6:26 (// Luke 12:24) and Prov 6:6–8', *JBL 108*: 497–98.
Heijerman, M.
    1994   'Who Would Blame Her? The "Strange" Woman of Proverbs 7', in Dijk-Hemmes et al. (eds), *Reflections on Theology and Gender*: 21–31.
Hepper, F. N.
    1992   *Baker Encyclopedia of Bible Plants* (Grand Rapids, MI: Baker Book House).
Hermisson, H.-J.
    1978   'Observations on the Creation Theology in Wisdom', in Gammie et al. (eds), 1978: 43–57.
Hildebrandt, T. A.
    1988   'Proverbial Pairs: Compositional Units in Proverbs 10–29', *JBL 107*: 207–224.
Hoglund, K. G.
    1987   'The Fool and the Wise in Dialogue', in Hoglund, Huwiler, Glass, 1987: 161–80.
Hoglund, K. G.; Huwiler, E.; Glass, J. (eds)
    1987   *The Listening Heart* (Sheffield: JSOT).
Hubbard, D. A.
    1966   'The Wisdom Movement and Israel's Covenant Faith', *TynBul 17*: 3–33.
Humphreys, W. L.
    1978   'The Motif of the Wise Courtier in the Book of Proverbs', in Gammie et al. (eds), 1978: 177–90.
Hurvitz, A.
    1968   'The Chronological Significance of "Aramaisms" in Biblical Hebrew', *IEJ 18*: 234–40.

Irwin, W. A.
   1961   'Where Shall Wisdom Be Found?', *JBL 80*: 133–42.
Irwin, W. H.
   1984   'The Metaphor in Prov 11:30', *Biblica 65*: 97–100.
Isaksson, B.
   1987   *Studies in the Language of Qoheleth: With Special Emphasis on the Verbal System* (Acta Universitatis Upsaliensis. Studia Semitica Upsaliensia 10; Uppsala: Almqvist & Wiksell).
Jamieson-Drake, D. W.
   1991   *Scribes and Schools in Monarchic Judah: A Socio-Archeological Approach* (JSOTSup 109; Sheffield: Almond Press).
Jastrow, M.
   1996   *A Dictionary of the Targumim, the Talmud Babli and Yerushalmi, and the Midrashic Literature* (New York: Judaica Press).
Johnson, J E.
   1987   'An Analysis of Proverbs 1:1–7', *BSac 144*: 419–32.
Johnston, R. K.
   1970   'Confessions of a Workaholic. A Reappraisal of Qoheleth', *CBQ 38*: 14–28.
Johnstone, W.
   1967   'The Preacher as Scientist', *SJT 20*: 210–21.
Jong, S., de
   1992   'A Book on Labour: The Structuring Principles and the Main Theme of the Book of Qoheleth', *JSOT 54*: 107–16.
   1997   'God in the Book of Qohelet: A Reappraisal of Qohelet's Place in Old Testament Theology', *VT 47*: 154–67.
Joüon, P.; Muraoka, T.
   1993   *A Grammar of Biblical Hebrew* (Subsidia Biblica 14; Roma: Editrice pontificio instituto biblico).
Kassis, R. A.
   1999   *The Book of Proverbs and Arabic Proverbial Works* (SVT 74; Leiden: Brill).
Kayatz, C.
   1966   *Studien zu Proverbien 1–9* (WMANT 22; Neukirchen: Neukirchen Verlag).
Keel, O.
   1974   *Die Weisheit spielt vor Gott: Ein ikonographischer Beitrag zur Deutung des mᵉsaḥāqāt in Sprüche 8, 30f*, (Göttingen: Vandenhoeck & Ruprecht).
Kidner, D.
   1964   *The Proverbs* (Tyndale Old Testament Commentaries; London: Tyndale Press).
   1976   *A Time to Mourn, and a Time to Dance* (The Bible Speaks Today; Leicester: IVP).
Kitchen, K. A.
   1977   'Proverbs and Wisdom of the Ancient Near East', *TynBul 28*: 69–114.
   1988   'Egypt and Israel During the First Millennium BC', in Emerton (ed.), *Congress Volume: Jerusalem 1986* (SVT 40; Leiden: Brill): 107–23.
Klassen, W.
   1963   'Coals of Fire: Sign of Repentance or Revenge?', *NTS 9*: 337–50.
Koch, K.
   1983   'Is There a Doctrine of Retribution in the Old Testament?', in Crenshaw (ed.), *Theodicy in the Old Testament* (Issues in Religion and Theology 4; London: SPCK): 57–87.
Koehler, L.; Baumgartner, W.
   1985   *Lexicon in Veteris Testamenti Libros* (Leiden: Brill).

1994   *The Hebrew and Aramaic Lexicon of the Old Testament* (Leiden: Brill).

Kovacs, B. W.
1974   'Is There a Class-ethic in Proverbs?', in Crenshaw (ed.), *Essays in Old Testament ethics* (New York: KTAV): 171–89.

Kruger, P. A.
1987   'Promiscuity or Marriage Fidelity? A Note on Prov 5:15–18', *JNSL 13*: 61–68.

Kugel, J. L.
1989   'Qohelet and Money', *CBQ 51*: 32–49.

Lang, B.
1979   'Schule und Unterricht im alten Israel', in Gilbert (ed.), 1979: 186–201.
1986   *Wisdom and the Book of Proverbs: A Hebrew Goddess Redefined* (New York: Pilgrim Press).

Lavoie, J. J.
1995   'De l'inconvénient d'être né: Etude de Qohélet 4, 1–3', *SR 24*: 297–308.
1996   'Temps et finitude humaine: Etude de Qohélet ix 11–12', *VT 46*: 439–447.
1990   'The Sage in School and Temple', in Gammie, Perdue (eds), 1990: 165–81.

Lemaire, A.
1981   *Les Ecoles at la formation de la Bible dans l'ancient Israël* (Fribourg and Göttingen: Vandenhoeck und Ruprecht).
1984   'Sagesse et écoles', *VT 34*: 270–81.

Leupold, H. C.
1974   *Exposition of Ecclesiastes* (Grand Rapids, MI: Baker Book House).

Levine, E.
1997   'The Humor in Qohelet', *ZAW 109*: 71–83.

Lichtenstein, M. H.
1982   'Chiasm and Symmetry in Proverbs 31', *CBQ 44*: 202–11.

Liddell, H. G.; Scott, R.
1940   *A Greek-English Lexicon* (Oxford: Clarendon Press).

Lipiński, E.
1988   'Royal and State Scribes in Ancient Jerusalem', in Emerton (ed.), *Congress Volume: Jerusalem, 1986* (SVT 40, Leiden: Brill).

Loader, J. A.
1969   'Qohelet 3:2–8: A Sonnet in the Old Testament', *ZAW 81*: 240–42.
1979   *Polar Structures in the Book of Qoheleth* (BZAW 152; Berlin: Walter de Gruyter).
1986   *Ecclesiastes: A Practical Commentary* (Text and Interpretation; Grand Rapids, MI: Eerdmans).

Loewenstamm, S. E.
1987   'Remarks on Proverbs 17:12 and 20:27', *VT 37*: 221–24.

Lohfink, N.
1979   'War Kohelet ein Frauenfeind?', in Gilbert (ed.), 1979: 249–58.
1990   'Qoheleth 5:17–19: Revelation by Joy', *CBQ 52*: 625–35.

Loretz, O.; Kottsieper, I.
1987   *Colometry in Ugaritic and Biblical Poetry: Introduction, Illustrations and Topical Bibliography* (Ugaritisch-Biblische Literatur 5; Soest: CIS Verlag).

Lyons, E. L.
1987   'A Note on Proverbs 31:10–31', in Hoglund, Huwiler, Glass, 1987: 237–45.

MacIntosh, A. A.
1970   'Note on Proverbs 25:27', *VT 20*: 112–14.

Mack, B. L.
1970   'Wisdom Myth and Mythology: An Essay in Understanding a Theological Tradition', *Interpretation 24*: 46–60.

Maire, T.
    1995   'Proverbes XXII 17SS: Enseignement 'A Shalishôm?', *VT 45*: 227–38.
Malchow, B. V.
    1985   'A Manual for Future Monarchs [Prov 28–29]', *CBQ 47*: 238–245.
Maltby, A.
    1963   'The Book of Ecclesiastes and the After-Life', *EQ 35*: 39–44.
Marcus, R.
    1943   'The Tree of Life in Proverbs', *JBL 62*: 117–20.
Martin, J. D.
    1995   *Proverbs* (Old Testament Guides; Sheffield: Sheffield Academic Press).
McCreesh, T. P.
    1985   'Wisdom as Wife: Proverbs 31:10–31', *RB 92*: 25–46.
    1991   *Biblical Sound and Sense: Poetic Sound Patterns in Proverbs 10–29* (JSOTSup 128; Sheffield: Sheffield Academic Press).
McKane, W.
    1965   *Prophets and Wise Men* (London: SCM).
    1970   *Proverbs: A New Approach* (Old Testament Library; London: SCM).
    1979   'Functions of Language and Objectives of Discourse According to Proverbs, 10–30', in Gilbert (ed.), 1979: 166–85.
McKay, H. A.; Clines, D. J. A. (eds)
    1993   *Of Prophets' Visions and the Wisdom of Sages: Essays in Honour of R Norman Whybray on his Seventieth Birthday* (JSOTSup 162; Sheffield: JSOT).
McKenna, J. E.
    1992   'The Concept of hebel in the Book of Ecclesiastes', *SJT 45*: 19–28.
McKenzie, J. L.
    1967   'Reflections on Wisdom', *JBL 86*: 1–9.
Millard, A. R.
    1975   'עלץ "To Exult"', *JTSns 26*: 87–89.
Miller, D. B.
    1998   'Qoheleth's Symbolic Use of הבל', *JBL 117*: 437–54.
Miller, P. D., jr.
    1970   'Apotropaic Imagery in Proverbs 6:20–22', *JNES 29*: 129–30.
Miller, P. E.
    1982   'Rabbi Shemaria's Commentary on Proverbs 19:14', *JQR 73*: 146–51.
Moore, R. D.
    1994   'A Home for the Alien: Worldly Wisdom and Covenantal Confession in Proverbs 30,1–9', *ZAW 106*: 96–107.
Muilenburg, J.
    1954   'Qumran Fragment of Qoheleth', *BASOR 135*: 20–28.
    1961   'The Linguistic and Rhetorical Usages of the Particle ky in the Old Testament', *HUCA 32*: 135–60.
Murphy, R. E.
    1955   'Pensées of Coheleth', *CBQ 17*: 187–94.
    1982   'Qohelet Interpreted: The Bearing of the Past on the Present', *VT 32*: 331–37.
    1985   'Wisdom and Creation', *JBL 104*: 3–11.
    1986a 'Wisdom's Song: Proverbs 1:20–33', *CBQ 48*: 456–60.
    1987   'Proverbs 22:1–9', *Interpretation 41*: 398–402.
    1988   'Wisdom and Eros in Proverbs 1–9', *CBQ 50*: 600–603.
    1990   'The Sage in Ecclesiastes and Qoheleth the Sage', in Gammie, Perdue (eds), 1990: 263–71.
    1991   'Qoheleth and Theology?', *BTB 21*: 30–33.

1992   *Ecclesiastes* (Word Biblical Commentary 23A; Dallas, TX: Word Books).
1995   'The Personification of Wisdom', in Day et al. (eds), 1995: 222–33.
1996   *The Tree of Life: An Exploration of Biblical Wisdom Literature* (Grand Rapids, MI: Eerdmans).

Nel, P. J.
1977   'The Concept "Father" in the Wisdom Literature of the Ancient Near East', *JNSL*: 53–66.
1982   *The Structure and Ethos of the Wisdom Admonitions in Proverbs* (Berlin: Walter de Gruyter).

Neusner, J.
1998   *The Economics of the Mishnah* (South Florida Studies in the History of Judaism; Atlanta, GA: Scholars Press).

Newsom, C. A.
1989   'Women and the Discourse of Patriarchal Wisdom: A Study of Proverbs 1–9', in Day (ed), *Gender and Difference in Ancient Israel* (Minneapolis: Fortress Press): 142–60.

North, F. S.
1965   'Four Insatiables', *VT 15*: 281–82.

O'Callaghan, R. T.
1954   'Echoes of Canaanite Literature in the Psalms', *VT 4*: 164–76.

O'Connell, R. H.
1991   'Proverbs 7:16–17: A Case of Fatal Deception in a "Woman and the Window" Type-scene', *VT 41*: 235–41.

Oesterley, W. O. E.
1929   *The Book of Proverbs* (London: Methuen).

Ogden, G. S.
1984a 'The Mathematics of Wisdom: Qoheleth 4:1–12', *VT 34*: 446–53.
1986   'The Interpretation of דור in Ecclesiastes 1:4', *JSOT 34*: 91–92.
1987a 'Vanity It Certainly Is Not', *Bible Translator 38*: 301–307.
1987b *Qoheleth* (Readings. A new Biblical commentary; Sheffield: JSOT).

Pardee, D.
1987   *Ugaritic and Hebrew Poetic Parallelism: A Trial Cut ('nt I and Proverbs 2)* (SVT 39; Leiden: Brill).

Peels, H. G. L.
1994   'Passion or Justice? The Interpretation of bᵉyom nāqām in Proverbs 6:34', *VT 44*: 270–74.

Perdue, L. G.
1977   *Wisdom and Cult* (SBLDS 30; Missoula, MONT: Scholars Press).
1994   *Wisdom & Creation: The Theology of Wisdom Literature* (Nashville: Abingdon Press).

Perdue, L. G.; Scott, B. B.; Wiseman, J. (eds)
1993   *In Search of Wisdom: Essays in Memory of John G. Gammie* (Westminster: John Knox Press).

Perry, T. A.
1993   *Dialogues with Koheleth* (University Park, PA: Pennsilvania State University).

Peuch, E.
1988   'Les Ecoles dans l'Israël préexilique: données épigraphiques', in Emerton (ed.), *Congress Volume: Jerusalem, 1986* (SVT 40; Leiden: Brill): 189–203.

Ploeg, J. P. M., van der
1953   'Prov 25:23', *VT 3*: 189–92.

Preuss, H. D.
    1996   *Old Testament Theology* (Edinburgh: T & T Clark).
Rabin, C.
    1949   'מעט חבק ידים לשכב', *JJS 1*: 197–98.
Rad, G., von
    1953   'Josephsgeschichte und ältere Chokma', in Anderson, Bentzen, de Boer et al. eds, *Congress Volume: Copenhagen, 1956* (SVT 1; Leiden: Brill): 120–27.
    1962   *Old Testament Theology* (San Francisco: Harper).
    1972   *Wisdom in Israel* (London: SCM).
Reitman, J. S.
    1997   'The Structure and Unity of Ecclesiastes', *BSac 154*: 297–319.
Renfroe, F.
    1989   'The Effect of Redaction on the Structure of Prov 1:1–6', *ZAW 101*: 290–93.
Ringgren, H.
    1947   *Word and Wisdom: Studies in the Hypostatization of Divine Qualities and Functions in the ANE* (Lund: Hakan Ohlssons Boktryckeri).
Rogers, C. L., III
    1997   'The Meaning and Significance of the Hebrew Word 'mwn in Proverbs 8,30', *ZAW 109*: 208–21.
Roth, W. M. W.
    1965   *Numerical Sayings in the Old Testament: A Form-critical Study* (SVT 13; Leiden: Brill).
Rottzoll, D. U.
    1999   *Abraham Ibn Esras Kommentare zu den Büchern Kohelet, Ester und Rut* (Studia Judaica 12; Berlin: Walter de Gruyter).
Rousseau, F.
    1981   'Structure de Qohelet 1:4–11 et plan du livre', *VT 31*: 200–17.
Rylaarsdam, J. C.
    1946   *Revelation in Jewish Wisdom Literature* (Chicago: The University of Chicago Press).
Saebo, M.
    1986   'From Collections to Book: A New Approach to the History of Tradition and Redaction of Book of Proverbs', in Giveon (ed.), *The Period of the Bible, division A* (Proceedings of the 9th World Congress of Jewish Studies; Jerusalem: World Union of Jewish Studies): 99–106.
Salters, R. B.
    1976   'Note on the Exegesis of Ecclesiastes 3:15b', *ZAW 88*: 419–22.
Sawyer, J. F. A.
    1975   'Ruined House in Ecclesiastes 12: A Reconstruction of the Original Parable', *JBL 94*: 519–31.
Schneider, T. R.
    1986   'From Wisdom Sayings to Wisdom Texts, pt. 1', *Bible Translator 37*: 128–35.
    1987   'From Wisdom Sayings to Wisdom Texts, pt. 2', *Bible Translator 38*: 101–17.
Schökel, L. A.
    1988   *A Manual of Hebrew Poetics* (Subsidia Biblica 11; Roma: Editrice pontificio instituto biblico).
Schoors, A.
    1981   'The Particle כי', *Oudtestamentische Studien 21*: 240–276.
    1985   'Koheleth: A Perspective of Life After Death?', *Ephemerides Theologicae Lovanienses 61*: 295–303.
    1992   *The Preacher Sought to Find Pleasing Words: A Study of the Language of Qoheleth* (Orientalia Lovaniensia Analecta 41; Leuven: Departement Orientalistiek).

Schwede, J. G.
    1996   'The Horse Leech: An Enigmatic Figure in the Talmud of Babylonia, (Abo-
           dah Zarah 1', in Neusner, *Approaches to Ancient Judaism, ns v. 9*: 33–42.
Scott, R. B. Y.
    1955   'Solomon and the Beginnings of Wisdom in Israel', in Rowley, Noth, Tho-
           mas, 1955: 262–79.
    1960   'Wisdom in Creation: The 'Amôn of Proverbs 8:30', *VT 10*: 213–23.
    1965   *Proverbs; Ecclesiastes* (The Anchor Bible 18; Garden City, NY: Doubleday).
Segert, S.
    1987   'Live Coals Heaped on the Head', in Marks, Good (eds), *Love & Death in the
           Ancient Near East* (Guilford, CONN: Four Quarters): 159–64.
Seow, C.-L.
    1996   'Linguistic Evidence and the Dating of Qoheleth', *JBL 115*: 643–66.
    1997   *Ecclesiastes* (Anchor Bible 18C; New York: Doubleday).
Shead, A.
    1996   'Ecclesiastes from the Outside In', *Reformed Theological Review 55*: 24–37.
Sheppard, G. T.
    1977   'Epilogue to Qoheleth as Theological Commentary', *CBQ 39*: 182–89.
    1980   *Wisdom as a Hermeneutical Construct: A Study in the Sapientializing of the Old
           Testament* (BZAW 151; Berlin: Walter de Gruyter).
Shupak, N.
    1987   'The Sitz im Leben of the Book of Proverbs', *RB 94*: 98–119.
    1993   *Where Can Wisdom Be Found?: The Sage's Language in the Bible and in Ancient
           Egyptian Literature* (OBO 130; Göttingen: Vandenhoeck & Ruprecht).
Skehan, P. W.
    1967   'Wisdom's House', *CBQ 29*: 468–86.
    1979   'Structures in Poems on Wisdom: Proverbs 8 and Sirach 24', *CBQ 41*: 365–79.
Smith, J. Z.
    1975   'Wisdom and Apocalyptic', in Pearson (ed.), *Religious Syncretism in Antiquity*
           (Series on Formative Contemporary Thinkers; Missoula, MONT: Scholars
           Press): 131–56.
Snell, D. C.
    1983   'Taking Souls in Proverbs 11:30', *VT 33*: 362–65.
    1987   'Notes on Love and Death in Proverbs', in Marks, Good (eds.), *Love & Death
           in the Ancient Near East* (Guilford, CONN: Four Quarters): 165–68.
    1989   'The Wheel in Proverbs 20:26', *VT 39*: 503–507.
    1991   'The Most Obscure Verse in Proverbs: Proverbs 26:10', *VT 41*: 350–56.
Snijders, L. A.
    1954   'The Meaning of ZR in the Old Testament: An Exegetical Study', *OTS 10*:
           1–154.
Spangenberg, I. J. J.
    1996   'Irony in the Book of Qohelet', *JSOT 72*: 57–69.
Spina, F. A.
    1983   'Qoheleth and the Reformation of Wisdom', in Huffman, Spina et al. (eds),
           The Quest for the Kingdom of God: 267–79.
Staples, W. E.
    1955   'Vanity of Vanities', *Canadian Journal of Theology 1*: 141–56.
Steiert, F.-J.
    1990   *Die Weisheit Israels - ein Fremdkorper im Alten Testament* (Freiburger theologische
           Studien 143; Freiburg: Herder).

Strömberg-Krantz, Eva
  1996   'A Man Not Supported by God: On Some Crucial Words in Proverbs XXX
          1', *VT 46*: 548–53.
Terrien, S.
  1981   'The Play of Wisdom: Turning Point in Biblical Theology', *HBT 3*: 125–53.
Thiselton, A. C.
  1992   *New Horizons in Hermeneutics* (Grand Rapids, MI: Zondervan).
Thomas, D. W.
  1934   'The Root שנה in Hebrew', *ZAW 52*: 236–38.
  1937   'More Notes on the Root ידע' in Hebrew', *JTS 38*: 404–5.
  1949   'Note on בְּמַדָּעֲךָ in Ecclesiastes 10:20', *JTS 50*: 177.
  1953   'Note on בַּל־יָדְעָה in Proverbs 9:13', *JTS 4*: 23–24.
  1955   'Textual and Philological Notes on Some Passages in the Book of Proverbs',
          in Rowley, Noth, Thomas (eds), 1955: 280–92.
  1962   'אוּ' in Proverbs 31:4', *VT 12*: 499–500.
  1963   'Note on דַּעַת in Proverbs 22:12', *JTS ns 14*: 93–94.
  1964   'Meaning of חַטָּאת in Proverbs 10:16', *JTS ns 15*: 295–96.
  1965   'Notes on Some Passages in the Book of Proverbs', *VT 15*: 271–79.
Thompson, J. M.
  1974   *The Form and Function of Proverbs in Ancient Israel* (Hague: Mouton).
Torcszyner, H.
  1924   'The Riddle in the Bible', *HUCA 1*: 125–49.
Torrey, C. C.
  1954   'Proverbs, Chapter 30', *JBL 73*: 93–96.
Tov, E.
  1990   'Recensional Differences Between the Masoretic Text and the Septuagint of
          Proverbs', in Attridge (ed.), *Of Scribes and Scrolls* (Lanham, MD: University
          Press of America): 43–56.
  1992   *Textual Criticism of the Hebrew Bible* (Minneapolis: Fortress Press).
Toy, C. H. A.
  1899   *Critical and Exegetical Commentary on the Book of Proverbs* (ITC; Edinburgh: T &
          T Clark).
Trible, P.
  1975   'Wisdom Builds a Poem: The Architecture of Proverbs 1:20–33', *JBL 94*:
          509–18.
Ullendorff, E.
  1962   'Meaning of קהלת', *VT 12*: 215.
Ulrich, E.
  1992   'Ezra and Qoheleth Manuscripts from Qumran (4QEzra and 4QQoha,b)
          [Hebrew Texts, P', in Ulrich (ed.), *Priests, Prophets and Scribes* (JSOTSup 149;
          Sheffield: JSOT): 139–57.
Van Leeuwen, R. C.
  1986a   'Proverbs 30:21–23 and the Biblical World Upside Down', *JBL 105*: 599–610.
  1986b   'A Technical Metallurgical Usage of יצא', *ZAW 98*: 112–13.
  1986c   'Proverbs 25:27 Once Again', *VT 36*: 105–14.
  1988   *Context and Meaning in Proverbs 25–27* (SBLDS 96; Atlanta, GA: Scholars
          Press).
  1990   'Liminality and Worldview in Proverbs 1–9', *Semeia 50*: 111–44.
  1992   'Wealth and Poverty: System and Contradiction in Proverbs', *Hebrew Studies
          33*: 25–36.
VanderKam, J. C.
  1994   *The Dead Sea Scrolls Today* (Grand Rapids, MI: Eerdmans).

Varela, A. T.
  1976 'Note on Ecc 5:8–9', *Bible Translator 27*: 240–41.
Vawter, B.
  1980 'Prov 8:22: Wisdom and Creation', *JBL 99*: 209–16.
Verheij, A.
  1991 'Paradise Retried: on Qohelet 2:4–6', *JSOT 50*: 113–15.
Vos, G.
  1973 *Biblical Theology: Old and New Testaments* (Grand Rapids, MI: Eerdmans).
Waldman, N. M.
  1978 'The dābār raʿ of Eccl 8:3', *JBL 98*: 407–8.
Walsh, J. T.
  1982 'Despair as a Theological Virtue in the Spirituality of Ecclesiastes', *BTB 12*: 46–50.
Waltke, B. K.
  1979 'The Book of Proverbs and Ancient Wisdom Literature', *BSac 136*: 221–38.
  1991 'Superscripts, Postscripts, or Both', *JBL 110*: 583–96.
Waltke, B. K.; O'Connor, M.
  1990 *An Introduction to Biblical Hebrew Syntax* (Winona Lake, IN: Eisenbrauns).
Washington, H. C.
  1994 'The Strange Woman of Proverbs 1–9', in Eskenazi, Richards, *Second Temple Studies, vol 2* (JSOTSup 175; Sheffield: JSOT): 217–42.
Weeks, S.
  1994 *Early Israelite Wisdom* (Oxford Theological Monographs; Oxford: Clarendon Press).
  1999 'Wisdom in the Old Testament', in Barton, 1999: 19–30.
Weiden, W. A., van der
  1970 'Prov 14:32b', *VT 20*: 339–50.
Westermann, C.
  1971 *Creation* (London: SPCK).
  1995 *Roots of Wisdom: The Oldest Proverbs of Israel and Other Peoples* (Edinburgh: T & T Clark).
Westermann, C.; Golka, F. W. (ed.)
  1979 *What Does the Old Testament Say about God?* (London: SPCK).
Whitley, C. F.
  1979 *Koheleth: His Language and Thought* (BZAW 148; Berlin: Walter de Gruyter).
Whybray, R. N.
  1965a *Wisdom in Proverbs: The Concept of Wisdom in Proverbs 1–9* (SBTh 45; London: SCM).
  1965b 'Proverbs 8:22–31 and Its Supposed Prototypes', *VT 15*: 504–14.
  1966 'Some Literary Problems in Proverbs 1–9', *VT 16*: 482–96.
  1972 *The Book of Proverbs* (The Cambridge Bible Commentary; Cambridge: Cambridge University Press).
  1974 *The Intellectual Tradition in the Old Testament* (BZAW 135; Berlin: Walter de Gruyter).
  1978 'Qoheleth the Immoralist (Qoh 7:16–17)', in Gammie et al. (eds), 1978: 191–204.
  1979 *Yahweh-sayings and Their Contexts in Proverbs 10: 1–22, 16*: 153–65.
  1981 'The Identification and Use of Quotations in Ecclesiastes', in Emerton (ed.), *Congress Volume: Vienna, 1980* (SVT 32; Leiden: Brill): 435–51.
  1988 'Ecclesiastes 1:5–7 and the Wonders of Nature', *JSOT 41*: 105–12.
  1989a *Ecclesiastes* (Old Testament Guides; Sheffield: Sheffield Academic Press).

1989b   *Ecclesiastes: Based on the Revised Standard Version* (New Century Bible Commentary; Grand Rapids, MI: Eerdmans).

1989c   'The Social World of the Wisdom Writers', in Clements (ed.), *The World of Ancient Israel* (Proceedings of the 9th World Congress of Jewish Studies; Jerusalem: World Union of Jewish Studies): 227–50.

1990   *Wealth and Poverty in the Book of Proverbs* (JSOTSup 99; Sheffield: JSOT).

1992   'Thoughts on the Composition of Proverbs 10–29', in Ulrich (ed.), *Priests, Prophets and Scribes* (JSOTSup 149; Sheffield: JSOT): 102–14.

1994a   *The Composition of the Book of Proverbs* (JSOTSup 168; Sheffield: JSOT).

1994b   'The Structure and Composition of Proverbs 22:17–24:22', in Porter et al. (eds), *Crossing the boundaries*: 83–96.

1995   *The Book of Proverbs, A Survey of Modern Study* (History of Biblical Interpretation Series; Leiden: Brill).

Williams, D. H.
1994   'Proverbs 8:22–31', *Interpretation 48*: 275–79.

Williams, J. G.
1980   'The Power of Form: A Study of Biblical Proverbs', *Semeia 17*: 35–58.

1987   'Proverbs and Ecclesiastes', in Alter, Kermode (eds), *The Literary Guide to the Bible* (Cambridge, MASS: The Belknap Press).

Wilson, F. M.
1987   'Sacred or Profane? The Yahwistic Redaction of Proverbs Reconsidered', in Hoglund, Huwiler, Glass (eds), 1987: 313–34.

Wilson, G. H.
1984   'The Words of the Wise: The Intent and Significance of Qohelet 12:9–14', *JBL 103*: 175–92.

Wolters, A. M.
1988   'Proverbs 31:10–31 as Heroic Hymn: A Form-Critical Analysis', *VT 38*: 446–57.

1995   'The Meaning of kîsôr (Prov 31:19)', *HUCA 65*: 91–104.

Wright, J. .S
1972   'The Interpretation of Ecclesiastes', in Kaiser (ed.), *Classical Evangelical Essays in Old Testament Interpretation* (Baker): 133–50.

Yee, G. A.
1982   'An Analysis of Prov 8:22–31 According to Style and Structure', *ZAW 94*: 58–66.

1989   'I Have Perfumed My Bed with Myrrh: The Foreign Woman (ʾiššâ zārâ) in Proverbs 1–9', *JSOT 43*: 53–68.

1992   'The Theology of Creation in Proverbs 8:22–31', in Clifford et al (eds), *Creation in the Biblical Traditions* (CBQMS 24; Washington, DC: Catholic Biblical Assoc of America): 85–96.

Yeivin, I.; Revell, E. J. (tr.)
1980   *Introduction to the Tiberian Masorah* (SBLMS 5; Chico, CA: Scholars Press).

Zimmerli, W.
1964   'The Place and Limit of the Wisdom in the Framework of the Old Testament Theology', *SJT 17*: 146–58.

Zimmerli, W.; Green, D. E. (tr.)
1978   *Old Testament Theology in Outline* (Edinburgh: T & T Clark).

Zuck, R. B.
1991   'God and Man in Ecclesiastes', *BSac 148*: 46–56.

INDEX NOMINUM

INDEX LOCORUM